THE PØRTAL

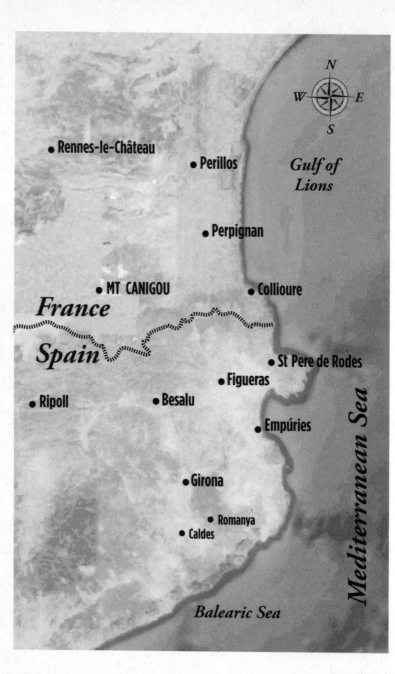

THE P⊕RTAL

An Initiate's Journey

into the

Secret of Rennes-le-Château

Patrice Chaplin

Theosophical Publishing House
Wheaton, Illinois * Chennai, India

Copyright © 2010 by Patrice Chaplin
First Quest Edition 2010

Quest Books
Theosophical Publishing House
P. O. Box 270
Wheaton, IL 60187-0270
www.questbooks.net

Cover design by Kirsten Hansen Pott
Typesetting by Wordstop Technologies

Library of Congress Cataloging-in-Publication Data

The portal: an initiate's journey into the secret of Rennes-le-Château /
Patrice Chaplin.—1st Quest ed.
     p.   cm.
ISBN 978-0-8356-0888-6
1. Chaplin, Patrice.   2. Spiritual biography—Spain—Girona.
3. Eglise Sainte-Marie-Madeleine (Rennes-le-Château, France)   I. Title.
BL73.C375A3 2010
204.092—dc22
[B]   2010014526

5   4   3   2   1   *   10   11   12   13   14

Printed in the United States of America

Dedicated to Lluís of L'Arc

Mt Canigou:

How high her plateau! How splendid her robes!
Dawn brings silver, the sun its finest gold
To keep her regal crown forever fresh.
Stars kiss her brow; then linger on as jewels.
And at times, it is said, travelling the stars
Seraphim stop to rest.

—Jacint Verdaguer

Cant de l'Amat

When you were not yet you
Nor I was yet I,
Remember, Beloved?
And the bells rang in your hair
And the blood sang in your veins—
Your smile that of an angel
From another time.

—José Tarres

TABLE ⊕F C⊕NTENTS

LIST ⊕F ILLUSTRATI⊕NS

ACKNOWLEDGMENTS

The author wishes to thank Madam Marta Andras,
Tove Frisvold, Ingerborg Zander, Señor Jaume Vialles,
and Josep Tarres.

Figure 1.1. The tower at Rennes-le-Château in southern France, built by the Abbé Bérenger Saunière in the 1890s.

CHAPTER I

The poor priest in a rundown church in a little-known village in the Aude district of southern France could hardly eke out a living. His account books showed a hand-to-mouth existence. Then one morning, without explanation, he became fabulously rich. The year was 1891, and he was thirty-eight years old.

How did he get the money? What had he done? The answer to those questions has been a mystery ever since and in the last three decades a source of continuing speculation, producing books, TV documentaries, and the basis for the novel and film of Dan Brown's *The Da Vinci Code*.

The priest, Bérenger Saunière, was born in 1852, in Montazels, a small village south of the medieval town of Carcassonne in France. As was customary in large families at that time, he went into the Church. Ambitious and intelligent, he seemed destined for a promising clerical career, but after a short term in the seminary in Narbonne, he was placed in the rundown parish of Rennes-le-Château. With a donation from a member of the Habsburg dynasty, Saunière began to repair and restore his church. In 1891, while removing the altar columns, he discovered four scrolls, two with coded messages. These, it appears, were the source of his wealth.

He took the scrolls immediately to the Church of St-Sulpice in Paris and, while they were being examined, was introduced to esoteric and secret societies. Was this where his involvement with a mystery unholy and still not resolved began?

On his return from Paris, Saunière continued the restoration of the church, discovering Templar emblems, gold, and ritual stones. A number of theories now exist that Saunière's great and continuing wealth was the result variously of alchemy, blackmailing the Vatican, or obtaining proof that Jesus and the Magdalene produced a child and thus began the divine bloodline that continued in France. It is also theorized that the Habsburgs were his paymasters.

Saunière restored the church in a manner that provoked curiosity and shock. He built the Villa Bethania, a substantial house in the Renaissance style, and the Tour Magdala, a neo-Gothic tower facing southeastern Spain. He created a park, a zoo, an orangery; he gave lavish entertainments and planned for a paved road down to the nearby village of Couiza. He lived a sumptuous and extravagant life. This country priest Saunière met intellectuals and celebrities who would not normally have crossed his path: Mallarmé, Maeterlinck, Debussy. Such celebrities became visitors to Saunière's home in Rennes-le-Château, and it was rumoured that he had a liaison with opera singer Emma Calvé, the Maria Callas of the time.

The Archduke Johann von Habsburg took an interest in Saunière's restoration, and the two men opened bank accounts with consecutive numbers. Saunière's maid, Marie Denarnaud, was dressed in the latest Parisian fashions and called 'Madonna' by the villagers.

Figure 1.2. The Abbé Bérenger Saunière.

By all accounts, Saunière liked grand things and important people. So why did he stay in a backwater? Was it because he *couldn't* leave? Did fear keep him in the rundown parish? He and his maid died without leaving any explanation of the source of his wealth; but I have been told more than once that his paymasters paid him too well for him to do as he pleased, and that they demanded he stay at the church and work as they needed.

Saunière did make short journeys for a few days at a time, but to where and for what? Did he go to Paris? Nearby Carcassonne? The parishioners said he crossed the border into northeastern Spain. Many years later, I came to learn that he went to the ancient city of Girona. This pre-Roman site, forty miles inland from the Costa Brava, has a vast old quarter, Arab baths, and monumental churches. Its predominantly Gothic cathedral, believed to have begun as a simple pagan temple, features a disproportionately large nave, and the fact that the building still stands at all is considered a miracle.

Figure 1.3. Girona's old quarter.

Bells ring across the forest of stone that is Girona every fifteen minutes, day and night. The old part survives—gloriously, with cobbled alleys, crumbling stairways, and deep arches leading to unexpected courtyards—all stone, medieval, or pre-Roman, with parts of the original city wall still standing as clumps of stone, four thousand years old. The buildings, huge buttresses of Roman skill, lean together across the strip of street, leaving only a shine of brilliant sky. The stones make the town echo and enhance all sound. Only the bells are free as they toll high above the old town. Girona holds onto its atmosphere and makes sure the past is there always, solid, unconquered by decay. It was to this city that the French priest came.

Nobody could have known the purpose of Saunière's visits in the 1890s, and they still wouldn't know it today if it weren't for an unthinkable, unacceptable, yet inevitable fact—people grow old and die. Facing death, the custodians of hidden material in Girona—those who held what the priest had come there for—needed conclusive outcomes. What had seemed beneficent in their youth and bound them

Figure 1.4. In Girona, the stones themselves hold secrets.

together in maturity became another thing altogether as they became more opinionated and despairing in the emergence of death's shadow. They disagreed. Secrets leaked a little. Suddenly, too many outsiders seemed to know something. This was in the summer of 2003.

In antiquity, before the Romans arrived, Girona had been an Iberian trading centre. The Iberians, the first-known inhabitants of the area, lived in the Catalan country village of Ullastret at least five thousand years ago. The Phoenicians settled in Girona province, leaving artefacts and sacrificial stones. The Greeks left a settlement along the coast:

Empuriés, a Spanish translation of the Greek *Emporion*, with rows of still-existing sculpted figures in some decay, looking out to sea. Along that coast, many villages have names based on the Greek influence.

The Romans built a large part of what is now Girona's old quarter. Charlemagne marched into the city and left his influence, as did Napoleon III. Girona won the Moorish contest but lost against Franco in the Civil War in the 1930s. Every invader left some mark.

Perhaps because so many cults and religions had flourished in Girona, not one of them is remembered exceptionally. The only visible sign of what has been so important there and then completely forgotten are the stones. Historical finds occur frequently, giving evidence of even older civilisations than local historians could have predicted; and today Girona celebrates this past with fiestas, legends, ritual, and theatre.

Situated between the frontier with France and the Catalan capital of Barcelona, Girona has always been a city of passage. Those anonymous travellers passing through it had left little trace, making it a good place to hide what must never show its name.

When I first set foot in Girona in the 1950s, I knew this was where I should be. I was fifteen, a bohemian, hitchhiking through Europe with my friend Beryl. We were travelling south, taking the roads as they came, running not away from anything but towards freedom. We wanted to be gypsies. On the evening we entered the town, the local craftsmen were lighting fires at the edge of the old quarter, and the sky was violet and flashing with huge, flat stars. The sun was setting behind the last bridge in a blaze of scarlet rage. The narrow streets were full of music, perfume, the smell of wood smoke. The church bells chimed as though for a celebration, and then all the lights of the city came on—hundreds of yellow eyes. It was a true welcome.

It was said that the stones of Girona had a magnetism that drew certain people back time and time again. Carcassonne, an ancient, fortified French town in the former province of Languedoc, had the same legend, and I heard it had to do with ley lines. At certain points across the earth, the energy builds up and creates a pull, a pulse, and in these places unusual and mystical things happen. In Girona, on certain days, depending on the wind, even the air was charged, producing an instant excitement. As I said in *City of Secrets*, you were seduced and changed into a different person, into the town's lover, because that's what the town wanted. You laid your heart on the narrow streets like a newborn child at a sacrifice. The town approved of offerings on a grand scale. A stranger could never really belong. It was a question of the stones, not the inhabitants. The stones housed the power.

The spirit of the town was what mattered. It had to approve of you; otherwise, you'd pass through that old quarter and it would show you nothing. I believe the spirit of Girona did approve of me as I was then. Of course it would not let me go; a town's love does not die. At the time, a lovely fifties optimism prevailed, and no political regime—even that of Franco's then tyrannizing Spain—could quite suppress that. The town was touched by dreams, dreams from other centuries that appeared in legends and were passed down in poetry, songs, and even the cries of birds.

The day I first entered Girona when I was fifteen, I remember standing on the side of the river that wound through the centre of the town knowing that if I crossed the clanking, iron bridge built by Eiffel and stepped onto the other bank, I'd be in an unimaginable land and changed forever.

The thought was providential. The first person I saw on the other side of the bridge was José Tarres. All the radios were playing a haunting Spanish song I thought was a flamenco chart buster. (It was in fact an advertising jingle for Torres chocolate.) The music was full of the melancholy and desire that Spain conjures up, and I thought it announced the beginning of a huge, even deadly, passion. How right I was.

Figure 1.5. José Tarres, 1950s.

As time went on, I could not have known that my unsurpassable feelings for this man and the town echoed those of another woman half a century before. A Frenchwoman, her name was Maria Tourdes, and she had been the lover of Bérenger Saunière, priest of Rennes-le-Château. She was surely one reason for his frequent visits to Girona, although he had others, as well. I think Beryl and I, as we first walked on that superb evening through those ancient streets, sensed the imprint of some of this intrigue, although of course we could glean nothing of its outer, knowable form and could not have put any of it into words.

José Tarres—charismatic poet, defender of his Catalan province against the rape of Franco's dictatorship, keeper of the old customs that had survived through the centuries—celebrated his birthplace with fiestas, dances, and language, making Girona come alive and unlike any other area of Spain. That was the part I knew. He himself was unlike anyone I'd ever met. Over the last half-century, that hasn't changed.

Beryl and I stayed in his small, family-run hotel, the Residencia International, behind the Ramblas. It was the heart of the old quarter and the base for considerable resistance against Franco's regime operating from Madrid. The guests passing through the hotel from France to Barcelona or for holidays on the then-untouched Costa Brava were sophisticated and well-off. Others stayed permanently on full pension and had work or business in the area. Local artists also made the Residencia International their home. Dances were held every Saturday night on the ground floor to live music with a singer of tangos. The hotel, steeped in atmosphere, had the feeling of being cared for and shown to advantage, its identity provided by José, who always brought out the essence of wherever he was. Jean Cocteau stayed in the hotel while making a short film about a poet in love with a local girl whose lost shoe in his hands turned into a rose. Umberto Eco stayed in a room behind the bar.

I knew José completely and utterly from the first glance and felt that the whole of my life until then had been merely a time of waiting. Over the years I understood he loved his town more than he could ever love a woman or, indeed, himself. If necessary, he would have protected it with his life. Catalan history was spotted with charismatic figures who, bearing the secret of the stones of the city, cherished and defended it. They were a product of the soil and of the myths and religions that had flourished there.

After dinner at Chez Beatrice (a small dining room run by two sisters) for forty pesetas, José and I would walk through the alley seething with stray cats into the old quarter, never tiring of the city's strong skyline with the cathedral, the Church of St Felix, and, oddly, an ordinary house with a rather grand neo-Gothic tower that stuck up incongruously amidst the ancient buildings. José said it belonged to a Frenchwoman and would say no more.

Cocteau set his film around that house with the tower. The Frenchwoman, Maria Tourdes, had lived there apparently alone since the 1890s. The garden was overgrown and treacherous with holes and tricky weeds. The surrounding walls, some of them forming part of the ancient city wall, were broken, and steps up inside this formation provided another entrance to the house. A huge royal palm tree gave a wonderful, deep shade for which we were grateful, its branches seeming to cover the garden. The tower, a mere hundred years old, was attached to the side of the house facing the sacred mountain of the Catalans, Mt Canigou. The house, much older, was built behind the cathedral, from which the organ music filled the rooms, shook the windows. The garden, known as the Black Cemetery, had been a burial ground for priests.

'Oh, this house used to be splendid,' said José's uncle, the cathedral organist. 'Here there was a superb garden, the talk of Girona in its time. The house was done in the Parisian style. They had a carriage and entertainments. Debussy came here.' He pointed to a sign over the garden entrance: House of Canons. 'The clergy always lived here.

Figure 1.6. Patrice, cast by Cocteau as the girl the poet loved.

The Frenchwoman was the first secular individual to own this house.'

At the time of my visit, Cocteau was arranging ladders to get inside the tower. He cast me in the role of the girl the poet loved, but I didn't think he really wanted to make a film. He wanted to be inside that house. He mentioned the 'society', and it seemed José wanted him silent on that subject. After Cocteau's visits, I used to climb into what I thought was a deserted garden, and when José found out he said I must never go there. I asked why. 'Because it is cursed' is all he would say.

In that time in the fifties, José enhanced life; he drew people close and had the power to transform them. He certainly transformed me. But he would suddenly be gone for hours, days, without explanation. I learned from the hotel cook that he was involved in a political group. When the grey police, the dreaded ones in 'blind cars'—cars without lights—raided the Residencia International, I understood that José was more than simply a poet. He was a Catalan Nationalist supporting fighters against Franco, hiding them in the hotel and helping them escape across the Pyrénées into France. I believed that accounted for the air of undeniable mystery around him.

But the issue of José's mysteriousness was much more complex. It took my discovery of a nocturnal group that faded away in the light of day for me to begin to understand his true identity. The group—which turned out to be the members of the secret society—was made up of established professionals: a banker, lawyers, a priest, Masons, a French industrialist, the wealthy, and the scholarly. They met at various locations, including the house of the Frenchwoman. José was the society's custodian. Much later, I understood that the role he'd taken had been in existence for hundreds of years. José's family had held the position for the past century, and as a young man he had been sent for two years to Ripoll, a small town in the mountains, to prepare for the responsibility.

The role was documented in the Middle Ages, when secret practices that had been known in ancient Egypt were further experimented with in Girona—practices that transformed life as it was understood. Considered unsuitable for public knowledge, the material had always been withheld and kept in the care of a private society. (In Catalunia, the classification 'private' was preferred to 'secret'.) The material was handed down and the group renewed when necessary with chosen members, the intention being always to keep the content hidden and not to make personal use of its properties. The prevailing sense was that a time would come perhaps when the world would be a more optimistic and safe place for such knowledge to be revealed.

Old documents held by the families of former custodians show that there was early contact between Girona and Rennes-le-Château, especially in AD 500. At that time the Visigoths dominated the area around the Pyrénées in both southern France and northern Spain, with much exchange back and forth. They also sacked Rome, and legend has it that they brought back the minorah that the Romans in turn had taken from the second temple in Jerusalem, supposedly created by the Knights Templar, many of whom were Catalans. In any case, Rennes-le-Château was then a powerful and flourishing community; the Visigoths made it their capital in the sixth and seventh centuries, before it was later abandoned and eventually forgotten.

The contact between the French village and the Spanish city mainly concerned the ley-line connection marked by two identical towers, one in each place. According to the society's documents, this line had been known since the creation of Girona at least four thousand years ago. Over the course of history, the two towers have come and gone. That there had been early reconstructions the documents implied with a reference to the seventeenth-century Italian Cassini, royal astronomer to the French king. Apparently, the two towers had been destroyed at that time. Cassini, who was also a mapmaker, had the skill to map the energies in the area and so to identify the spots where each tower should be reconstructed. At one point, he disappeared for two years. The speculation was that he was in the French towns of Perillos and Perpignan. But nobody knew for sure, and nobody knew why. It is not known whether the two towers were reconstructed according to Cassini's findings, although it is understood that those findings were eventually consulted. Nor do we know whether a Girona tower existed again until the society rebuilt it in 1851, after which Saunière rebuilt the other at Rennes-le-Château in the 1890s.

In 1792, the priest of Rennes-le-Château was a man known as Abbé Antoine Bigou. Before fleeing the French Revolution, he hid four scrolls in the altar columns, two of them coded, it was said, for some future initiate to find and understand. He then crossed the border into Spain, and not much more was known of him. But in Girona the private society of that time certainly knew of him; they took care of him in a house adjoining a private church in the middle of a forest west of town.

The four scrolls that the Abbé Bigou hid were, as one might have guessed, the same ones Saunière found during his restoration of the church a century later. Once he had decoded the parchments, he lost no time following in Bigou's footsteps. At the time it was known that in the Middle Ages Jews had formed a nucleus in Girona and that there the great Cabalists had performed some of the mystical experiments never openly heard of before. Girona was the birthplace of the great Rabbinic scholar Nachmanides, who wrote *The Book of Splendour*. Cabalists Azriel, Ezra ben Solomon, Jacob ben Abraham, and others from Narbonne, including Isaac the Blind, practised the sacred ritual text in the twenty-four houses surrounding a courtyard in the shadow of the Girona cathedral. Present from the eleventh century until the Expulsion in 1492, this nucleus of devotees so preserved and advanced Cabalistic wisdom that the period was considered 'The Golden Age'. After the Expulsion, the area in Girona known as the Jewish Quarter was closed down and sealed by order of the Church. It seems that the Cabalistic material was again made available only in the nineteenth century.

So Girona wasn't just an atmospheric city with a splendid cathedral, Arab baths, a long eventful history, and an unspoiled, extensive old quarter. It had been the very centre of Cabala in the Middle Ages; and, when the priest from Rennes-le-Château slipped into the city in the 1890s, the Jewish presence was still remembered. But by the time I arrived, during Franco's regime in the fifties, the subject was closed over as completely as were the houses and courtyard in the old Jewish quarter, having survived only in local street stories.

The Jewish presence, however, was not really a secret. Instead, what was secret involved the transformation of time and space. It was a secret that had been in existence long before the Jews made a practice of Cabala, and much of it was said to have originated in pre-Christian times.

So when did that secret originate? And how? It took many years and visits to Girona before I discovered even the smallest trace of this mystery, and that discovery had a price; it changed my life. Quite early on, though, I did become aware of a link between the Catalan city and Rennes-le-Château.

It happened this way: José took me with him to meet the writer Salvador Espriu in the fishing village of Arenys de Mar. 'Was the affair Saunière settled?' the writer wanted to know. It seemed that Noel Corbu, the new purchaser of the priest's French property in Rennes-le-Château, wanted to turn it into a hotel; and, to attract business, he had gone to the press to draw attention to the deceased priest's wealth and possible hidden treasure. Treasure seekers were already arriving with shovels. 'Do something,' Espriu said, speaking as if he expected José could. But why should José, living in Girona, have any power over what happened at Rennes-le-Château?

Figure 1.7. Patrice and José on the cathedral doorway step.

The first time I had visited Girona, José had asked me to be his fiancée, or *novia*. I felt so high and so joyful that I ran into the street and danced along the dark alleyways in celebration. Soon, and without thought, I arrived at the house with the tower. I balanced carefree along the wall and swung on a branch of the palm tree. Looking in a window, I suddenly realized that the house was not empty. Behind the broken shutters a ceremony was taking place. I could partially see men in the flickering candlelight intoning off-key phrases relentlessly, and among them I was sure I saw Cocteau. On the long table was placed a substantial engraved piece of stone, a scroll unrolled, a metal bowl. The sound grew louder, as though forcing my head to expand, and soon became unbearable. Later, I remembered it as hypnotic, in a way that I could only run from. Did this group represent a part of the secret society?

Later, I discovered that other members of the group I had seen through the Frenchwoman's window included Lucia Stilman, who always dressed in gold and got away with it. Her beauty was quite unlike that of any other, and I was so fearful that she'd take José.

'Why do I wear gold?' she laughed, repeating my question to her. 'It goes with the territory. You could say that here in Girona, all that glitters *is* probably gold.'

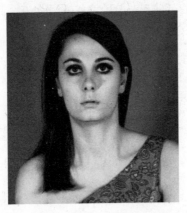

Figure 1.8. Lucia Stilman.

And then there was the priest and scholar Quim Carreras—elegant, erudite, deadly—who was probably also a member of the group. He was on his way to South America and wanted different outcomes for José, as I learned to my dismay only later.

The place to meet was at the Arc Bar. José's close friend Lluís, nicknamed 'the Wolf', who spoke several languages, opened the bar opposite the cathedral steps. It became the spot for the fabled, nocturnal life of the fifties and sixties, its jazz music sweetly reaching into the night. And at this bar, in the near darkness, sat the occasional celebrated writer or actor, quite at ease amongst the young unknown and those who wanted—as I did—adventure and freedom. The young unknowns may have been there because they had to have an acceptable reason to obtain a visa to cross the border, and many could not get out. Lluís himself, on the other hand, and unlike most, did travel abroad.

His Arc Bar was quite unlike anything else in Catalunya. Before opening it, he had worked at the cathedral as a guide for the infrequent foreign visitors at that time. The bar was his project and became his life. He loved jazz, the night hours, gossip, politics, irony, Gitane cigarettes. The atmosphere in that bar was not to be forgotten. Courtesy of Lluís, it had appeared as richly and simply as the deeper and explosive phenomenon that José held secret.

When I met Maria Tourdes, I thought she was the cleaning woman. I assumed she was too old to be the little-seen *femme fatale* they talked about in Lluís's bar. Once when I was walking along her wall, she asked me in to the kitchen for tea. I observed that the tower didn't match the house and asked why it was built.

'Why indeed?' she said. 'That's a question many would like answered.'

She was a woman of quality and substance and could so change that she was virtually transformed. When she put on her glamorous clothes and makeup, I didn't recognise her. I thought she was no older than fifty. It turned out she was nearly eighty. She was kind, and I felt during the short time I knew her that I could tell her about my love for José. During my last visit, she was moving photographs and trinkets into a case. I realised she was packing. Organ music from the cathedral drowned out every sound in her house. When it subsided, she said she was going to Paris. It seemed she had no choice.

Figure 1.9. Maria Tourdes, the Frenchwoman.

'You see, I once loved a priest,' she remarked cryptically.

Later, certain people warned me about Girona. Lucia told me to be careful. So did Carreras. They all warned me that nothing there was as it seemed. But I ran out of luck even before I encountered any danger. On short notice, I had to leave Girona. It seems that Franco's undercover assassins, the grey police, had infiltrated the city. José, being a Catalan Nationalist helping many to escape into France, was high on their wanted list. He insisted that it was safer if I left right away. Without him? I objected. We would meet in Paris, he promised. He gave me some money and helped me hitch a ride on a lorry headed north.

We were to meet in Paris two days later at the Gare d'Austerlitz. But José couldn't be there. I did try to wait for him, but the money ran out. Paris was a hard city in which to be broke and homeless. After having known José for less than a year, I restarted my life in London. But that's wrong: in essence, I'd known him all my life.

In the late 1950s, I began revisiting Girona whenever I could, and the affair with José did not diminish. I was now at the Royal Academy of Dramatic Art and working as an actress in London. My future seemed to be in the direction of Hollywood. José came twice to London and promised me that I belonged in Catalunya. During one visit to Girona in the mid-sixties, I discovered that the house with the tower had been pulled down stone by stone. Even the royal palm tree had been dragged up by its roots. I was shocked by the devastation. Maria had died in Paris in 1964. José was upset.

'They didn't find what they were looking for, poor thieves in the night,' he said. He was referring to a treasure that had already been gone for a long time. I asked who 'they' were. He stood by the angry hole the tree had left and didn't answer, swearing only, 'I will look after this garden. They won't touch it again.'

'They?'

'I'll go to Quillan. That's where she came from. I'll make sure there is nothing else for anyone to get.'

Quillan was near Rennes-le-Château, and I went there with José and a doctor who was a member of the society. They searched a house that Maria Tourdes had stayed in, and then we drove up the hill to Rennes-le-Château. In the church there, I had an experience that I could not dismiss as a dream, a hallucination, or simply the way the light fell. It would remain with me for the rest of my life. I could only say it was beyond anything that belonged in this world. Was the figure I saw a ghost? It did not wish me well. His eyes, like swords, swung into mine, filled with a power built up from hundreds of years of unimaginable existence.

The experience was so potent that I almost missed seeing the tower Saunière had built. But of course, I'd already seen its almost identical twin in Maria's garden.

I was later to learn of many surprises that rivalled the one I had seen that day in the church. Saunière, for instance, had come to Maria's garden in Girona to get the exact measurements of her tower. He'd written asking her and José's uncle for the architect's plans. It was essential to him that the tower in his parish was erected; there had to be two towers, one north at Rennes-le-Château and one south at Girona, situated on their common ley line and equidistant from Mt Canigou. The documents held by the society mentioned this requirement frequently. But why?

The walls of Girona were so substantial and uncompromising that they suggested nothing could be behind them, so it was with some amazement that in the 1970s José opened up an eighth-century wall and discovered behind it the medieval Jewish site that had been Nachmanides's palace and synagogue. In the Middle Ages, the site had been famous as a centre of learning excelling in jewellery, medicine, scholarship, and, among other things, Cabalistic studies. José found it remaining much as it had been when the Jews had been forced to abandon it during the the Spanish Inquisition in 1492. Previously a wasteland for stray dogs, so hidden no one had even guessed its existence, the site became an important discovery worldwide. José restored it as a shrine to entice the Jews to return to Catalunya—once known as the 'Mother of Israel'.

Lucia said, 'Of course he didn't just happen to knock through a wall. Ever since we were children, he had always known the place was there.'

In the 1970s and '80s, the restored site, having become a museum, attracted thousands of visitors. José set it up, and then one day he left it, simply moving on from his years

Figure 1.10. The courtyard of the Jewish Centre, Isaac el Cec, restored by José, now the Museu d'Història dels Jueus a Catalunya.

of involvement. Whatever he had sought from it, he had found.

In 1976, opposite the Frenchwoman's garden, a vision said to be the Magdalene was witnessed by many people of Girona. In scores they rushed to the hill just a few yards from what was still the garden's entrance. The appearance could not be explained, but the observers said they felt a sense of calm, of healing. But in spite of all the witnesses, the Church and the establishment did not support the validity of this appearance and said it must simply be forgotten. Only the Church alone could authenticate a vision or miracle. Even the press didn't mention it. The vision of the Magdalene in the garden did, though, have an effect in the secret society. What had really occurred that night? What had brought forth this vision? It took some years for me to find out.

In 2003, after José Tarres had a heart attack, a decision had to be made as to the society's future. A senior member, a woman, was terminally ill. Others, who were old and uncertain about into whose hands the guarded material would fall, wanted it disposed of, finally. The matter of the vision in 1976 should have been warning enough, they argued. As I then learned, the appearance of the Magdalene had been called forth by a ritual held by initiates for society members. The initiates considered the vision successful in so far as a presence known as "The Lady with the Cup" had appeared splendidly. The problem was, though, that it had not appeared in the specific area they'd intended; indeed, they had had no control over where the presence manifested. After this experiment, the rituals were stopped.

The society was further divided by its more modern-thinking members. Lucia Stilman, for one, believed that secrets were elitist and gave their holders too much power; she wanted the truth made public. Some of Saunière's money had passed to her through Maria, and since Lucia had also inherited from her father, she was rich enough to command being heard. Quim Carreras's view, in contrast, was that all evidence of the society, dating back to a timeless past, should be given to the Vatican. José Tarres, the custodian, wanted some aspects of the society made public. Its care had mostly been in the hands of his relatives, who were canons of the cathedral.

All of these eventualities are part of the history that Beryl and I innocently stumbled upon decades ago and that has continued to hold me in its thrall ever since. As it turned out, José and I did not marry; perhaps marriage, in its everyday habits, would have killed the ecstatic resonance between us, and that was one death I could not allow. José eventually married a Breton sculptress and rarely left Catalunia. They had one son. I myself was twice married, had two sons, and had followed my career in the United States and Europe. But work kept bringing me back to Girona, including a film of one of my books, the performance of a play, and presentations of my books based in the Catalan town. José and I didn't see each other often, but when we did meet, it felt as though we'd never been apart.

Figure 1.11. Patrice and José, during the restoration of the Jewish Centre.

So what was the secret of the Cabalistic mysteries guarded so well by the ancient stones of Girona? As I have said, it had to do with transformation.

In 2003, José introduced me to a new part of the society's activity. 'You have to do what initiates have done in every century,' José said. 'You have to make the journey. It is the journey that matters, not the destination.'

'Will it have an effect on me?'

'Oh, beyond doubt.' And he laughed, dryly, as he used to when I first met him across the river.

'Remember what Maria told you. And remember the two towers.'

What journey, where? He must have seen me hesitate. I'd start asking questions next. He avoided any of that.

'Make the journey,' he simply repeated.

Figure 2.1. The barraca door.

CHAPTER 2

When José first mentioned the journey in 2003, I thought he meant something that led to a state of realisation. Other people thought other things. We were all wrong. The journey led to the unexpected and unbelievable, beyond the laws of this universe as it is normally understood. Not surprisingly, the truth and nature of the journey were kept hidden. Society members through the ages had defended the material with their lives.

Shortly after José had raised the subject, I spoke with the local hotel owner, Señor Mons, who said that one began the journey at the barraca—a small stone hut on a stretch of land José had inherited that happened to adjoin the property of the Frenchwoman. Señor Mons hadn't been on the journey himself but had heard it wasn't exactly a tourist excursion. He said the people who came back from it were changed by the experience. I asked if it was religious.

'Not to do with the Church. You can be sure of that.'

'Black magic?'

No, he didn't think the kind of people who were purported to be involved would be associated with magic. So who were they? People of standing? Señor Mons didn't know, at least when I asked. When he spoke in terms of 'the ones who came back', I asked what had happened to the others. His answer wasn't satisfactory.

'Was it like the pilgrimage to Santiago?'

'No, nothing like that,' he replied in a tone that dismissed the subject. Then he introduced a few ironic Catalan jokes to get my mind off what he clearly thought it shouldn't be on anyway.

The Catalans were not keen on the occult or mysticism in general. Even their visions had to be confirmed by the Church; otherwise, those who witnessed them were considered lunatics or drunks. The Church approved only of visions associated with the local stones or the appearance of water, as in the vision at Lourdes. The favourite condoned myth was that of St Narcis calling up swarms of flies to drive back the French in the seventeenth century.

The Catalans for centuries had considered themselves down-to-earth and materialistic—people who dealt with the land, food, money, and survival. Until Franco's death in 1975, they were dominated by the Church, the military, the police, the bureaucracy. They acquired property if they could, and land. They were not like the French, who had a long history, style, and culture, as well as an enviable aristocracy. Catalans had always felt inferior to the French, and they are still dealing with the complex even now. The Catalan rich—and there were always rich ones, whatever the circumstances—amassed land and the people on it, huge houses in the country, and palaces in the cities. These land owners were minor aristocrats, but, as the historian Lluís Maria de Puig has said, 'They were not exciting and grand like the European aristocracy farther north, and they knew it.' Nor were these minor aristocrats any more interested in the occult than were the ordinary citizens.

So, apropos the journey of which José spoke, the Catalans would not have believed in the subject matter the private society guarded, in any case. They did not make journeys except to work, to church, or to the bank or bar.

Naris, who had built up a good business exporting fruit, understood that Señor Mons was a member of the Freemasons and had received his information about the journey from them. After Señor Mons's sudden death in 2004, his widow said he'd actually only known of one person who had made the journey; it was from that man that he had heard of others and their experiences. The idea had interested Señor Mons for a while, but it had not been for him, and his widow certainly didn't want to talk about it. It was all in the past and didn't happen anymore.

While doing research for my book *City of Secrets*, I found records of journeys made in the 1890s. They hadn't happened often and were usually for the purpose of a ritual experience or for the initiation of a new member of the society. It was clear that the French priest had been on such a journey.

Why did the experience begin at the barraca—the hut on the land José owned—and how many sites on the journey were there? Where was the destination? After a while, I understood that it didn't have to do with 'where' but with 'what'. I was told not to involve myself in the process but to stick to writing my book; that alone presented enough obstacles. But I could not heed this advice and kept trying to find out more about the journey. Apparently it followed an unchangeable route and entailed, along the way, a great deal of physical and spiritual preparation.

The barraca had hardly changed over the centuries. A tough little building, it stood alone with a solid roof, well-crafted chimney, and two friendly windows. Thick trees kept it private. Many things over the years had been

Figure 2.2. Roger Mathieu, the tower at Girona in the background.

hidden in this one-room stone hut, including people. By some lights it belonged in a fairytale. The land was variously used for keeping small animals and growing vegetables, and José had cultivated the garden without losing its wildness. For a while it was a place for celebrations, with lights in the trees, dancing to live music well into the night, and lamb and sausages cooking on the wood fire. But essentially it was a hidden place on the slope amongst the trees at the junction of two tracks. Few people even knew it was there. Neighbours passed without seeing it. There was no electricity or running water, the latter having to be carried up from the fountain on the rough path to the village San Daniel.

But even though the barraca was relatively unknown, it was not without historical importance. It had been one of the original outposts of the city, and Charlemagne had rested there in AD 785 on his stealthy journey into Girona. The legend stated that he'd had a strange experience while at the barraca and had later placed a sundial on the grounds. In the 1960s, the sundial was still there and had odd markings that seemed to change with the light.

The first track leading to the barraca reached up from behind the cathedral, passing the Frenchwoman's garden to the broken Torre Gironella—another legendary landmark, especially during the nineteenth-century Napoleonic war. The other track, steep with sliding stones, passed the fountain to the agricultural neighbourhood known as San Daniel. It was by this approach that Charlemagne had marched into Girona, then under Moorish invasion. The Moors hadn't expected this cunning French attack and so were defeated within days.

The barraca was always kept swept and clean with a stone floor, table, a bed, a stove. José had inherited it from his uncle, and it pleased him more than any other place except the Frenchwoman's garden. He would stay there in silence, giving himself time to write, to reflect.

The barraca didn't change. It was said a ritual had been performed in the eighteenth century to keep the place safe and secret. The land could not be sold or exchanged but had to be handed down through the family or from one member of the society to another. It was believed that to try and make a profit on the property would bring bad luck. In 1870, the hut had been designated as a place to sit in silence, reflect, and prepare for the journey. A list of questions in French was kept beneath the stone floor:

'Am I strong enough to be a member of the society? Am I able to fast? To be alone? To cut from those I love and need? To keep the secret?'

In the fifties, José's nearest neighbour was still Maria Tourdes, but from the barraca he could see only the tower of her house. Once when he and I were at the barraca together, I commented that the tower was a strange addition, neo-Gothic, a young intruder in the midst of such a feast of history. José made no response then, but later I discovered the tower's purpose, and it certainly didn't have anything to do with grandiosity on the part of the house owners.

It was also in the barraca that José would reveal the story of Maria Tourdes and Bérenger Saunière to me. One day in the mid-nineties, I had just come from a visit to Rennes-le-Château and was showing my literary agent and his wife the French garden. They had read my books on Girona and were keen to see the city. The heat was suddenly terrible, and I took them towards the shade of the cathedral. I would not have seen José at all if a wind from the south—always lucky for me—hadn't started up and made me turn to enjoy the sweetness, and there in the distance was a figure I'd know anywhere walking along the path leading to the barraca. He was carrying a large string bag of oranges and a bottle of water from the fountain. I called his name and in spite of the heat hurried toward him.

'I've been to Rennes-le-Château,' I said.

'But Rennes-le-Château is here. You'll find nothing there.' The kiss he gave me was polite and formal, but his eyes were fixed on mine in a way I will remember until death.

My agent and his wife were quite impressed by this meeting and its sheer improbability. Just minutes before we started our walk, Lluís of the Arc Bar had told us that José was out of town with his wife.

'Oh, José's always the first person I see,' I said, nonchalantly enough, now that I knew the love between us was still in place. Suddenly, I wasn't the same person the agent and his wife had met an hour ago. Octaves of high happiness had made me unrecognisable.

'We're on a magnetic path, aren't we?' José said offhandedly, trying to explain the surprise, the excitement, away.

The barraca was cooled by the abundance of trees growing densely together, and gratefully we sat in their shade and drank fountain water. José showed us Charlemagne's sundial. 'It's made in the French way. When he wanted privacy, Charlemagne used to sit here in the cool evening and listen to the music from the cathedral, which was smaller in those days.'

The next story just came out of José without his customary caution. Was it the surprise of our meeting that made him so free with the facts?

'Of course,' he went on, 'Rennes-le-Château is here. That's why the priest came here. Girona always held the secret. A place like this, with all its resonance, would of course have something as powerful as that.'

'What secret?' my agent asked.

'The one they keep trying to find across the border in France.'

'So the priest came here?' I asked. It was the first I'd heard about it. Bestselling books had been written on the subject, yet José had not ever said one word about it to me, until now.

As José then explained, sometime in 1892 Saunière had brought Maria from Quillan to Girona as a very young woman, still in her teens. His purpose was to install her in the house he had bought here to be a front for him. To begin with she had stayed out of sight. Her supposed gardener, Guillem, was in fact her chaperone. Saunière visited frequently in the late 1890s and kept material in Maria's house that would no longer be safe in Rennes-le-Château because his well-known wealth made his parish the subject of too much curiosity. He also entertained guests of importance at Maria's for the same reason.

'So yes,' José concluded, 'Saunière came to Girona to see the Frenchwoman. It is well known here. My cousin Geli, the organist of the cathedral, knew all about it and looked after her. He did not know the priest, but my grandfather did. In truth, the French priest came here to get that which was never in Rennes-le-Château.'

'But what about the parchments, the ones that were found in his church?' my agent pounced, having turned from a tourist to a tiger. He knew the smell of 'bestseller'.

'They contained coded instructions indicating the location of the material, but it wasn't in France.'

'*Material?*' We all had a turn at that one.

'Documents. The ritual. The . . .' He stopped and asked if anyone wanted an orange. Nobody wanted anything except for him to keep talking. 'It's unlikely that the parchments today are the originals. They would have been copied and changed several times since 1891. Saunière would have seen to that.'

'Who put them in the church if the secret isn't there?' my agent asked.

'Abbé Bigou. He was the priest of Rennes-le-Château in the eighteenth century and got out of France before the Revolution. He had certain information that linked Rennes-le-Château with Girona.'

'Where did he go?' My agent, soft and persuasive, moved closer to his prey. Before the sun went down, José could get a glowing book deal.

'Here. He came here and to a village nearby. And he had to get out certain information that had been left in the French church. It was 1792.'

José had now also completely changed, just as I had done upon seeing him on the path. I would have said the change had to do with his pride in claiming the importance of his city.

'Any documentary evidence?' my agent asked, carefully.

'A correspondence exists between Saunière and Maria Tourdes.' And then José would say no more.

How did Saunière get the secret encoded in the parchments? And what was it? (I understood he'd taken the scrolls to St-Sulpice in Paris to have them decoded. People have puzzled over them ever since.) My agent asked the questions and we all wanted the answers, but all we got was another orange each and a sightseeing tour through the old part of the city. And that was that.

Later, I realised that José had just been throwing us a small, unimportant part of the truth. Although the mystery of the French priest had filled books and documentaries for decades, it was nonetheless at the periphery of the *real* mystery.

The next time I saw José, I asked him why, when he had known of this material all along, he hadn't told me until now.

In typical fashion, he would say only, 'I don't think it's a subject for discussion.'

Was that his way of saying he didn't trust me?

It took a few more years, until I was researching *City of Secrets* in 2004, before I understood more about the journey. Why was the barraca such an important place? Why start the journey there? José said it had always been a site of reflection and enquiry, so what better place to begin?

And things could be well hidden there. In the 1790s, when Bigou came to Girona, a hiding place had to be found for the documents and artefacts he carried. The society members in disagreement spent many stressed weeks seeking the right place.

'The solution was there under their noses,' José exclaimed. 'The barraca was warm and waterproof, and safe from movements of the earth, sudden floods, or robbers. Some members of the church, aware of Bigou's presence in the city, compromised his safety. For days afterward, he was kept in the barraca before being moved to a house adjoining a private church in a forest in Palera outside of the town Besalú, west of Girona.'

I asked if Maria Tourdes visited the barraca.

'Only to hide with Saunière when Roger Mathieu arrived unexpectedly.'

I asked who he was.

'Her husband.'

It was the first I'd heard of Mathieu. I asked why Maria married him if she was in love with the French priest.

'Perhaps she saw that there was no future with that particular person.'

Roger Mathieu was a silent participant in the story, and I got little information about him from José or anyone else. What I do know is that, at some unknown date towards the end of Saunière's visits, Mathieu, described as a man of letters who travelled in Europe, made Maria's acquaintance. They married sometime before the onset of World War I. Mathieu had a house north of Girona in Lansa, near the French border, but the couple stayed mostly at the house in Girona, with him travelling frequently. He was the worst choice Maria could have made according to José's relatives, including those in the Church who got to know him. Friends of Maria, especially Lucia's mother, said the same; and Maria's letters to Pepita, presumably another friend, show that she was not happy.

Secretly, Mathieu worked for the Vatican, and his intention was to trap Saunière by proving the source of his wealth and the extent and nature of his activities. The common assumption in Girona was that Saunière's occupation had little to do with the Catholic Church. Society members discussed the situation, and José's uncle, the cathedral organist, observed that the French priest had been 'too wily' to be caught and knew how to deal with his enemies.

It would seem that Saunière still visited Girona, in spite of Mathieu's presence. Maria's friends said the three-way relationship was a source of consternation to her. Mathieu was considerably older than Maria; when he died in 1940, the Vatican gave him a burial of honor. After the funeral, a letter from Maria's closest friend Gloria again confirmed that the marriage had not been happy.

José kept an envelope of Maria's letters to Saunière and of those from him to her. Saunière's letters were often matter-of-fact, concerning his arrival in Girona and entry by the city wall, the plants he was bringing, the architectural plans he wanted of his tower, and proposed visits to Girona by his brother Alfred. In 1964, when an unnamed contingent, whom I later understood was deadly, pulled Maria's house and the tower down stone by stone and dug the palm tree up by its roots, José thought it prudent to hide any information that might be of interest in the barraca.

When I photographed this small hut for my book *Happy Hour*, I had no idea it played such an important part in the Girona story. On José's table in the hut, letters were lying quite casually as he sorted through them determining what I could use. The paper looked well preserved and of good quality, the writing stylish. Maria had written several to the priest about the house; he must have returned them to

Girona with other papers at the end of his visits around 1910.

'Why does she ask him how he wants things arranged? It's her house,' I asked José.

'Perhaps she thought she should. He paid for it.'

José went on to explain how Saunière had set her up in the house sometime at the end of the 1890s. She had been the first secular person to own it. Before then, it had always belonged to the canons of the Church, and a sign over the entrance reading 'House of Canons' was still there. José had the deeds of the house showing that a lawyer named Saguer had put the deal in his name since Maria had been too young—probably just seventeen at the time—and Saunière could not have his name appear anywhere on any document. José's grandfather had looked after both Saunière and Maria, taking care of their practical require-ments in this foreign Catalan province. On other occasions, José's cousin Geli told me of Maria's need of company, and the butcher's daughter spoke of having done errands and tasks for her.

Among those initiates to the secret society who had made the journey that began at the barraca was the late nine-teenth-century Catalan priest and poet Jacint Verdaguer. By his poetry, Verdaguer brought back Catalunya's pride in itself, uplifting the mere labour of those working the land into an activity to be extolled. This vision was the basis of his depiction of Catalunya and influenced other artists and writers of that time, especially the group known as the Revista of Girona, which wanted a new province separate from the overbearing dictates of Spain. Verdaguer brought back the Catalan language into a Catalunya where at the time Castilian had been the official tongue.

In the documents, I saw references to Verdaguer's accounts of the journey as 'Walking with the Great Bear' and 'Treading the Seven Stars'. It is not clear who first referred to the Great Bear, but later I understood from the Cabalists that its inclusion was as old as the material itself. And in every case, the first step of this passage into unknown dimensions had been in a humble hut hidden on a slope among the trees at the edge of an ancient town.

So the stone hut still had an importance, even as in the time of Charlemagne. In the journey directions, it is described as 'the hidden'. A Cabalist later confirmed that it was on an advantageous ley line. Although it was a place of mystery and enquiry, no one asked questions about it. José's friends saw it as the ideal fiesta location, with lights strung through the trees. I myself remembered it as a place of love and ecstatic promises. José and I had our secrets, even as Saunière and Maria once had theirs. But I had no idea just how many others had secrets beyond the barraca's low door, or what those secrets were. In 1964, when Salvador Dali talked about an initiation in the rustic hut, was he referring to the barraca?

Figure 3.1. The cathedral and the Girona
tower, rebuilt by the society in 1851.

CHAPTER 3

The two documents in the society's care detailing the journey were originally in Catalan. They were translated into French in the 1950s so that new society members from outside the province could read and understand them. The first document recorded the process by which, in the 1890s, the then-custodian of the private society, Mossen Avila, guided Saunière through the journey to 'the invisible'. Eleven places were mentioned. The journey seemed to be broken into two parts, and only segments of the document were available. Throughout the account, a previous journey was mentioned—that of a law student from Paris who in a rare bookshop had discovered details of 'transformation' taking place in 'Girona, northeastern Spain'. The student gave up what could have been a lucrative profession and went to the town in 1820. To find the journey's secret, he set out by foot and then horseback to follow the path of 'walking the bear'. (Again this reference to the bear; I vaguely understood that it had to do with the constellation of the Great Bear or Ursa Major, which contains the smaller constellation known as the Big Dipper.) The student's expedition had taken several weeks.

The first document further stated that the journey was known in the fourteenth century, when the alchemist Nicolas Flamel had also come from Paris to seek from Jewish scholars the secret he had found in an 'archive'. He later returned from Girona and became an extremely wealthy man.

The eleven places that made up the journey were predominantly Catalan and were situated on both the French and Spanish sides of the border. I asked José if I should follow the same instructions others had used.

'You should,' he said. 'If you want the experience of true change, you have to do the traditional journey.'

'But they're unrecognisable now, those places.'

'You have to follow the suggestions. And then you would surmount the modern changes that at first seem to have irrevocably altered the place.'

'Would it work?'

'It did in the fifties. Places change mostly on the surface. Their energies don't.'

'How do you know?'

'I did the journey.'

'I wish I'd done it with you.'

He shrugged, as he often did when uncertain. 'You need a good person to guide you. First, you have to decide if you want to do it.'

I said I did. I sensed the journey was something out of the ordinary that I certainly hadn't found in my research for *City of Secrets*. Taking it would be a continuation of that work. José said he would find somebody to escort me. It sounded simple enough. He said he was suggesting it because I had already touched on much of the material in my writing and was interested in other dimensions. I was also now mature enough.

Mature enough? Did he mean old? This conversation took place in 2004, decades after I had first met him.

Two days later I was ready. The start was the barraca—
'the hidden', 'the place of Reflection and Enquiry'. I sat
alone at the table writing, as José had asked me to provide
my guide with a brief note about myself as an introduction. The door was open, and in the garden I could see
the sundial inscribed by Charlemagne. In the grey light it
seemed to leave the secrecy of the trees and come forward,
its markings dark brown and curly as though the stone suffered a disease. I had heard that barren women sat against
it and became fertile.

I was waiting for the person to arrive who would accompany me; José had said earlier it would be at noon. Nobody
came. Newly built houses farther down the track to San
Daniel were occupied, and I could hear domestic shouts as
though neighbours were quarrelling bitterly. The Spanish
always sounded dramatic. They were probably discussing the price of sausages. A woman struggled with heavy
shopping bags to the first house without even looking my
way. Was the barraca invisible? I drank a little hesitantly
from the bottle of fountain water José had placed on the
table and tried to decide whether I should go and eat. I left
a note and started along the track to the cathedral. What
if the person showed up and wouldn't wait? I went back
to the barraca, ate two apples, and tried to translate documents from a worn leather case under the bed.

Saunière's name was mentioned. There were diagrams
and groups of numbers that always added up to 360. At
four o'clock, I left another note and hurried to the nearest restaurant in the Calle Forsa. By five o'clock I was
back in the stone hut. No one had come. I tried to be calm,
to breathe deeply, to get a sense of this journey. I drank
the last of the fountain water. Then, agitated, I started to
walk up and down the track. Did José have no sense of
time? I knew the answer. The sky darkened; a storm was

approaching. This was not going to work. I sat on the bed and closed the door.

Two more hours passed. Then a woman pushed her way through the trees, her feet crunching the bracken and small stones. She was naturally blond, her hair streaked even lighter by the sun, her skin radiant from life in the fresh air. At first she seemed youthful. Then I saw her face. She must have been at least sixty-five. She was robust and well built. I asked what she wanted and said that José was not there. The cathedral clock struck seven.

She waited until the last chime. 'Seven. That is a very special number.' She spoke English with a mid-European accent. 'You will understand seven. So let's start.' She put down her rucksack.

'Where is the guide? He isn't here.'

'But I am here.' She laughed and stepped into the barraca as though it was familiar. She swept the papers on the table to one side and sat down with a surety that made my heart sink disagreeably.

'But José said you'd come at noon.'

'But it's seven. Do you know the meaning of the number seven?'

I didn't answer.

'It's the sacred number of the peak of Canigou. And of this city. You will learn about the number seven.'

I said I'd been waiting for a guide since noon.

'You should never wait.'

Did I want this person as my guide?

'Let's see if I will take you,' she said, suddenly.

Was she a mind reader? I'd expected an attractive, young, charismatic man with the same qualities as José and the poet Verdaguer. I hoped I was concealing my disappointment.

'Let's see what you've experienced between noon and seven. Tell me how you feel about waiting.'

44

I made it clear that I didn't like it and would waste no more time.

'What does José's idea of "noon" mean to you?'

So she did know him. His lack of sense of time was legendary. She finally persuaded me to revisit the ambivalence, exasperation, anger, indecision. She summed it up as 'helplessness'.

'It's useful to recognise how helplessness manifests in you. You'll get some experience of it on this journey. But you did look after yourself. You went to eat. You looked through some of the material.' She'd noticed the open document case. She looked swiftly at my personal resume. 'But you haven't put down "Expectation" here. You expected me at noon. Don't expect. An expectation is resentment in the making. I think to be open to surprises would be wiser.'

She lingered over her vowel sounds as though she loved them, her voice full of cadences and drama. I decided she had an Austrian accent. She could have been a theatre director making each point clear through her skill with sound. I asked who she was. Her name was Liliane. She'd studied cabala and many other subjects, sometimes with Ingrid, the German Cabalist who'd helped me with my research for *City of Secrets*.

'So you know José?' I asked.

'Well, of course, my friend. How else would I know where to find you?'

Naturally, José wouldn't send a charismatic man. Jealousy had made him pick out this woman. I felt better immediately. Liliane walked to the edge of the land on which the barraca sat and pointed to Mt Canigou. 'What do you think of that?'

'It's the sacred mountain of the Catalans.'

'What else?'

'I used to live in the foothills on the French side and saw it in all its moods.'

But that wasn't what she was interested in.

'It is diagonally opposite the wall of the Frenchwoman's garden, where the tower used to be,' I tried again.

'You should never take anything for granted. Not on this journey.'

'So what should I do?'

'Question it.'

It was getting late. Should I go back to my hotel room? I did. I stayed in the Hotel Cuidad by the river. I suspected Liliane would have preferred me to spend the night alone in the barraca without food or running water, or lights, or clean sheets, or sanitary arrangements. Not to mention that the heat would have required opening the windows, thus allowing animal or human prowlers to climb in and join me without problem. I was filled with fears and had never been so appreciative of an ordinary hotel room with lights that switched on, a lavatory, a running bath, bottled water. I was sure Liliane disapproved of the hotel and would much rather have had me out of it as part of my evolvement.

She'd showed me documents relating to José's journey in the fifties—how he'd spent days and nights alone in the barraca as well as how that preparation had helped him in the days that followed. She'd asked me to consider what the term *to reflect* meant. She'd asked for concentration on the tower. I had learned something about it during the research for *City of Secrets*.

The tower had been built in 1851 by the private society using a Señor Massaguer as the cover purchaser. The purchase documents that later disappeared from the archives stated that Massaguer had paid for it 'out of his own pocket', as though this practice was unusual. As I've said,

Saunière had come to Girona to copy the tower and had written to Maria Tourdes and José's uncle to acquire the architect's design. In 1903, Saunière reproduced the Girona Magdala Tower in Rennes-le-Château.

The next morning, after a delicious breakfast in the hotel, I tried to reach José to ask him about my guide—if she was indeed the guide. For my meeting with her at the barraca I arrived late, expecting that she would be offended as I had been the day before; but she was sitting calmly at the table looking at a sheet of paper. I watched as she drew a triangle with its top lopped off. The top was suspended above with a measured space between the two shapes. In the centre of the lower, larger shape, she wrote the number 49; in the higher, smaller shape, the number 1. She worked with an exactness, a certainty, as though the drawing was something she understood, controlled, and enjoyed.

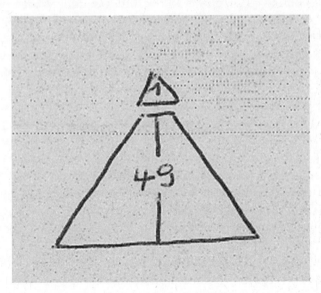

Figure 3.2. Pyramid with detached capstone.

'So what do you see?' she asked.

'Placed together they would form a perfect triangle.'

'This relates to the Great Pyramid of Khufu, of which you will have heard.'

I understood that the pyramid's construction was a continuing mystery. I asked where she came from and what she normally did.

'Research. It doesn't matter where I'm from.' And that was all I was going to get to know.

'So what do you see?' she repeated. She didn't wait for me to answer. 'The top of the Great Pyramid is missing. That's the part with the number 1, the missing part that extends into the next world. When it descends from heaven, then the pyramid is complete. Its descent is celestial. Man cannot bring down this missing part and so make $49 + 1 = 50$. It descends by divine grace. Girona itself could be a completed pyramid. You will find that for yourself.'

'So what have you discovered about Reflection?' She continued working on the beheaded triangle.

I said I'd gone so far with my research into the private society but that there was much more information I'd like to . . . I hesitated over the next word and nearly said 'claim' but changed it to 'experience'.

'That is an intention. Not a reflection. Have you heard of magic squares?'

I had not.

'There are several kinds. For example, there is one for the moon and another for Mercury. And Saturn. This particular journey fits into the Venus Magic Square. We deal with numbers. Have you heard of Pythagoras?'

I had.

She explained that the magic square was a copy of a celestial pattern currently being studied by quantum physicists. I'd met one or two after the publication of *City of*

Secrets who were working on magic squares and sacred numbers in a way I could not begin to understand. They had wanted to check out my information on the two towers. Apparently, scientists were also researching the energies at Mt Canigou, although they preferred to remain anonymous as their interest could damage their credibility among their mainstream colleagues.

'A number to remember is 360,' Liliane pronounced. 'We will come back to that on occasion.'

She wrote more numbers at the side of the separated pyramid: '49 + 1 = 50 Sirius.' Then she added the word *Teba*, preceded by a wavy sign. I thought Sirius was a solar system that had given us our intelligence. About Teba I knew nothing. My ignorance did not surprise her.

'*Teba* is the name in the Cabala for the Ark of Noah,' she said. Then she went on, 'The journey begins in Girona. It is a Venus journey, which is fortunate, the energy of Venus being lucky for you.'

She added that here in the barraca I would do exactly as the travellers before me had done. I should prepare for the journey as they had, making use of the wisdom recorded in the documents. First, I should list the qualities I must seek and practise during this preparation.

I hoped preparation didn't include spending the night alone in the hut. I had a new consideration: rodents. I asked how long this preparation would take. She did not answer directly, but said we would follow the path of four documented journeys that started exactly where I was standing.

'*El pozo*,' she said, pointing to a well I had never noticed. Covered with a rusty grille disguised by shrubs, it was deep with no sign of a bottom. I dropped a coin through the metal bars and counted to five before hearing a distant splash.

The four documented journeys that mine was to follow had been made by men, each in the care of a guide. José had travelled with his master from Ripoll in 1955. Saunière, with the priest from St Feliu. The Catalan poet Verdaguer had made the journey with his patron, the Count Comillas, sometime in the 1880s. Comillas was an extremely wealthy man owning a shipping company, 'The Transatlantic'. He took the poet with him as the family priest on his world-wide travels. Finally, the French law student had started his journey in 1825 under the guidance of a rich and vener-able Mason. We would make use of all their experiences.

Liliane told me the journey had a pattern that I would discover as I followed it. I asked if it was from the Cabala. She said it was from another time and space altogether. Again, I asked who she was.

'A traveller like you,' she laughed. She had a good laugh. She gave me some sheets of paper and a pen. 'This is the first stage. The Enquiry. So write the qualities you must seek and practise.'

When I'd made my list, probably too quickly, she asked what I'd discovered about the towers. 'And remember that the peak of Canigou is on the same meridian as St-Sulpice,' she said. 'So there is another part of the pattern: Girona, Canigou, St-Sulpice. Remember the name St Sulpicio.'

I remembered that Saunière had gone with the newly discovered scrolls to St-Sulpice. I, too, had gone there to visit one of the priests who knew of the two towers and of how 'the South always had to disappear'. In the *City of Secrets*, I described the German Cabalist Ingrid telling me of how the North and South have to be integrated, and then the south point always disappears, with the North remain-ing. When I'd asked why, she replied, 'because the South had done its work' (meaning its journey). In Egyptian sym-bolism, the North is Aset, the Serpent, Isis, and the South is Nephthys, the Vine. That Saunière knew of the subject led me to suspect that he had a connection with the Girona secret society.

I plied Liliane with questions, needing facts: Given that Saunière had gone to St-Sulpice, was Paris part of the journey? How long would it take? 'Let's see how you get on at this stage. Forget Paris,' she answered. She read my list of qualities to seek and work on. 'You've left out serenity.'

'It hadn't occurred to me.'

'It will.'

She didn't comment on the ones I'd not left out. We sat for a while not speaking. If José had taken this journey, then I would also do it, and fully. If it would be life-changing, thrilling, then I'd go for it. I realised my aims might seem a little cheap to Liliane and hoped we wouldn't have to examine them.

'Expectations won't save you,' she said quietly.

I asked what she meant. The bird-filled trees were so loud I could hardly hear her.

'You run on expectations. For instance, you expected I would be impatient because you arrived an hour late. Where does that come from? Yourself? The way others have behaved to you? You can't fit that onto me. You don't know me.'

I could only agree.

'Expectations will have to go. Try being in the moment, each moment. Change your thinking.'

'How?'

'Breathing. Chanting. Contemplation.' She told me how to practise the exercises. 'And now for the first step: Enquiry. Make the enquiries. Let's start with what you know about the two towers.'

I understood from the Cabalist Ingrid, who had much original knowledge on the Rennes-le-Château enigma, that the two towers were the point of the story, creating as they did mathematically a golden mean with Mt Canigou. The energy that traversed from one to the other marked the centre point.

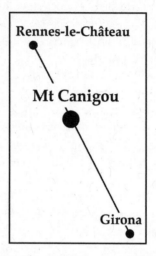

Figure 3.3 The two towers mark the centre.

She stopped me. 'What is there? At Mt Canigou?'

'I have been told it is the site of an awesome and un-explained occurrence that has been known of since antiquity.'

'And before,' she concluded, enigmatically.

She asked about Saunière, and I said he was acting under orders, apparently from the Habsburg family. She asked what he had been doing.

'No one understood why Saunière built his tower. What purpose did it serve? They put it down to grandiosity. I put it down to having to use up some of his fortune. He didn't know what to do with all that money. But then I did my research. It seems that nobody in France knew anything about the opposite tower in Spain.'

'The two towers united North and South,' Liliane said, 'which was one purpose of Saunière's work in Rennes-le-Château. Later, we'll go into why the second tower had to be built. What about his journeys here?'

'His frequent short journeys were another mystery. His parishioners stated he crossed the border from Perpignan into Spain on numerous occasions at the end of the 1890s into the first decade of the new century. His maid covered his absences.'

Liliane asked if I'd been to the peak of Mt Canigou, and I remembered reaching it with José many years ago.

Abruptly she asked why I was here.

'To start the journey.'

'Where is the start?'

'In the hotel,' I assured her.

She sighed.

'I can't and won't be here alone. Not at night.'

'But Charlemagne did it! Right here in this garden. At that time Girona was losing the battle with the Moors and under siege. Charlemagne did the ritual breathing, the enquiry, and then the transformation. A visible chemical change took place. A cross of fire appeared right over there.' She pointed farther than the cathedral toward the Pyrénées. 'He led his men up this track ready to take the town, but the invading Moors had fled. The cross of fire had terrified them. Charlemagne, his patience conquering his fear, saved Girona.'

'So he could by transformation create a chemical change at some distance from him?'

'What do you think a ritual is?'

And I realised she had no fear. That was what was so different about her.

After lunch in the traditional bar in San Daniel with its simple food and overloud television, Liliane translated the record of Saunière's arrival in the barraca. He had been prepared to travel with a member of the Church from St Feliu until the time he should be joined by his guide. In the house with the tower, Maria Tourdes had prepared bread smeared with tomato and tortilla wrapped in paper, as his journey would be by foot through countryside. She added two litres of good light wine. The two men would pass through the village of los Angels up to Romanya de la Selva high in the hills, where an unknown ancient civilisation had left an arrangement of sacrificial stones not unlike those at Stonehenge, though much smaller. Liliane said the journey would have taken several days. In Romanya, Saunière would meet his guide and from there they would travel by horse and carriage to the next site. The priest was used to striding through the countryside for hours at a time and was strong, fit, and quite able to sleep under the stars.

'He showed no fear, having had experiences that had burnt it out of him. So let's see what gets rid of yours,' Liliane challenged.

'But he knew what he wanted,' I said. 'He knew the intention of the journey.'

'Exactly.' She was pleased. 'But not how to fulfill it. His problem? He thought he knew it all.'

'Why did he do the journey?'

'It was essential to become an initiate if he wanted to join the private society.'

So the first part of the preparation in the barraca was enquiry. Then I had to examine my intention in making the journey. That was easy: José had told me to do it. But that reason didn't quite suit my teacher.

'You are still in love with him,' she said, as though diagnosing a fatal illness. (She might well have been.) 'And that is why you are here.'

'Absolutely untrue,' I protested, even though it could not have been more true.

'You want to get some magic from this experience and get him back.'

I didn't answer. The idea of magic was not unappealing.

'What do you know about the journey?' she asked.

'Only the little I've just read.'

'Why don't you make reclaiming your lover your intention?'

I felt this to be a trap. 'Everybody has something in their lives.'

'In your case it would seem to come under the category of illusion.' She gave her lovely laugh and I tried to hide my fury. How could I let go of something God-given years ago that was still true until death and after?

'I would prefer to keep personal matters out of this exchange.'

'He is married.'

I had never for a moment believed in that marriage. Liliane and I had quite a discussion about that.

'Your relationship with José is a jewel in your past,' she said, suddenly. 'And his. Can't you leave it like that?'

I made my enquiry. Liliane said that we would allow two weeks and that the journey followed a pattern which would be explained to me. How did I see the journey? As a spiritual exercise, I decided. Its purpose? To expand my consciousness, heighten my level of involvement, give me freedom. I wished to be reborn.

But what were the practical aspects of the journey? Where would it take me? For how long? How would I travel? I liked walking as well as the next person did; but, having read Saunière's account, I didn't feel up to the first stretch—the one between the barraca and Romanya—as it was uphill and had been exhausting even for him.

Liliane left me some water, some fruit, and accounts in French of the meeting with Saunière and the priest from St Feliu and their discourse on the journey to Romanya. From the notes I could tell that Saunière had received better treatment altogether than I was getting. Liliane told me I was to practise the breathing exercises, stillness, chanting. And look at the stars. Lie back on the grass and absorb the night sky. When had I last done that?

I found José by the Arc Bar as the light was going. In the old days I would have clung to him. Now, in our new circumstances, we stayed a polite distance apart. He hadn't changed. Had I?

'Will you stay tonight with me in the barraca?'

He hesitated.

'I can't do it alone,' I said.

Softly, he refused. His wife—the problems it would produce with her. He would have done it in the old days without a second thought.

'Then why don't we just be in the old days,' I said. 'After all, this journey seems to go into the past. No clocks on this route.'

His eyes were the way they once were, and as I always remembered them to be. He'd made a decision.

'I'll come to you at nine,' he promised, 'but I have to get the last train to Flaca.' The village of Flaca was where he was now living in a vast, old house that he was restoring with his son.

Nine o'clock. Footsteps along the track as the cathedral bell sounded the hour. I'd know that walk anywhere. He brought a parcel of food, some wine. He said he'd tell me about his journey, the first segment, but we sat under the trees and talked about our past. That was the lovely time. Around midnight he prepared to leave and laughed at my fear.

'You'll be all right with my thoughts around you as that cross and chain once were. Remember?'

In the fifties, when I had left Girona for Paris the first time, he'd taken off the cross and chain he always wore and put it around my neck. He'd walked with me as I'd gone to hitch my first lift.

'It'll keep you safe.' He had said as he touched the cross. 'Don't lose it.'

As though I'd ever lose one little thing about him.

That night in the barraca, by candlelight I read some of Saunière's notes and what he hoped to find on the journey. He needed to traverse what in metaphysical language is known as the 34th line, pass through *shin*, unite North and South within him. His handwriting was small and private. He wanted 'The Tear of Isis' (the inundation of the Nile) to complete the 360-degree circle. Through the power of the Grail, the Phoenix would be consumed by fire and resurrected from the ashes in its previous beauty. For this experience he needed 'the doorway' in Girona to be 'the flame'. For the Grail to transform the Phoenix and he to take the passage through the flame he had to cross square number 34 and continue the journey to 44.

Not one thing made any sense to me. While I accepted the existence of such unknown ideas and constructions beneath our reality, I questioned why they should have been shown to me. I had enough trouble with the everyday stuff.

Saunière had spent some part of the first night in the barraca garden. Someone else had written he'd spent the entire night there in preparation, without sleep, fasting, drinking only water. The priest from St Feliu had arrived shortly after dawn and Maria had come with the food.

On the journey to los Angels Saunière had asked his companion about the chalice made of a rich gold beyond belief. It had been used in the 'sixth ceremony'. There were numbers and diagrams throughout the short account.

José's report of his own journey was shorter. His aim was to walk away his obstructive qualities and to know the humility of his guide. He'd go to any lengths to reach the sublime path. He, too, had spent the night without sleep. He'd prayed between sessions of meditation.

Both accounts commented on the peace of the barraca, the sweet air. Neither man had eaten lunch or supper and had drunk only fountain water. They used breathing exercises that had come from the East.

On my night at the barraca, the moon was up and the air sweet, as described in the accounts I'd just read. Nothing much had changed over the years. A rustling made me jump back. I could see gleaming eyes, a long tail. I was out of there and along the track faster than Charlemagne had charged. I got to the hotel with a speed I had not managed for years.

The next morning, Liliane was accepting of my cowardice and I was disappointed with myself until I remembered the rat.

'But it's from the country,' she pointed out. 'It's safer. It's not like the city rats you know in London.' And that brought the subject to an end.

I had asked José about her. He said she'd lived in the mountains for years. She was wise and ageless. Looking

58

back at the beginning of my experience with her, I didn't think I'd accomplished much. I'd only been made aware of what I didn't know and couldn't achieve, especially in terms of the level of physical activity it seemed to require. Had I waited too long to make the journey?

Figure 4.1. Part of the original city wall of Girona.

CHAPTER 4

'What is old?' asked Liliane.

'The city walls, four thousand years old,' I answered. I was proud of this information.

'Time! You have no idea of what it is. Remains of artefacts have been found in Girona that date back to 8,000 BC, when it was inhabited by Celtic tribes. Moreover, a mandible was found in the pre-Neanderthal town of Banyoles supposedly two hundred thousand years old.'

I had no idea what a mandible was, but I would not ask her. I changed the subject, but a few sentences later she brought it back to mandible. I didn't react one way or another.

She laughed. 'You are proud.'

No, that wasn't it. I didn't want to be with her; I wanted José. For a moment, I felt all wrong about this journey.

Then she said, 'You will have to learn to ask.'

I shrugged.

'The journey will certainly teach you that.'

Liliane took me out of the barraca, locked the door, and put the key in the agreed place so José could find it.

'How long do the others stay?' I asked.

'A week, a month.'

'But they're men.'

'Not all.'

I hadn't even lasted one night.

She admired the way the garden curved and dipped, finding its own rhythm. We now started on the local stations of the journey. The next building could be seen only a distance away on the track—the Torre Gironella, broken and crumbling, with its own legends and miracles. Next Liliane led me toward the Frenchwoman's garden. On the left, we saw the shrine on the small hill where in February 1976 the vision of the Magdalene had appeared, witnessed by dozens of Girona residents. Naturally, I thought we would stop there. It must be a pivotal point in any journey, must it not?

But no, without stopping Liliane continued on to the 'Garden of the Frenchwoman', as it was now known; it was even so commemorated with a plaque on the wall. It was in a poor state—walls broken in places, completely open to the public. When I'd visited in the fifties, the garden had been uneven with rocks, holes, and tall tough weeds, overgrown and unkempt. Earlier, at the turn of the century, it had been a place of elegance. Liliane sat where the royal palm tree had been uprooted by those determined to find information. I assumed the Vatican had been behind it.

'José is going to look after the garden,' said Liliane, pointing to a fountain in the process of being restored and to gas lamps being repaired. 'He'll get it as it should be.' For once, I agreed with her.

'What did they want here?' I asked. 'Those who destroyed the house?'

'What had been kept hidden for centuries. You can't dig for this. You have to let it come to you.' Without pause she told me my itinerary. There were eleven stops on the journey. 'When Saunière made it he was fit, José young. You're more mature, so it will be modified and we'll go in part by car or train. You'll walk a little more each day. You will always keep within the limits of what you can do. Do you know your limits?'

I doubted it. I asked why the location of the vision was not a stopping place. Surely it was the most otherworldly happening that Girona had experienced in recent years.

'The shrine to the vision is in honour of something that did not happen. Go and have a look. Then we will discuss what really happened.'

Alone, I crossed over to the small slope. It was an elaborate shrine, well kept with fresh and artificial flowers. An engraved account on a white tablet described how a local woman had seen a vision of Jesus: 'The markings on the earth were the footprint of Our Lord.' The date and time of the vision were recorded.

Across the track, Liliane was measuring a part of the city wall and writing numbers in the notebook. 'From this garden, Maria Tourdes could see across to Mt Canigou.'

'Is that important?'

'Essential.'

I asked why she was measuring the wall.

'In search of something that has never been discovered,' she replied. 'Did Saunière find it? Is that why his visits stopped?'

I had no idea what she was talking about.

She asked what I thought of the shrine. I thought it was synthetic, the materials cheap, but I didn't want to be disrespectful.

'The engraved account is wrong. It was not Jesus who appeared. It is not his foot they have made an imprint of.'

She described the event I have mentioned of the vision occurring in February 1976: a vision of *La Dona con la Copa*, 'The Lady with the Cup', had appeared on that hill lasting perhaps an hour before midnight. It was said to be the Magdalene, and she had previously appeared by the Lake of Banolas in 1902, a mere hour's journey away.

Figure 4.2. Shrine of the Lady with the Cup.

'The appearance can only happen in certain places, depending on the power of the ley lines, or pulses of energy, in that precise area,' Liliane explained.

'Did you see it?'

'Not at all. I was in the Pyrénées. There were dozens of people hurrying to that small hill. When they saw the spectacle they were quiet, awed. They said later that the form was beneficent, holy, never to be forgotten. Spectators farther away said it was a patch of light in the sky that didn't move. Then it faded and was gone.'

I told her I couldn't understand why that place, so beyond our world, was not used on the journey.

'It never has been. And that place is nothing special. The cause of the vision happened somewhere else. Once this house and its tower were torn down, the society could no longer have ceremonies here; this garden is now a public space. So where did the members go? To the barraca. They use the barraca garden. It's on the same energy line. (You'll start to understand "energy line".) The night in question, they carried out a ritual, something that hadn't happened for some years. Enough initiates were present and the activity provided changes in the atmosphere exactly as had happened with Charlemagne. The initiates called up the "Lady with the Cup", as they had in the past, although not often successfully. This time the resonance was right and the Lady took form.'

'So she appeared on that hill but was not called up from there?'

'Exactly. She actually arose from behind the hill. But because she was at least twelve feet high, her viewers thought she was hovering over it. So crowds go every month to the hill and pay respects to an event that did not happen there and did not concern the revered figure recorded on that plaque.'

'So it is deliberately confusing? Who put the plaque there?'

'One woman who saw the vision was deeply affected by it and afterward saw markings on the hill. She placed a cross and some flowers on that spot, and many came to pray there. She insisted that she'd seen the Magdalene and it had healed her. On the ground were undeniable traces that were difficult for the disbelievers to explain. Something had definitely happened there, but what? The woman's wooden cross and sign were removed from her makeshift shrine, and she was put in a mental hospital. They changed her story for her. She was told in no uncertain manner that the figure she had seen was not the Lady with the Cup but Jesus and that, if she accepted that truth, she'd be let out. It was they who put up the shrine for her—the shrine to Jesus.'

'They?'

'The Church, supposedly.'

'Where is the woman?'

'Oh, well, that's impossible to know.'

'But all those other spectators?'

'They said they'd seen something and left it at that. Why get into trouble and be shut away? The mental hospitals can always find a bed.'

I wanted to know who the people were who had been so against this vision that they had to falsify evidence and get rid of a witness. Liliane said, 'You wouldn't want to know.'

'But they didn't mind it being Jesus. So whoever they are they accepted that something had taken place.'

'So what do you conclude from that?'

'That the appearance of the "Lady with the Cup" was the problem.'

'Yes, one of them. She has been seen before—in 1902, as I mentioned earlier—but at a different location. Questions were asked. And in 1890 there was yet another sighting.'

Liliane looked into her tight, leather document case and found a newspaper cutting preserved in plastic. She had good control over objects, things, the outer world. 'Here is the report. It is in Catalan, so I will translate it for you. In 1890, the witness was a restaurant owner passing along the track late one evening towards his home in San Daniel.

He was alarmed by a sudden silence, so immense it was as though nothing existed; not even the trees made one creak. Then a dog growled and that was that. He said it was unnatural. He thought evil spirits were trying to approach and prayed to the saints. Then he heard voices chanting and, scared, he ran all the way to San Daniel.'

Now Liliane chose another document. 'And here is what a witness said in 1976: "There were crowds gathered around the hill. You could hear a pin drop. And then a dog barked and I prayed to Saint Michael who symbolises the unknown from the other world. He protects against evil."' Liliane closed the document case. 'So in certain places it is wise to use spiritual protection, which we will discuss once outside of Girona.'

'So the rituals calling up the "Lady with the Cup" had to stop?' I concluded.

'Of course. The society could not risk that amount of attention. The locals complained that the Frenchwoman had disturbed the spirits and caused all sorts of sightings.'

'Why is it always the "Lady with the Cup" that appears? Why not some other spirit?'

'Because she is the Magdalene, of course. Because of the tower, and then, after 1903 and more powerfully, two towers. The towers themselves are called either 'Magdala' or 'Magdalene', and between them she can be apparent.'

'What does she bring?'

'Oh, that's another thing altogether. You're not there yet.'

And then I got a good idea. 'Why didn't the society move the ritual to a more private place?'

That produced laughter. 'You can't just do a practice on that level anywhere. Its happening at all depends on the energy and vibration of the area. And here, just where you are now, is a main pulse point.' She moved me against the imprint of the tower's remains on the decaying wall. 'There are more pulse points, but they have less power. This was what the French priest was interested in—just where you stand now. For a while in 1902, the practice was moved to a forest near Lake Banolas; and the Magdalene with the Cup was seen by enough respectable citizens, including a nun, to warrant an investigation to be called for. Because the vision was identifiable, all activity was stopped until 1955 and then again in 1976, when the society used initiates to perform the ritual. You make the action and prepare the ritual, which can take four hours. Then it is true that a transformation can occur, but there is no control over what comes through, or where. Remember that. Better yet, write it down.'

I said I'd heard once or twice in Girona that the ritual came from Catalan practices in the Middle Ages.

'Yes, but you have to be at the energy points. Remember the two towers. A group of high initiates can be powerfully transforming the texts, but if the place has no resonance then nothing happens. So reflect on this place: what you have learned about its history and what you personally re-member. You have never seen a vision, so reflect on what a vision could be and why it appears in the first place.'

For a moment a memory did stir unpleasantly. I recalled my visit with José and Dr Mascaro to Rennes-le-Château in the mid-sixties and how a figure had been present in that church that could not actually be there. Yet it had been more startlingly *there* than any other person or object. That day I hadn't told the two men who had tried to calm my hysterical flight anything about it, and I had never talked about it since. Nor did I tell Liliane anything about it now.

Following her direction, I first did five breathing exer-cises, then some clearing of my subtle energies by chanting, and lastly a short meditation. The reflection on what a vi-sion could be happened quickly. Immediately in my mind,

I saw a figure made of smoke. It could be a woman with a headdress or long hair held up with ornamental clasps. It softened, becoming a coloured cloud. The woman carried an object, possibly a goblet. It depended on how you looked at it. It could be just cloud. I waited, but unlike a cloud it did not dissolve or change shape. Also, I did feel a sense of calm. The ornamental clasps faded, and I thought I could discern eyes. From them came a warmth and sweetness, and I felt as though I were filled with sugar. I felt, if anything, too sugary. I suspected that all of this was happening because my companion was sending energy or thought waves or something else to make it possible. Then Liliane spoke, and the cloud began fragmenting softly and was gone.

What had I seen? Could I recall it? Yes. Made from my imagination? I didn't think so. She told me to open my eyes and drink water. And then she described how information from another source beyond ours could be channelled.

'You attune to your highest level. You invite. You receive. It can be described as an imprint. It is more vivid than any thoughts and is instantly recallable and unchanging. If it were merely created by the imagination, it would be hard to recall. It would not appear to come from outside you. The real test is that the imprint is not made up of a person's usual thoughts but instead is "foreign" to them.'

I felt that I had experienced something instantly recallable, as though coming from some other place. My thoughts seemed to be suspended, and the image imprinted in their place. Then Liliane asked me to do an experiment: I must close my eyes and in thought summon up José. I surely knew him well enough. I got him for a second, and then other thoughts of all kinds came in that added to and took away from the image. Then I saw his mouth. Then I couldn't get it properly. The whole experiment took effort. It was not at all the same experience as the one of the woman made up of smoke. In that case I had only to think of her and she was instantly there, unchanging.

'And she always will be,' said Liliane.

For the first time since meeting her, I thought I'd done something right. I asked if she had projected the image of the woman into my mind.

'And how should I do that? If I had that power, I'd run the world.'

Just then a tourist photographer came up the steps into the garden and took shots of the walls. The house had been constructed so that the city wall formed one side of the house and its garden. The tower had been in the corner; its remains were still visible.

'The locals must have questioned these visions,' I said, after the photographer had passed.

'They thought they were ghosts and some told the priests,' replied Liliane. 'But not often and not in the past. Seeing spirits in the nineteenth century was considered blasphemous.'

I asked what had happened.

'Nothing. The Girona inhabitants in general did not believe in visions and ghosts, so if you saw one, it meant that something was wrong with you. Indeed, the same is true today. Also, it depends on whether or not the Church officials validate the vision. If they do, then it's claimed as a miracle.'

Liliane paused a moment and then suddenly added, 'So the terrain here does one thing. What is it?'

'It allows sights to manifest that would normally not be seen.'

'And why should that be?'

'Because of the ley lines, the energy pulses.' I was pleased not to be at a lost for an answer. Of course, she'd already mentioned these things.

For a while, Liliane didn't say whether I was right. She gave me a notebook and asked me to list everything I remembered about the garden and house. My reply was not popular.

'But that will take ages.'

'Why do you want to do this journey?'

'My answer is the same as it was when you last asked the question.'

'I hope not.' She put the notebook on my lap. 'You're right about the energy pulses allowing another dimension to intrude. But you've forgotten the towers.' She spoke slowly. 'They cause the space between them to be charged so it becomes lighter, more transparent, like a worn-out curtain. The air isn't so thick. If I describe it that way, do you understand?'

I said I did. I didn't.

'So there is a long charge of energy between here and Rennes-le-Château.'

Before we left the garden she asked me a testing question. 'Close your eyes and recall the woman of smoke. Describe everything.'

I did. She was still there.

'What does she make you feel?'

I thought the feeling was of being loved and safe, as though I were a beloved child. No, it was bigger than that. I was sure Liliane was somehow projecting this figure and its effects.

This was only the second stopping place and already the third day. I felt she was fed up being my guide. I wasn't handling the situations well enough. She was used to high initiates. The Great Bear and the Seven Stars? I couldn't even get off the ground.

GERONA = 57   Plaza Independencia   M. P.

Figure 5.1. The Girona cathedral visible through
one of the town's many archways.

CHAPTER 5

Liliane and I sat outside Lluís's place, the Arc Bar at the bottom of the cathedral steps, and the table was spread with food and drink. I asked for another portion of chorizo with bread. I'd known Lluís before he had opened the bar in the fifties. Originally, it had been a food shop.

Liliane asked me what I felt about this place. I told her how in the fifties and sixties the Arc Bar had been the nucleus, the heart of the city after dark. I remembered its jazz escaping out sweetly into the night along cobbled, broken streets and passageways as far as the thick, stone walls that locked in the Barrio Chino, a seething area of run-down houses, prostitutes, and bars that never closed. The walls were so thick that they sealed in the huge noise of competing music, street cries, and drunken brawls inside the Barrio; you wouldn't even guess it was there.

'The Barrio was a kingdom of debauchery. It was packed with customers, yet the walls held all the noise in. You didn't hear one sound.'

'Oh, the walls hold a lot,' Liliane said.

73

In those past days, Lluís, wearing tinted glasses, had stayed behind his bar, smoking the essential cigarette and recounting the gossip, the politics, and the city's intrigue with irony. He was clever and eloquent in several languages. He had a definite poise, and there was no one like him. José called him 'The Wolf'. What Lluís called José was not known. Later, it turned out to be 'Snow White'.

Figure 5.2. Lluís and José.

The bar had been thick with black tobacco smoke, wood smoke from an open fire, the smell of sausages cooking, girls' competing perfumes. The crowd had gathered around Lluís, the artists, the local personalities, anarchists, and the not-infrequent celebrity. Dali liked it there. So did the American stars making movies on the Costa Brava, including James Mason and Ava Gardner, who'd earlier made *Pandora and the Flying Dutchman* near Girona. Visiting flamenco dancers came—Antonio, Rosario. And the music heated up and the fire roared and we felt removed from the city, as though on a boat starting out for fabulous adventures.

The Catalans wanted an ideal province. If Lluís was their impresario, their leader was José, the instigator of change. It was that time in the late fifties when everyone was getting higher on little alcohol and much optimism and plans were being made for a better future.

'So what does this place represent?' Liliane asked.

'Freedom. A way to get it?'

'Through drink? Substances?'

I was thinking of the past, the beloved past. You got high on life. It was enough. But I didn't tell her everything and would not.

'We used to dance "The Madison". In a line in the bar. It had just come out.'

Figure 5.3. The sign for Lluís's bar.

And it had absolutely been the best time. I looked around at what there was today. The buildings were the same, but everything else was too changed, as though all the lights of the world had gone out. The town was too rich and the inhabitants had lost their identity, become global. I realised that thinking about the happy times made the present look kind of lost.

'Everything changes,' Liliane said, again linking into my thoughts. Perhaps she was a mind reader as well as a hypnotist.

'And what a fuck-up that is,' I observed.

'What stays the same?'

I pointed to the buildings.

'They are going through a crumbling disorientation. The atmosphere pervading them inside and out is completely changed since you first came here. Are you the same?'

I thought in some moods I was. Liliane looked as though she doubted it. I asked why she kept pushing me back into the past.

'Because that's what it is, this journey. The discovery that nothing is lost. We just get lost in time.'

She said I should sit in the Frenchwoman's garden and do the exercises as she'd asked. 'You seem opened up by remembering this bar, so you will find writing about Maria Tourdes and the house with the tower easier. Use reflection, enquiry. And start now to absorb where you are, wherever that is. Take it in.'

As we stood up to leave, Lluís—still, after all these years, the host of the night—came to the doorway and told me the latest news. It involved a sex scandal in which the participant said that, *au contraire*, he had been cleaning up the town. There was nothing about Girona that Lluís didn't know and couldn't sharpen up with his wonderful wit. From his bar he sent out dry malice repeated across town until it reached his prey. It was never without a nugget of wisdom and instigated more change than did many press editorials.

Figure 5.4. Lluís, still holding forth in the twenty-first century.

He didn't seem to know Liliane, so I introduced them. I told Lluís I was visiting the garden of the Frenchwoman.

'I never met her,' he said, 'although she lived right up there.' He pointed to the path behind the cathedral.

Liliane was joyous. 'But it is incredible that this foreign woman lives in a house for years and you don't remember her.'

'I came to the bar at night and stayed till dawn. She and I obviously had different hours. She didn't come here.'

'She must have been given the cloak of the invisible one.'

Lluís nodded and pointed farther down to St Luke's Church. 'The invisible ones came in and out of that door. That's where you went for the messages they had left.

We needed credibility at that time.' He was obviously talking about something else, and I assumed it was political.

'She had a gardener called Jacint,' Liliane said.

'I remember Jacint. I think the woman you mention had quite a good life but before even my time. Perhaps the French garden gives a certain invisibility. They say it gives many things. Even money.'

And that's when I remembered Lucia, that striking superb girl dressed completely in gold—shoes, dress, earrings, bag—vital and rich, like a gold bar. Gold of such a high quality that you couldn't afford it and could only covet it from a distance. Lucia was out of the range of most people. Even her make-up was gold, and her shoes with their skyscraper heels were like gold ingots. She reminded me of a mythical city of gold from ancient times. Her laughter was full of coins. She would walk into the bar, as she did one night in 1959, and I could only watch as José moved up to her, not even thinking to disguise his pleasure. That was during my second visit to Girona. She had a little liquor high that made her eyes sparkle, and Lluís talked to her ironically and made her laugh.

'She is as fragile as a golden butterfly,' Umberto had said. He was not too sober, either. Nobody was sober that night.

But amidst it all, Lucia found a moment to caution me. She was suddenly very clear. 'Remember. Girona is not called the city of illusion for nothing.'

It was that night when the priest and scholar Quim Carreras questioned me about the cross and chain José had given me at the end of my first visit. He assumed I still had it. Where was it?

'Perhaps José has it. It's his,' I said.

'No,' said Quim Carreras, 'he doesn't wear it anymore.'

'Do you check his body for lost jewels?'

That got a laugh, and it was then that Lucia started to like me.

'Did you give him the cross?' I asked Carreras, unwisely now. 'Should I pay you something for it?'

'You couldn't.' He tried to hide his anger. 'It is beyond price.'

I tried to remember what it looked like.

'Where is it?' he asked, softly.

Paris had been tough, and I'd given the cross and chain to a man in Montparnasse for the price of a meal. He had said to give him something in exchange, and it was all I had. José hadn't made me aware that it had any special value.

'I never had it,' I said, and to distract him started talking about the Frenchwoman. I wondered if the cross was valuable because of to whom it had belonged.

'She had had a real love affair,' Carreras was saying. 'It makes contemporary ones seem threadbare.' He asked how I knew her and I said I had seen her in Paris.

'But she's not in Paris,' José said, tapping my leg in warning.

'Oh, but she is,' said Carreras, looking at me. 'What did she say, by the way?'

'She said how much she liked you. She said it was a pity that you're a priest.'

Lluís got a good laugh out of that. They all did. Carreras was now an enemy. I felt that his assessment of contemporary love affairs as "threadbare" was aimed at mine with José.

'Why did Maria have to leave Girona?' It was my turn with the questions.

'Ask Miss Midas.' Quim Carreras pointed to Lucia. 'She has all the answers. Actually, Paris suits Maria. There are people of her quality in Paris. This is so provincial.'

'Why did she ever live here, then? This certainly isn't Paris.'

Lluís answered that one. 'Because she couldn't leave.' And then he added, 'Until she was told to.'

'Oh, we don't talk about that here,' and Lucia raised her glass. 'Why do you think I am covered with gold? This is the place for it!' And that's when she again warned me to be prudent.

Now, forty years later, I was essentially still at the Arc Bar during that night in 1959. The past—that was all that concerned me. I was certainly absorbing *that*, whether or not I was as good at absorbing the present moment, as Liliane had instructed.

What was it about that night that I had not understood?

Liliane went ahead of me back to the garden and chose where we should sit. She went back to the old subject of absorption: 'Absorb the place. Still your mind and let the atmosphere in. Keep your eyes closed. Feel with your hands and fingers the ground around you. The leaves, the stones, the gravel. Absorb the feel of these things. Don't give them names. Hear the wind, the bells, and now hear the less obvious sounds. First those near to you. Just observe, then absorb. Then the sounds farther away. The sound of the train. Now identify each smell. Absorb the many different odours that make up this garden. As far away as the olive oil cooking in the Arc Bar. Pick out the rhythms of the garden. The way the wind fills the trees and sighs its way out. The sound of water dripping. Now open your eyes and take in this place deeply. Forget time. Take as long as it takes. When thoughts come in they will always try to take over. Let them pass with no reaction and go back to stillness in the garden.'

Liliane's voice was hypnotic enough for me to have done exactly what she asked and not once questioned myself doing it.

'Watch the shadows on the wall. They make up a language, another reality. Go deep into their ever-changing existence. Absorb the shadows. What do you expect from this journey?'

'Nothing.' It came out without thought.

'Good. What worries you about absorption?'

I didn't think anything did. She got to work on that, clarifying the experience. I was frightened of taking in something that might harm me or that I couldn't get rid of. Or that would change me.

'So you're frightened of losing control.'

It wasn't so in every case.

As she left then for some hours of personal business she observed, 'You have very little trust.'

Alone in the garden, I picked up the document of Saunière's preparation for the journey. The notes were made by a companion, practical and precise. Liliane had made remarks in pencil. Saunière knew where he was going and for what purpose, and was prepared to be patient. The notes documenting his progress indicated that he was calm about his parish affairs, having stated that he'd be away on retreat. At the beginning, he, too, had sat in contemplation in this garden, aware of all that was around him. He had had trouble with recurring intrusive thoughts, worried that someone unnamed would get to what he wanted.

What was this journey, and should I be on it? I felt it was time to seek out the one who'd suggested it. Being in this semipublic garden alone was not pleasant. I read the exercises Liliane had given me for the evening: contemplate, concentrate, meditate. Sit in reflection. Practice breathing. Sustain chant on F-sharp; she'd left me a tape of the sound. Finally, the Enquiry. I was supposed to remember everything that had happened in the Frenchwoman's garden and write it in the notebook; but the place was so different, so sadly changed, I felt bereaved.

Maria Tourdes had had such warmth and delicacy. She was bright and clever and seemingly at ease in herself. I had first seen her when I was fifteen and had been walking on her broken wall. She had come out of the house, watching me, and I had told her I would work in a circus. I could still see her now clearly, with those bright black eyes like currants. I was looking at a mark on the tower to keep my balance. Was it a watermark from a high rising flood? I remarked to her that the tower must be old.

'Not at all. It was built in 1851.'

This memory of Maria shattered as sightseers climbed the steps and ran around all over the place, exclaiming loudly as they peered through the narrow slits of the defensive city wall through which arrows and later bullets had torn apart the enemy climbing the steep hill.

I left the garden and hurried down the cathedral steps, suddenly concerned Liliane might somehow know, perhaps by attunement, that I had not followed instructions. 'Stay with the shadows.' The sun thankfully had gone in.

I was making this journey because I loved José. I passed the Arc Bar, but he wasn't there. The second-hand bookshop in the Calle Forsa was closed. The Jewish Centre that José had unearthed and restored was crowded with a line of sightseers waiting to get in. I expected he would be in a bar on the Ramblas. The waiter had not seen him. I crossed the Eiffel Bridge toward the Calle Nou.

What made me stop at the Savoy Bar next to the Hotel Peninsular? Nostalgia? Because it had belonged to Señor

Juli Lara, whom I had liked very much? It used to be a spacious bar, dark, retaining the atmosphere of another time. The banquettes had been black leather and well worn. Engraved mirrors had hung around the walls, some with advertisements. The table tops, each with a central, identical pattern made of embroidered linen, had been covered with glass. The floor had been of polished stone. Now, almost all of its past elegance gone, it was like anywhere else.

He was sitting at the back, reading a newspaper. Before approaching, I paused in honour of my love. For this man I'd crossed continents, left marriages. My love for him, too big for my small heart, had sent me hurtling into churches, asking God to take it from me. Yet he blamed me in the end for our inability to stay together. I couldn't stay because I didn't trust. He might have had something there.

José saw me and smiled, amused. 'Your journey seems a little unusual. You've lost your guide and you're in a bar.'

'Come with me.' I was surprised at how much passion I still had. 'Let's do this together.'

His answer wasn't a surprise, but he said it gently. He had to follow his—I think the word he used was *obligations*.

'Should I do it?'

'You did the book. You've done research and you're involved. I think you must do it while you have this chance. And then we will meet for sure. I will come for you wherever you are.'

I asked what he'd received from the journey.

'Oh, look, each person is different. Why fill your mind with my experience when you can have your own?'

I asked what I could expect from it.

'You will see everything anew. You'll never forget it. But don't tell Liliane I said that. She won't want you to have expectations.'

I asked why Saunière had come to Girona.

'To follow the instructions left in code by the Abbé Bigou, his predecessor. To find the society's ritual material and to use it. The tower was the key. He gave Maria Tourdes enough money to acquire the house at whatever price from the Church. A lawyer, Saguer, fronted the deal.'

I asked about the pharmacist Señor Massaguer who'd built the tower, and José remembered him as being part of the society. 'Saunière copied that tower and also called it "Magdala" after Mary Magdalene, but it couldn't have been perfect, because he planned to enlarge it later in life. He brought money into Girona and Maria had to invest it. In her garden he could meet people he could no longer see in Rennes-le-Château. He'd attracted too much attention there. He or his brother Alfred brought documents to Maria for safekeeping. After his death nothing was found in his parish. But Saunière went too far.' I asked what he meant, but he did not reply.

'Why are you in this bar?' I asked suddenly, surprised.

'I am from time to time.'

'But it's not the same.'

'Not on the surface, but Maria used to come here. She took care of some Free French from the Second World War. They used this bar. I often think of her.' His voice became caressing.

'We could just *fou le camp*,' I said, suddenly. 'Get the hell out of here.'

'We could. But he didn't. Monsieur, the priest.'

Going back up the narrow street, the Calle Forsa, the main vein of the old part of the city, I kept hearing José's last remark. It put me into the group, the secret. Was I now one of them? 'We could just leave, but he didn't, Monsieur, the priest. But then there was too much for him to do and acquire in Girona.'

By Ruiz's second-hand bookshop, I met Juan Puig from the town hall, who had helped me with research the previous year. He asked why I was back, and I said to find out more about the vision in 1976. I did not mention the journey. He recalled that the woman who'd insisted on the shrine and her witnesses had felt an approaching divinity, a lightness beyond anything known. The feeling had lasted some hours. 'So they locked her up and changed her story for her. But she stayed with her version. She'd seen the Magdalene.'

I asked about the unusual markings on the ground.

He thought lightning had struck and left a mark on the earth like a sign. I asked where the woman was now. He didn't know.

'She said the experience healed her, changed her life.'

'Who put her away?'

'A doctor.'

'To keep her quiet?'

'Definitely,' said Juan, quiet and serious. 'For some reason they didn't want the Lady of the Cup mentioned.'

'They?'

'Obviously it coincided with something else that was happening. Maybe that something stirred up the appearance. I have heard that a few times from surprising people.'

I thought his remark itself was surprising coming from an employee of the municipality. I felt strangely on the edge of something I had perhaps been part of and certainly unknowingly had passed through. Yet I didn't know enough to be able to protect myself.

Figure 6.1. The Frenchwoman's garden as it is now.

CHAPTER 6

Sometime in the 1890s, the house of the Frenchwoman was filled with music. Debussy was present, somewhere among the guests in the garden.

A sudden wind from the south lifted the scents of the flowers, dispatching them with a true superiority amongst the conflicting, man-made perfumes of the guests. It set up a virtual blaze of heady exuberance almost competing with the music. Older women, a little overcome, fanned their faces briskly. 'What a summer.'

The French priest stood seeming to admire the acacia from Constantinople as it fluttered generously, enjoying the last of the breeze, and the women behind their fans admired him. He was well made and drew every eye. The bright yellow heads of the huge flowers were dazzling dangerously, as though another minute of sun would transform them into gold. These exotic plants had been personally brought from France. The Spanish flowers stayed in a line against the wall in the shade, as though shy. Orange trees and lemon trees gave of their best, and then, just when it seemed there could be no more splendour, all the bells rang, celebrating the hour. The eau de Cologne the Spanish men put in their hair intensified in the heat, and the summer insects droned and fluttered as though it were their last moment.

'Delicious,' said the French priest.

'A gift from God,' replied the Italian musician.

And the champagne sparkled for once discreetly, for once staying in its place on this afternoon given over to other, often not as noticeable, liquids and waters. Girls in lace aprons served the cooling lemon juice; and it seemed that, in this garden, nothing could go wrong, ever. Even the slight presence of the Madonna lily promised that all was well. But in spite of the bounteous colour and scents, the exquisiteness of this day, I was aware of one thing—the smell of freshly dug earth.

The scene was absolutely real, and yet for a moment I knew that I was asleep and that this was simply a too-

Figure 6.2. The opera singer Emma Calvé.

powerful dream; I must get myself awake. A chamber group moved into the shade and introduced a short German recital. A French singer stepped forward under the royal palm tree, her voice soaring effortlessly, marvellously, until the guests shivered with the sheer thrill of it. The handsome priest applauded. 'Brava, Emma!'

Pleased by his approval, Emma Calvé—for she was indeed the famous opera performer—suddenly switched to a passage that would be difficult for any singer. Pride made her lift the stanza in staccato steps, each with an elongated vowel, followed by a deft pause. She might have carried it off had not the unthinkable happened: The birds in the palm tree imitated the sounds, especially the slight tremor of her top range, and her face flushed as the guests struggled to hold down the inevitable terrible laughter. The birds, confident now, mocked her voice and its steps to the highest note, which they ravaged in their failure quite to get there. Her finale was torn to shreds with squawks and raucous shrieks. The birds were the ardent amateur at the audition, just missing the top C badly.

At first the guests could hardly believe it. They hoped they wouldn't have to believe it. It couldn't have been worse if a band of yokels had come to the garden gate and with unimaginable insolence mocked, even jeered, at the French singer.

'The bloody birds!' The young Duke de Charente called the gardener Jacint to deal with them. Jacint bashed into the low branches of the palm with a long broom, convincing some hoarse-voiced, greasy, feathered black interlopers to flutter unwillingly to the next tree. The violinists tried to make up for the noise; but the audience, who longed to laugh, to howl with laughter, turned away, hiding their faces. Some of them, shaking and bent forward, sought privacy down the steps to the garden entrance with its sign

'House of Canons'. The singer brought the song to a swift end and made a clever retort to the birds, which everyone expected of her. Actually, she wanted to shoot the lot, birds and gigglers, and she avoided the priest's eyes, not wishing him to see her anger and understand her disgrace.

Servants carried ornate trays of champagne and French delicacies brought by carriage from the border that morning. The singer, breathing too deeply in spite of her corsets, did not risk alcohol. Things had gone too badly wrong. Enraged, she asked only for water with freshly squeezed lemon juice and ice.

'This is better for you.' Jacint said, pouring her water from a jug. 'It's from the fountain.'

Emma thought he meant the fountain in the garden and looked displeased.

Jacint laughed. 'No, the fountain by the barraca. They say it is visited by the Magdalene. It brings healing.'

The priest toasted the singer. 'Even the birds envy her.'

A guest spoke too loudly. 'It would have been better if they'd shat on her head.'

Upstairs, Maria Tourdes lay on her bed sobbing convulsively, holding a scroll the priest had hidden and trying to rip it with her nails. 'You come from the devil!' she cried. The wallpaper was the purest, most innocent blue ever mixed. It came from the first dawn of colour. She could see downstairs to where Emma Calvé was standing close to the priest. 'My love, you are not holy.'

'This place is cursed,' said Emma. She was leaving for Paris.

'It's cursed because of Monsieur le Priest stirring things up.' The Duke de Charente spoke clearly, used to being believed.

'It's the black cemetery,' said the organist from the cathedral, trying to smooth things over.

Still in my dream, I went to and fro the house and garden, sometimes walking, sometimes suspended in space and bouncing up and down like a balloon. I felt drugged. Of course, the priest and his colleagues had slipped me something. They didn't like the uninvited. Yet it seemed I was not visible to them. I'd fallen into another time altogether. Could I ever come back to where I belonged? This was no dream; I was not dreaming.

Cold forced me back, and not without horror I found myself lying on rough ground crawling with tough insects. I felt certain that the inexplicable experience I'd just had was more real than any dream. I didn't feel anything was safe. I could see stars spiralling into deep distances that Liliane would enjoy. The exuberance of those unguessed-at worlds took away my fear. I had never seen so many stars, and I was ready to acknowledge the reality of so much more matter than just this planet, which I now condemned to the suburbs of the galaxy. I felt hypnotised by the night sky, opening up as it did a space and magnificence that for me had no end. *Had* I been dreaming? I remembered that after I had practiced chanting in F-sharp the day before, I had asked the same question Verdaguer had asked: 'What am I meant to see?' He had written it in pencil on a half-page in his account of his journey along a mountain ridge near France. Then I had been stolen from my life and floated back there to the afternoon party in the garden, to a time that was past and yet not unfamiliar.

I sat up and with dismay discovered I was lying in the Frenchwoman's now-abandoned garden. Might it be empty, or not? The lights of the city were out. It was well into night. I had never before seen a crescent moon that was blue. Liliane would be pleased that I should open up enough to see a moon differently.

Figure 7.1. The well in the Frenchwoman's garden.

CHAPTER 7

Liliane and I left the barraca in the morning at a mad hour, but any sense of reality I might have had was reduced by the previous night's experience. Emma Calvé had stepped forward to sing an aria with the birds in the palm tree doing their version; the priest, robust and handsome, was applauding; and upstairs, in a gilded bedroom, his other mistress was lying desperate, unhappy. The whole scene was more real and forceful than anything around me was now, inside or out.

I was never at my best at such a time of day and rarely witnessed it except in some emergency. Little sleep, no coffee, washing in a bucket of fountain water, and trying to crouch in bushes instead of using a lavatory made me reconsider the whole thing.

'I was never in the Girl Guides.' I tried again to clean my teeth. 'Sleeping rough is not for me.'

My guide seemed calm and obviously well slept.

'Enquiry. What is yours?'

I was suddenly furious and couldn't answer.

'Reflection? Well, you say you've been here long enough.'

I think I stamped my foot. It was as bad as that. 'I don't know how you came into my life. I sincerely hope there's a good reason why we have to leave at this unearthly hour. Are we getting the very last plane that will ever fly to the pyramids? It had better be something like that. It's only 6 a.m. I will not do this.'

'This?' She was unmoved.

'Travel rough. There's no reason for it. Is it because they did it?' I pointed to the document folder she'd left with me. 'Or did they? The French priest had it pretty well set up. He didn't wash in a bucket.' I remembered him, immaculate and at his best, from my reality-challenging vision in the garden.

Where had I ended the night? I'd crawled up from the Frenchwoman's garden to the shrine. It should have been safe there. It wasn't safe. It felt, like everything else, terrifying. I'd ended in the barraca garden. Liliane asked me why I hadn't asked the woman of smoke for help. It hadn't occurred to me. I was too exhausted even to seek her image. Maybe she wasn't on my side. Was it the woman of smoke who had caused my too-vivid reverie?

I complained again about the spoilt male travellers. 'Verdaguer. He seemed to fall on rich patrons. Buckets? Not for him. And my darling José. I know him well enough. Sweet comfort all the way for him.'

'You don't have to do it.'

I stopped, surprised.

'All you have to do is say you won't do this. I've suggested you follow the path as it's been trod before. But never once have I said you have to do what is unacceptable to you.'

'But you didn't say stay in the hotel and I'll meet you at breakfast.'

'Why didn't you say it?'

I was too furious with her to continue.

'You have to start making your boundaries. If it's unacceptable, say so. Well, you have made an enquiry into following the path that previous aspirants, including myself, have followed in this way. It upsets you. So don't do it. And later we will ask why it upsets you. It's not lifethreatening.'

'It's unnecessary.'

'It's a way of letting go of what you deem necessary.'

'I do definitely deem my choices necessary.'

My toothbrush had gray scum hanging to the bristles. I threw it away savagely. 'I want to go to the hotel and shower, have breakfast, pack properly.'

I thought Liliane looked down to hide possible laughter, but her voice was steady. 'To walk as the predecessors have done is unnecessary at your age and in your condition.'

'Oh, excuse me. I am in good condition and can take care of myself.' I could not entertain insult on top of everything else.

'That is good news.' She didn't believe it. Her tone told me that. 'This is new for you, so keep a notebook and express your resentments and surprises.'

I told her again I'd been on the pilgrimage to Santiago. She made some reply and lifted my bag and the document case. I *had* gone to Santiago, but I had left a lot out in the telling. It certainly hadn't been on foot all the way, and it was thirty years ago. Trains and buses came into it, as I remembered.

She took my hand, and we stood by the barraca pond. Her hand was surprisingly comforting.

'We have decided that on this journey you do not do anything you consider too much for you. You question yourself fully first. Am I too tired? Do I want a better result?

Is this frightening? That's a start.' She squeezed my hand and let go. We walked towards the town. 'Reflection?'

'Oh look, whatever I reflect or decide is pointless. The private society wants me to do this journey. They need for me to be involved because of the research I did for the book. So I'm in it whether I want to be or not. They don't know what I know or what I've uncovered. Maybe it's dangerous for them.'

'So you've come to a state of suspicion and lack of trust.'

'It's better than paranoia.'

'Do you still want to go to the hotel?'

'Definitely.'

I felt better when I'd taken a hot bath and cool shower, changed my clothes, and enjoyed a satisfying breakfast alone. When Liliane came back, I told her immediately that a hotel each night and three meals a day were necessary. And I took my mobile phone.

She nodded. 'For now.'

I asked what that meant exactly.

'This journey is in part about letting go. Some people experience it as loss. You came into this world with nothing. You keep nothing. You go out the same. What do you actually have?'

'Myself.'

'Oh, really? But that self changes every moment. Are your body and your mind really yours? You can't keep them as they are now, not even for five minutes. You, my friend, will have to let go or feel loss to reach this journey's destination. It might be wise to start thinking of the woman of smoke. I am surprised that you passed such an uncomfortable night but didn't think to recall her.'

'What could she do?'

'She made you feel valued and loved. Only yesterday. Your turnover in lovers must be something to see.'

It was the first time I had heard her be sarcastic. We happened to be standing outside a clothes shop, and I rushed in and bought two shawls, a red and a pink. At the pharmacy three doors along, a skin-care travelling case and a dozen toilet articles joined the purchases. Walking shoes came next.

Liliane sat outside the Café Grand Via, waiting. The sun was up by this time, the air acrid with heat. I now needed a coffee, some water, a visit to a normal lavatory. It would be necessary to have lunch next. She asked what I was going to do with all the purchases.

'Use them.'

'Who carries them?'

I said I would. I knew she wanted to ask why I needed them, and I had my answer ready. 'They keep me as I should be. Make me even better.'

'So they are tools for your life?'

'I wouldn't go as far as that.'

'How do you feel without them?'

'I don't allow myself to be without them. What is our first step?' I had to have some control in this.

'You eat lunch.'

Late in the afternoon, we walked out of Girona and took the curving path toward los Angels. I kept stopping because of the heat.

'Exactly,' Liliane remarked. 'That is why we were going to start early.'

I am a grandmother, in good shape in my opinion, if not in reality. On that walk toward los Angels every arthritic flaw in my body made itself felt; then dizziness had its turn. I sat by a most welcome fountain and bathed my feet. Liliane decided to take off to the left on the flat land. We were going to the hamlet of Romanya de la Selva, in an area little changed over the centuries called Les Gavanes. Our destination was the summit of a steep hill, its atmosphere pastoral and calm.

'Do we stop on the way?'

'Yes, at Caldes de Malavella.' It was the spa village where curists took the sulphuric waters. It was twenty minutes by car south of Girona.

I knew Caldes and it pleased me.

'Let's see if you will know it a little differently this time.' We sat on the dry grass in the shade, and Liliane brought up again the subject of the purchases.

'Look, I'm not some shopaholic,' I replied. 'I need these things.'

'Can you do without them?'

I thought of my creams, lotions, vitamin pills. 'Why should I?'

'So they make you who you are. Perhaps they're your identity.'

'Don't you clean your teeth and look after yourself?'

'Certainly.' She did look composed and clean, her hair plaited at the back. She had good colouring by nature. Perhaps fountain water was all that was needed. I explained that I was a city girl and that make-up was a must.

But Liliane wouldn't let it go. She said it made me who I thought I wanted to be.

She suggested we now started the programme of preparation that we could do daily. Together we did the stretching exercises; the five minutes of breathing; the contemplation, meditation, and chanting on F-sharp. The experience of the night before of being present in that garden with the priest and Emma Calvé kept forcing its way into my thoughts. Had it been a dream? A visit by chance back in time?

Suddenly I told Liliane all that I'd witnessed and how I'd certainly not been visible to the people in the scene.

'Perhaps you were there in that time, at that occasion.' She spoke seriously. 'That's something you will ask: "Where was I after my last death and before this birth?"' Then she read from Saunière's documents about his own journey.

'He forced his way through his tiredness and enjoyed as always using his body. He found the landscape pleasing. He questioned the priest accompanying him continually about one object.'

'Which was?'

'The golden cup.' Liliane turned more pages, and I asked if this was the only copy of the document.

'Oh, there are a dozen or more. Everything was copied out by hand in those days. The writing is always elaborate.' She asked me to read a paragraph.

'But it's in Catalan.' I did my best.

She said Saunière believed the golden cup of great weight, richness, and power would make itself known on the journey.

'He believed it was the grail?'

'It would seem so. He had heard from several sources that the Magdalene appeared in the vicinity. He wanted the physical object, which was left behind on this earth as it could not traverse other planes of existence any more than other physical matter could.'

'Was it the cup used at the Last Supper?'

'It was in existence long before that.'

We started walking, and I said I would stop at the next bar or café. I needed a drink, some food. I was full of needs.

Liliane asked, 'If Saunière sought the cup and it was an integral part of his journey, what do you look for? What is your cup?'

I didn't have an answer, so I asked her about the grail.

'The grail or chalice has always been part of the Catalan myth, so there must be a point to his enquiry. Perhaps it added to his own concept.'

'So he was afraid someone else would claim it.' I remembered reading something to this effect in one of the short accounts.

'No. To the contrary, he thought they who knew of it were too scared of its power. He was not.'

'But what do you look for?' she persisted. 'Is it the shops, cafés, hotels along the way? Do they comfort you?'

I hadn't thought of it in this way.

'You said you wanted to be free.'

I promised myself that I did.

'What would that feeling be like?'

We agreed it would not be the need of going into a shop.

I felt that what I sought was to run faster and faster, arms lifting, until I could spring higher and higher into the air and, once up, to dog-paddle my way against the pull of gravity so that I could stay up and, as though swimming, fly. It was to push my arms down, down, legs furiously pushing against the air, until I lifted up and could soar. And then I could spin and somersault like a golden, free being, light and weightless as though on the first bright morning that ever was.

'Don't you do that in your dreams?' Liliane asked.

Crossing the countryside towards Caldes, I talked to my confounding guide, not because I wanted to or because she was my usual sort of friend or even a friend at all. I talked because she was there. Liliane kept everything in the present or referred only to the precise past that the other initiates had experienced. I realised that they were all one thing I was not: apart from being men, they had all been intellectuals.

By a forgotten, broken-down signpost for the village of Cassa de la Selva, Liliane searched the ground and lifted a small rock. The law student from Paris had found something exceptional exactly in that place. Scratching the earth and dust with her foot, she exposed another small rock and asked me what I saw. Just a rock. She scraped its surface but it didn't help.

Then she knelt down and pointed out a dark weal across its side as though it had been burned. Had I seen it before? I had not. And then I remembered the black mark on the ground where the Magdalene had appeared above the hill. Liliane said it was the same. I could make out a pattern. She said it was a cabalistic sign. Did I want to know its meaning?

To my nod she replied, 'Daleth. Portal.'

Figure 7.2. The Hebrew letter *Daleth*,
Cabalistic sign for 'doorway'.

At a bar in Cassa we drank coffee and tried the freshly baked local cakes—*ensyñadas*. Then I heard Liliane order a taxi.

Had I failed so badly? Worse than I thought. We weren't going to Caldes but back to Girona.

'Why?'

'You haven't met Isis yet.'

Figure 8.1. *La Nuit,* by Villalonga.

CHAPTER 8

Evening was the time for the barraca; it brought out all its best colours, the bird-filled trees, the sweetness of the air. I sat by the pond and, as requested, read the reports of each of the four men's departures from this hut and the enquiries they had made. I suspected the text had been edited, and Liliane didn't disagree.

The poet Jacint Verdaguer had asked who prepared the journey. In his reflections, he'd understood it was formed before our knowledge of time and history, when the human element still belonged to the etheric—before the descent of the human being into matter, with the pull of gravity bringing us ever farther down. What answer had his guide given him? The Count Comillas was silent on this subject. Verdaguer referred to a state of being light years distant for which he longed and to which he believed he belonged. Liliane asked what I knew about Atlantis; I said I thought it was a land mass that might have existed, once joining the continent of America with Europe.

Liliane replied, 'The existence Verdaguer refers to is before Atlantis. The concept of the two towers comes from that time. It was a superb time, a time when this planet was inhabited by man as pure spirit. Belief in that existence is documented by the private society and has been held by the members for centuries.'

I asked if there were any evidence for that pre-Atlantis time.

'Of course, there have been past sages and seers and spirits entering this sphere who brought back from that past the knowledge of our predecessors.'

What if I didn't believe it? Would that be a problem?

Liliane said no and pointed to the sky. 'Look at that now. If all you knew was this clear blue, opaque sky, and then I described how it had looked the previous night— dark and filled with galaxies endlessly forming—but you didn't believe me, then there might be a problem.'

'So what I see and know is not all there is.'

My reply hadn't been a statement or a question but more an acceptance of the innocent, unmarked blue sky and the other one dark and raging with endless spiralling activity. The idea set in motion a thought about reality that I almost grasped and then it was gone. I rarely had those thoughts.

Verdaguer's account mentioned Saturn and Saturnian beings having been present on earth at the time when man was, as Liliane described, pure spirit. Old Saturn's withdrawal from this planet was caused by the approach of dark elements–elements that did not include Lucifer, who, contrary to common belief, was not evil. I ventured to suppose that Verdaguer had accepted the concept of 'the Fall' from Catholic doctrine and its continuing vibration that brought humanity ever more into dense mass and matter. After all, he was primarily a priest. She disabused me of that idea. Apparently, Catholicism had not been his source. If I wanted more available information I should try not the Church but Eastern religions, the Theosophists, and, especially, Rudolph Steiner.

At the end of Verdaguer's account, he stated that he had received information from a shepherd in spirit who had looked after the barraca and its land. The two towers unifying North and South and signifying the doorway would be matched in the etheric realm.

Of all the accounts, Verdaguer's was the most compelling and mystifying. José wrote of a bygone time that had been replaced by inferior and brutal elements. He asked again for the ladder by which he could ascend into light. I hoped—oh, how I did—that his account would include some mention of my arrival in his life.

The law student had been concerned with sacred geometry; in his account, certain numbers had to be worked through and understood. He had obtained a scroll and was trying to decipher a message that linked Girona's position with Canigou and Rennes-le-Château.

Saunière asked about the cup.

Liliane took the documents away. 'We go back to the design I have drawn.' She lifted out a sheet with the beheaded triangle and the numbers 49 and 1. 'This drawing relates to Isis, the Egyptian goddess. The Egyptian pyramid of Khufu. Girona comes under Isis; Isis is number 7—'

'But before you said the North is Isis and the South, Nephthys, so how can Girona be Isis?' I was pleased to have remembered this detail.

'The *tower* at Rennes-le-Chateau is always Isis and the *tower* at Girona is always Nephthys. But the *town* of Girona is under the influence of Isis. The contradiction is only apparent; in the deeper mysteries, all is resolved.'

'So,' Liliane went on. 'Girona is number 34 on the Venus Magic Square. The numbers three and four together give seven, which is the same square number as Canigou, linking the mountain with Isis. There is yet another connection: Girona is ruled by the Hebrew letter Daleth, the value of which is 4 and which symbolises Doorway or Portal. Daleth relates in turn to Venus, bringing us back to the Venus Magic Square.

She allowed a silence before she next spoke.

'I am using sacred geometry and Cabala, which the previous initiates understood. She looked at me. 'You have understood nothing.'

I said she was right.

'Good. Why did there have to be two towers? Because two enhances the energy needed to promote an alternative state of consciousness. A technique exists to achieve this goal. The Girona tower was Nephthys, the South. The tower in Rennes-le-Château was Isis, the North. They have to be connected. For this connection to happen, you need the heart chakra. As I said earlier, the South always disappears, the North remains. You know some of this from your research. The North is our past, our origins. We are moving from the North towards the South. Everything is impermanent.'

She drew a circle with a cross underneath. 'This is the sign for Isis. Girona is also related to the Ark of Noah. Each site has its influences, its numbers, references, energies.' She went back to the original drawing. 'The numbers in these two triangles add up to 50, which equals Sirius.' She drew other signs and numbers and then added the word *Teba* and a curving line. 'You, however, will not study either Cabala or sacred geometry.'

I felt as if I'd been let off a prison sentence.

'I show you these examples in order for you to understand that the journey is not simply a walk from village to shore to town to mountain. It is a magic square culminating at the peak of Canigou. It reflects the celestial realm. It coils into a powerful finale, so you will need to work on strength and patience to assist you.'

When I asked if the numbers were a code, Liliane was outraged. 'They are sacred numbers and patterns that define the energy connection between this earthly plane and other realms.' She jumped up. 'So now you start.' Her tone was different. She seemed wired, running on electric current. She had masses of energy in her department. In mine, I was weary beyond words, but I decided to fight through it and make an effort of which she could only approve.

'At each stop on the journey you will practice five techniques. Controlling the breath, chanting, contemplating, meditating, and then absorbing. As we move on, other practices will be given to you. For example: at the later sites you will renounce, experience giving in, receive. You will attune to the place and look for the message.'

'What am I supposed to see?'

She clapped her hands and laughed. 'That's exactly the question you have to ask: *what am I supposed to see?*'

I asked other questions but got no laughing answers. She was only going to show me one piece at a time.

I did the practice in the barraca garden. To contemplate was not easy. I decided I would always be honest with her. Why waste time trying to please? She moved me in front of Charlemagne's sundial and said to look at it and concentrate, but in a state of near daydream. See the associations that arose in my thoughts. The exercise wasn't successful. To absorb the atmosphere of the place felt easier. I could hear, look, smell, and touch, and from the sounds hopefully receive a message. I didn't push it because I didn't know if my imagination was filling in the gaps. It was a practical set of exercises and attempts such as I would expect in a meditation retreat.

'Now we go to the second point.' Liliane decided.

The light was fading, and I reminded her of our agreement that when I found the work unacceptable I should stop.

'But we must start. And before dark.'

'What have we been doing most of the day? All the walking! Wasn't that a start?'

'That was simply preparation. To test your stamina. So that you understand what's required.' And she started towards the Frenchwoman's garden. I asked how old she was and expected she'd lose a few years in her answer. I would. She said it didn't matter. I told her she was in good shape. 'I work at it.'

Again, the exercises and the sitting in silence, the space for contemplation filled with thoughts of the past. I remembered going into the house for the first time when I was fifteen, entering through a broken door. I had been told the place was uninhabited. There was a mosaic floor and a chandelier with half its bulbs broken. I was drawn to newspapers in a corner: French, yellowing, and racing with ants. They dated from some time in the 1890s until 1917. There was a silent grandfather clock, an art nouveau mirror—and this was only the hallway. The chairs belonged in a palace. The main room was covered with dust, although the long table was polished with a mean gleam. The shutters were tightly closed, but there was enough light to see that this house had once been stylish. An upright piano, its lid open, was piled with sheet music, its keys covered with bills, letters, money.

Then I could hear my friend Beryl shouting from the wall, telling me to come out. We could always use this place to camp in if worst came to worst, as it had before on some of our carefree, Bohemian journeys. Even though we never had money, we sometimes danced in the street just for the joy of it. The passers-by misunderstood and threw us money, which was the best they could think of to match the joy of freedom we had then.

The kitchen was from the thirties. The house didn't feel empty. Why weren't the rooms filled with stale air? On the draining board were two big china cups, cracked, and they'd been recently rinsed and were still wet. I turned quickly, expecting someone, the worst figure my imagination could conjure up.

Beryl banged on the window. . . .

Liliane said, 'What date is it?'

I saw the pile of French newspapers in the hallway. 'October 1917.'

I sat in silence between the two realities and let the present come back into my senses, into itself. And I found myself crying for all the happiness that was gone. I was bound to José. He was father, lover, god to me, and I so wanted him. He could make anything magical. The highest moments with him had been enriched with something from the past, a past I was not sure belonged to this century at all. It hinted at other, more sensuous times. He once said we'd known each other before. The supernatural was a dimension of life not even to be questioned. 'But how do you know?' I had asked. 'Oh, I have proof,' he answered lightly. 'Life gives it to me.'

Although the hotel bed was clean, the mattress comfortable to my body, the window open, and a bottle of trusted mineral water beside me, still I could not sleep. I heard the cathedral clock chime the quarter-hour. It was after 3 a.m. All those men had done this process, contemplated, walked, received visions. But they had been young.

Then, in my mind, I was back in the house of the Frenchwoman; I could even smell her perfume—*Je Reviens*, by Worth. The fireplace was filled with half-burned papers.

On a sideboard was a scattering of tinted photographs, sepia snapshots, trinkets, quill pens. The ink bottle was dried out. There was a large ring that looked antique, blackened as though scorched in a fire. I could still see the initials: B.S. Bérenger Saunière?

In another room, the floor in the middle was dug up. The earth and clay piled at the side of the deep hole were not dry. It had the air of a dark, alarming drama that I should not investigate. Tiles had been smashed in this unholy digging, which made the room smell rotten. What were the diggers burying here? I hoped I didn't have to find out.

In my half-dream state, I realised I was asleep yet still conscious. Why, when Liliane asked me the date, did I say October when, in fact, the present month was April? The French newspaper at the top of the pile in the hallway, crawling with ants, had been dated October.

I would not do this journey, I resolved. It was too much for me. Then I fell into deep sleep.

The morning was sunny and fresh as Liliane and I walked up the Calle Forsa to the Arc Bar.

'So, do I practise the Enquiry here?' I asked.

'You have breakfast here.'

When we'd eaten, she said we would walk through the old quarter, stopping at the local stations of the journey in Girona, and then leave for Romanya in the afternoon, when it was cooler. She asked me to sit in silence and absorb the atmosphere of the bar. We would go inside.

'But why? It's fresher out here.'

'Because inside was where you always sat. It was like a cave, you said. They didn't put tables out here until much later.'

'Is this one of the stations?'

'No.'

She told me to close my eyes, and I could hear the sounds of the bar: discordant, overimportant. This was where Quim Carreras had challenged me about the gold cross and chain, where Lucia had made her marvellous golden appearances and where she warned me about the deceptive appearance of others. It was here that Lluís had always given me the gossip. All I ever wanted was to know about José. There were the good times and the bad times: when he was with me, and when he was with his wife. But the bad times were merciful, and even then there were reflections and echoes of the good, enough for us to strike up that old magic. Of course, there was the passion, but it was really that other feeling—nostalia, belonging to earlier times—that trod the paths to other places, not part of this present life. José and I did go to Paris many times. Oh God, don't think about that.

'I always thought I was happy here,' I said.

'Sit down,' she said.

I was standing up, probably ready to run.

'It's not about happiness,' she said, almost gently for her. She asked if I wanted anything to drink.

I got out of there fast and into the sun. Over the heads of too many tourists, I saw Liliane's retreating figure and tried to reach her, as if I were a ghost telling of other times; but she kept walking quickly away, down the Calle Forsa, in a precise present against the eighth-century walls. Not without horror, I saw that an old cantina had been turned into a posh shop selling bath tubs with gilt taps. Liliane stopped by a closed building I did not immediately recognise and opened the side door, squeaking and rusty and leading into a yard at the back of which was an overgrown garden. Then I remembered the smell of it and breathed deeply. It was the old Hotel Centro, which had originally been a medieval palace.

It was also one of the local stations of the journey, my guide informed me as she cleared dust off an iron bench. 'Aspirants stayed here for some hours or days.'

'But it's so near the barraca. What's the point?'

'Near? What has near to do with it? The energy is not the same at all.'

I sought out the smell—a blend of eau de Cologne, wood smoke, and must—which brought back a hundred memories while she told me something of the intent of the journey.

'This is a place of renunciation, of letting go. The journey includes a second site of renunciation, which comes later with good reason. The journey is not your personal journey. It is not about your gaining power to reclaim the loss that your heart tells you is yours. Or to make up for that terrible disappointment by acquiring powers to benefit you materially or amorously, or to increase your domination of others and get what does not belong to you.'

I said I agreed with all that. I didn't. I was now in a bad mood.

'Why do I have to renounce anything?'

'To give space.'

'Why?'

'To allow purification. To bring in a new state of being.' She put the accent on 'new'. 'It is a rite of passage. You pass through the states of mood and note them, but you don't rest on them.'

'What do I get instead? I want to know. I don't want it to be anything worse.'

'Freedom.'

The Hotel Centro had been the last old hotel left, with huge, lofty rooms, peeling green paint, and old-fashioned bathrooms with pedestal sinks and china cupids. The place had housed my love for José because I could sit

112

there and wait for him in the peace of that long-lost era that Maria Tourdes had known. Is this how she had felt, remembering back to the time she'd shared with the priest?

Mostly the rooms were unoccupied, their blinds closed, doors slightly open. And in the vacancy, there was a definite, lingering sense of a time gone, of romance heady but undeniably over. It made me sad, because wherever I went in the town, or in the country, or in whatever place I visited, that romance would not be found. And even if I could have found it, could I have held it? Could it ever be more than a sweet, tantalising fragrance forgotten in an out-of-date hotel? There were long, pale-green winding corridors and a palatial silent dining room with moulded ceilings, turn-of-the-century lamps, and pendulum clocks. It stayed this way because there was no money for modernisation, for which I was grateful. The wind howled around the end of the corridors, banging the shutters, and the hotel sign creaked and swung. The breakfast room where José and I had once sat was still full of oily, dark green paintings. The tablecloths were bleached by sunlight. The huge china cups gleamed, giving off a pale, milky light in the dim room. There was nowhere in the world I'd rather be.

The rooms were all pale green, and the lace curtains made the light soft. For a moment there was always the cold, thrilling, damp atmosphere I remembered from the early times, when I would open the window onto the lovely and unknown Hotel Centro garden. Since few people ever stayed there, few knew of the garden's existence.

'Look at the shadows,' Liliane said, pointing to the wall. 'Just watch them and let your thoughts go. Tell me about this place.'

'This was part of a palace. The water was always cold. The dining-room ceiling was vaulted, as though in a church.

113

It was a work of art, decorated with a scene from the old quarter, including the house with a tower.'

The room keys had been huge and made a great rattling noise as though opening the last cell in a disused prison. I wasn't looking at the shadows.

'Absorb what is around you. Let the atmosphere in.'

'But it's gone, it's changed.' I was almost crying again. I hated the loss of something that should not be lost, that was too beautiful.

'The place may be changed, but not the energy, the essence, the spirit. That is the same and holds all memory of what happened here. Nothing is lost.'

'That certainly isn't my experience.'

'Oh, you'll find evidence enough,' she said, casually. 'Maria Tourdes felt as you do.'

That took me by surprise.

'She had been too happy with the priest, and nothing else quite did it for her. That's what she said.'

I realised Liliane still carried the document case because it was there all of a sudden on her lap. She took out a folded sheet of Maria's thick, coloured, expensive notepaper and chose what she would read: '"Sometimes in the evening I sit on the wall and look over to Canigou and remember all that was in this garden. It seems from another world, and the person I was then I can hardly reach now. It only makes me sad if I do. To think I had so much and now can reach it only by memory, which is uncertain. Was he wrong or right?"'

Liliane folded the document back into the case and took out a flimsy sheet of 1950s Spanish paper. She said it was a letter from a man named Narcis to a friend in Girona saying he was worried about Maria and didn't see her out anymore.

'"Recently she told me that she still thinks about the French priest",' Liliane read from Narcis's letter. '"She said that there could never be anybody like him, but he had not wanted to give up his vocation". Maria had asked if Narcis thought Saunière was good or bad,' Liliane went on. 'And in an earlier letter, she had written to a friend in France . . .'

Liliane looked in the case but couldn't find the letter in question, so she quoted Maria by memory: '"I love Girona, I feel so alive. So fortunate."' Liliane paused. 'This was in 1896. Maria went on to say how Saunière had arrived on Wednesday and they had stayed in the garden until well after dark. And that he was forever delighted by the bells, this city of bells that he found glorious. "I feel transformed when he is here, as I should be. I do not know what will happen and for once I don't care."' Liliane continued, quoting from memory confidently: '"We laugh a lot, which will seem very inappropriate—yes, insanely so—but that's how things are when we're together. And then he always has to leave and I feel terribly alone."'

I remembered Quim Carreras in the Arc Bar saying that Maria Tourdes had had a *real* love affair. Quim had an edgy charm and always said what he meant to say. He was too precise by far.

After Maria had left finally for Paris, José had told me, 'It broke her heart to lose this house, but she couldn't go on living here.' I'd asked why. 'Too many memories. What had been so glorious and was now gone caused such pain.'

In the hotel room, the shadows had gone. Liliane suggested I do the five practices of preparation. For the contemplation, she placed an empty glass bottle in front of me. It caught the new burst of sunlight and gave off a marvellous brilliance, as though filled with gems.

'We begin with intent of renunciation: First, I release my hold on material needs,' Liliane said, quite naturally. 'Second: I release my hold on the people I love.'

I repeated the statements.

'What is renunciation for you?' she asked.

'Letting go of . . .'

'Of what?'

'Something I want or have. Or do.'

'Such as?'

'This old hotel.'

'Three of the men we have read about made the intent to give up their need for power over others. The fourth, to give up an easeful life.'

She wouldn't tell me which intent José had chosen and, oddly, I couldn't tell.

'Now we go for a good lunch.' Liliane decided.

Figure 9.1. Café Antigua, early twentieth century.

CHAPTER 9

In the afternoon we stopped first by the Jewish Centre, then at the place where José's family's hotel had been, and thirdly at the Café Antigua. Afterward, we went to the Eiffel Bridge and the Savoy Bar. Later, as the heat faded, we would take off toward Romanya.

Only the Café Antigua had remained unchanged from the 1950s, or even earlier. Under the stone arches of the Placa de Vi, opposite the town hall, the café was still lively and popular. Liliane said that at the time of Saunière's visits the café had been a favourite place to enjoy good coffee and exchange gossip. Customers used to watch from the café's quite private view the goings on to and fro the town hall opposite. Visitors from the surrounding towns and villages, wanting authorisation for their disputes or land purchases, tired and hungry, would cross to the café and enjoy good, freshly baked bread, tortilla, ham, olives, and anchovies from Palamos. And the women could accompany them to this establishment and enjoy plain ices with biscuit and chocolate. The Café Antigua's easy atmosphere was rare in the formal, bureaucratic Girona of the 1890s. It was rare for women, even accompanied, to be seen in a café or bar.

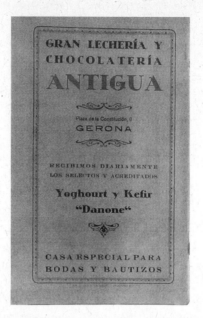

Figure 9.2. The Antigua was a favourite place
for gossip, coffee, and—always—chocolate.

Certainly they would not frequent the Café Vila nearby,
which was exclusively for the men.

At the end of the 1890s, the Antigua was the nearest
café to the Calle Forsa. There, Maria Tourdes would join
the newly established Catalan group of artists and writers without drawing too much attention and so relieve her
hours of solitude in the house with the royal palm tree. Her
papers showed that she was eighteen. Actually, she was
younger, and it was unlikely that she would have gone
out to the café alone. It was there, by chance, that she met
her friend Narcis, a photographer and perhaps the only
person not placed deliberately in her life by the private
society. From Maria's notebook that Liliane had photographed, it was understood that Narcis would run errands

and occasionally accompany Maria to entertainments, out of sight of her guardians. Liliane believed it was the same Narcis who, forty years later, wrote to his friend that he hadn't seen Maria and was worried for her health.

Members of the society casually met and drank coffee at the Café Antigua, feeling easy in the company of that place. The proprietor in 1905 was friendly to the private society and thought its members were trying to restore the culture of the province. Later it was said the group was part of a sect in France, possibly being Rosicrucians from Narbonne. The proprietor didn't think there was anything wrong with that and occasionally took messages to be passed to other members. It was a gay place of chance encounters and was still much the same a hundred years later.

'What does this place offer?' Liliane asked. Answering herself, she went on, 'A chance to be carefree, to meet new people, exchange ideas, feel safe, enjoy coffee, be in welcoming surroundings. What did they on the journey absorb from this atmosphere? Human warmth and spontaneity. A chance to drop one's guard, exchange with others, and enjoy basic nourishment,' she concluded.

She didn't ask what I remembered of the Antigua or if I myself had absorbed anything there. As she didn't ask me to do the preparation exercises, I assumed the café was not one of the local journey stations. I remembered the last owner in the 1970s—a sturdy, ruddy-faced man with an admirable moustache curling out to the sides. How I had enjoyed his friendliness! He had repainted the walls, but otherwise nothing had been changed since 1955. I had no unhappy feelings about the Café Antigua. You only got good food and good things there.

The Residencia International, José's family's hotel, had been closed for years. In 1991, the mayor, Joachim Nadal, had had it reopened as a youth hostel. I would certainly have fitted in with that locale when I arrived, a complete bohemian, with Beryl all those years ago. Now I stood by its new doors—it was unrecognisable—and couldn't even think, let alone talk. Farther along there was a passage, Carrer d'arc, and halfway down an old window still existed in this otherwise modernised building over an arch where I'd first stayed. The room had been simple and clean, and through that window had come all the sounds of the city. I used to hear José's footsteps going to one or another of the entrance doors. He'd sing or whistle and call goodnight to the concierge, but it was the footsteps I remembered. No one walked like him.

There used to be the alley with the torn chocolate poster from the 1940s or earlier, leading to the small dining room run by Beatrice and her sister. I could not, would not, relive that time. I was more than ready for the walk to Romanya.

'But this is a local station, this spot here in Girona.' Liliane's voice was melodious, her vowels long and emotive. 'You have to do the breathing, the chanting, the contemplation, the meditation.'

I stood with my hands over my ears, an undoubted look of horror on my face like Edvard Munch's picture of *The Scream*. Liliane told me of how the journey travellers had all dealt with the unacceptable.

'So what happened?'

'They learned to accept.'

'But they didn't feel like this. They haven't been through my experience, exactly.'

'But exactly. This city, bearer of power, magnetism, and ley lines, affects everybody, joyfully or otherwise. We all have memories, even love affairs. The other travellers didn't get off lightly.'

The light in the alley was extraordinary, melancholy, and brought back a sense of the past that was gone yet too strong to be extinguished.

'But of course,' my guide continued, speaking rapidly. 'Powerful events took place here. Powerful forces came into being here. Girona is square number 34; therefore, Daleth 4; therefore Portal. Girona is under Scorpio—Girona's symbol—signifying direct knowing of the Divine.'

I understood that to comprehend these numbers and symbols would be impossible on this short journey but that I should at least know, if simplistically, what the other travellers had known in depth. My memories of the past that day had left me ravaged, and Liliane wanted me to become more assured. 'Why don't you ask for the woman of smoke to come to you? Just make the attunement. Think of her; let the imprint be present.'

I tried to do as she said, but everything clashed at once: The memory of the alley in the fifties and the chocolate poster and José, so beautiful, nothing more to be said. And the desires simultaneously to run away and yet stay put on the off-chance of seeing him again. He was certainly on his journey to old age, at once unrecognisably yet undeniably him. The lady of smoke didn't stand a chance.

I told Liliane that this was a crash course in psychic change that should take years, that it was plastic surgery of the soul, that I could not do it.

'But we don't have years.' Her chortle of approval surprised me, all her sounds dancing—high note, low note. 'You couldn't be standing more on the spot.' She took my hand and pushed me gently backward until I was under the dirty arch with the disused room above in which I'd known so much enchantment.

Of course, she'd try to get me away from my searing nostalgia, but only José's appearance during these terrible

123

moments would have spared, me. Of course he was not now the same person whose step had been so unmistakable along the alley to Chez Beatrice; he was merely the continuation of the same soul. He, no more than I, could repeat one of our actions with the same effect. Even holding hands in those early days had been more ecstatic than the full act of lovemaking with another man in later years. Nevertheless, José could still share those early moments with me as I recalled them aloud; he could comfort me, hold me. How I wished he could come along the passageway now.

How had Maria dealt with the death of Saunière? What had she done with the ever-arising memories of what had once been so joyous? I had read some of her letters; in one she described sitting on the wall of his garden looking at Canigou and remembering all that had happened in that place: the richness, the joy. It all seemed from another world, and the person she had been then she could hardly reach now. If she did, it only made her sad. 'To think I had so much and now can reach it only by memory, which is uncertain. Was he wrong or right?'

I assumed she had meant Saunière. José had said there is another way to reach what has been, where time is not linear. 'But dare you do it?' he asked. 'And it certainly isn't dependent on memory.' Later, I came to know what he was talking about.

'This must be the most charged point in Girona,' I observed to Liliane.

'But no.'

So I asked what was.

'The barraca. And another place.'

'Which is?'

'We're not there yet.'

I told her I thought the tower of the Frenchwoman's house was the strongest point.

She said. 'That is the south tower, Nephthys. The north tower, the one Saunière constructed, is Isis. What did I tell you about them?'

'The North always survives and the South disappears. So the Girona tower's destruction was inevitable.'

Liliane led me toward the Jewish Centre—obviously a local station. Renunciation? Although José's courtyard remained with its Star of David, little else from the past did. The atmosphere was changed beyond recall. There was nothing to mourn here. It was packed with sightseers taking photographs. By the wishing well I did the exercises. The absorption was odd, and one memory even odder: In the 1970s a bird had interrupted a concert of Jewish songs arranged by José. It had mocked the soprano, leading me back to the Frenchwoman's garden in the 1890s as I had experienced it in my dream of the previous night. Was the parallel just a coincidence?

Liliane and I moved on to the Eiffel Bridge, that iron, clanking construction by the Frenchman who'd designed the Eiffel Tower. We crossed it slowly, marvelling at the skyline, superb in all lights. Finally, we stopped at the Savoy Bar in the narrow street Calle Nou next to the Hotel Peninsular, which had once been the social centre of the city. That stop was a surprise. These places were both sites that had provided powerful insight for the male initiates before me.

'Maria Tourdes used to bring people from Paris here,' Liliane informed me. 'It was the smart bar. People said that it was the meeting place for the private society and that Saunière had hidden the golden cup here.' She produced a sheet of paper, for once not from the document case but from her pocket. 'This diagram is a magic square. Venus: 7 x 7.'

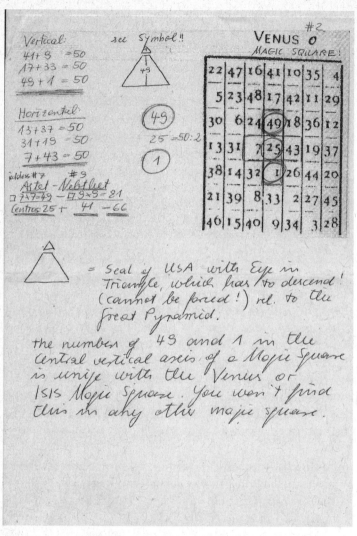

The handwritten notes read:

Vertical:
41 + 9 = 50
17 + 33 = 50
49 + 1 = 50

see Symbol!!

△
49

VENUS ♀
MAGIC SQUARE!

#2

22	47	16	41	10	35	4
5	23	48	17	42	11	29
30	6	24	49	18	36	12
13	31	7	25	43	19	37
38	14	32	1	26	44	20
21	39	8	33	2	27	45
46	15	40	9	34	3	28

Horizental:
13 + 37 = 50
31 + 19 = 50
7 + 43 = 50

49
25 = 50 : 2
1

jaldes #7   #9
Astet - Nebtleet
□ 7×7 = 49 — □ 9×9 = 81
Centros: 25 + 41 = 66

△ = Seal of USA with Eye in
Triangle, which has to descend!
(cannot be forced!) rel. to the
Great Pyramid.

the number of 49 and 1 in the
central vertical axis of a Magic Square
is uniqe with the Venus or
ISIS Magic Square. You won't find
this in any other magic square.

Figure 9.3. The Venus Magic Square.

126

As she described, there were 49 numbers: 7 horizontal, 7 vertical, 7 diagonal. The square was filled calmly with numbers that seemed unrelated. It was like some kind of lottery.

'Do I have to stop at each one?'

She laughed and took the paper back. 'There you are! Already making a presumption. Stop at each one? Why don't you just say, "I don't know what this means to me yet"?'

'Are they all the same? Magic squares?'

More sheets came from the rucksack. The first was Saturn: 3 x 3. Jupiter, 4 x 4; Mars 5 x 5. The Sun Square is 6 x 6; Mercury, 8 x 8. I wished we were doing the Moon Square, 9 x 9. It felt calm and safe. She said I could use the Moon Square to go to Santiago de Compostela. And then she produced the large one, Celestial Jerusalem: 12 x 12. Why were we doing Venus and not another?

'Because that's the journey.' And my guide placed the sheets in a folder and back in the rucksack as quick and skilfully as a conjuring trick. 'So what worries you about a magic square?'

Did I look worried? After the afternoon I'd just been through, worry was a luxury. To visit those sites and expose the loss of what was once so perfect and life giving had been anguish. Unperturbed, Liliane was calmly explaining the magic square in the simplest way.

'A magic square is an extremely rare configuration of numbers displayed in rows and columns where the sum of each line—vertical, horizontal, and diagonal—adds up to the same number. In the Venus Magic Square, for instance, the sum of each row, column, and diagonal is 175. A magic square also has astrological qualities and divinity. It is a talisman. Philosophers and sages have spent years of their lives on the mathematical feat of trying to create new squares. Magic squares were known in ancient Egypt, India, Persia.'

She asked if I could name one aspect of the Venus Magic Square. I said the Great Bear because that was the design we were following. Wrong!

'A magic square is definitely given from another dimension. It was known of in China by mathematicians in 650 BC. But there are various earlier dates of origin. I have said that in the Venus Square you have what is called the *sigil* or "signature" of the Great Bear constellation in which can be identified eleven sites, the number of which constructs the journey.'

'Are they all portals?'

'No, but all are energy points and hold great power.'

I thought it was my turn to show I could think, too, so I said that presumably a mathematician could create a magic square and it wouldn't have to be divine. She was ready for that one, of course. Had I heard of Josép Subirachs? I had not.

'In Barcelona in the Sagrada Familia Church.'

'Yes, I know this church. It was designed by Gaudi.'

'Josép Subirachs had created a magic square in which all columns and rows add up to 33. Christ, of course, had been thirty-three when he died, and Subirachs had actually created this square at Easter—The Passion of Christ!'

That put divinity back into the argument. I said crossing the square would be like celestial hopscotch and that I'd do it.

Figure 10.1. Romanya de la Selva.

CHAPTER 10

We were heading southeast toward Romanya. Two hours walking along the circling road and then into the forest left little energy for questions. Liliane made sure I rested before I became tired and stretched to relieve cramp and stiffness. She had agreed to follow that course of action each day. I was glad to leave Girona and all that unexpected pain.

As we walked, I began to process the information I had received over the past days. I asked how the cup could be held by the visionary lady, probably the Magdalene, and yet be in the Savoy Bar (if indeed Saunière had hidden it there). She explained that the cup was both here and in the seventh realm. During its journey through this planet since the beginning of time, it had collected more and yet more power and energy. It became heavier, the gold of the highest possible degree, and then changed in part into a white powder that some thought to be dust. A vehicle of divinity—because this was its true nature—it had a subtle body that passed into the next realm, the spirit realm, and higher, beyond our comprehension. And it came to those initiates who could resonate at that high pitch, which was said to be an F-sharp and to bring healing and divine change. But resonance with that level was rare.

Again Liliane decided I needed to rest, and I lay back on the cool sheltered grass. It was unlikely we'd get even close to Romanya that evening.

'Saunière naturally wanted the cup. Did he get it?' she asked. 'At that time, the earthly object was rusted over like an old tin can. He overlooked it for the one of his guide in St Feliu. That one was rich, exquisite, and very heavy.'

'Why? Why was the real one a tin can?'

'To disguise it from him. The society made sure of that.'

'They didn't trust him.'

'They knew of his coming. It had been predicted years before. But he had work to do. He was given a huge task.'

I didn't hear the rest. Later I woke up with some surprise; once again I was looking at stars. It was well into the night.

Liliane had covered me with her coat and my two shawls and put the document case under my head. I knew she hadn't slept but had sat watching over me. Was it because I was a traveller and she cared? She gave me some water. Another night without the necessary hotel.

After washing in a stream the next morning, we left the forest and walked uphill to a bar for coffee and freshly baked bread. It was 7 a.m. and cool. From here Liliane collected a friend's car, having already made provision for any feebleness on my part, and we drove across country to the steep locale of Romanya. There we sat outside the church, high on the hill, and she invited me to choose one of the journey points so far for us to clarify. This was the place for that. She explained that we were now outside the dynamic pull of the journey; we'd left the Venus Magic Square and were in a resting place of neutral energy, where one could get out of the time and the pace of development. Personally, I didn't think I'd developed much.

There were two restaurants beside the church and she chose wisely. 'The locals eat here.'

First we did the practices and she increased the timing. She gave me three different breathing exercises, and the chanting was more complicated. For the contemplation she went back to observing shadows, such as the leaves of a tree against the pale stone wall. The meditation was preceded by deep relaxation. Absorbing the atmosphere was often difficult and interrupted by constant thoughts.

'You are restless.' She didn't miss much.

The wind was silky and pleasant. The view was worth the climb. The few buildings were old and pleasant. 'There's not much to it. So not much can happen.' I concluded. Terrible answer! I knew it as soon as I said it.

'So you look for what is there in matter and make an assessment.'

'Dramatically. Not materially. If there were a curious tree or odd gateway, or the remains of a fire or . . . but this is just nature.'

How wrong could I be? I was going to find out. Liliane made me get up and stand on the north side of the church for some minutes, and then on the south side. I was to concentrate on the energy of each space. In what way were they different? I didn't know. I could only comment on the temperature, the wind, the smell.

'I felt more secure on the north side.' At least I thought I had.

She led me to a space on the north side. 'Take your time. Attune to the energy.'

I thought that here I did sense a mere moment of change. Perhaps a mood? Fear? Something that happened in that place? I didn't need to take time for that. 'Where will I feel this energy?'

'You will have a resonance with it and it with you.'

'Have I so far in these three days?'

'No.'

We sat quietly looking out at the view and it was pleasant enough, uninterrupted, unspoiled, unchanged for centuries. I asked what the travellers found here.

'Peace.'

Liliane went to get the keys for the church from a nearby house. I had not joined this journey as a mystic. I was not seeking to become an initiate. I wanted a profound experience. Yes, that was it. When she came back, I told her some of this and she said: 'What was it about the house of the Frenchwoman in your sleep experience that you didn't understand?'

'There was something about the house I'd missed. Something that should be there that wasn't.'

She gave me a few more exercises. In the future, my meditation would now be focused on that house and garden as they had been in the previous century. 'Just be there and note what you feel. What is happening? Is there something you feel impelled to do? You will ask these questions.' She made it sound simple.

She unlocked the church door with a huge, clanking key and put a euro in the box to bring on the lights. We sat at the back—was I supposed to pray?—and she began talking in the same manner as always.

'We have passed through the Enquiry, the Reflection, and the first step of Renunciation. We are now at a resting point that offers peace, a peace that nurtures. So allow it to give you its blessings. I would make the most of it, because next comes Purification.'

I knew I would not like Purification. I could see the hotels fading into a necessary dismal distance. More nights with a hundred insects under a thousand stars. Food would have to go, and I anticipated fasting and drinking only water. My guide didn't give me bad news directly anymore. Her new technique was to talk about what the others had done. 'Everyone starts on "the hidden", which is also a good place to hide things. Safely they make their enquiry. Verdaguer used the barraca to prepare to fast, to be alone, to test himself. For him, the barraca was a retreat. Saunière's companion, the priest from St Feliu, was asked if his charge was fit to be a member of the society. So they gave the French priest that question to reflect upon: "Am I fit to be a member of the society?"'

'What did he decide?'

'To go ahead. Whether he asked the question is another matter.'

'Didn't they like him?'

'He was too rich. And many of the priests succumbed to the lure of the money, took it, and so disliked him more. The student from—'

I stopped her. 'Everyone else had a guide, but Saunière had a companion. Why? Then he reached this place and met his guide. Who was his guide?'

She didn't answer.

'You told me this. He walked with the companion until he met his guide at Romanya and then continued by horse and carriage.'

'I'm glad you have a good memory. I can't tell you who his guide was.'

I asked why not, and she said it was a private matter.

I remembered that Lucia didn't like secrets. She said they harmed the holder, damaged the true self. I said as much to my companion.

'There are some things that you will be told not now but later, and others that you will not be told.'

Liliane continued on the subject of Enquiry and Reflection and of how the student from Paris in 1820 had enquired if he was strong enough to be a member. Saunière decided immediately that the barraca was a place to avoid treachery and escape trickery. He had had enough of those things in the house with the tower. Naturally I asked why. 'Because of who followed her—Maria—into the house. The barraca was a safe place for Saunière because Mathieu didn't know about it,' she concluded.

I asked if Liliane knew who the law student from Paris had been.

'Quim Carreras's ancestor.'

That made me quiet. I realised I was not sure of Quim Carreras and never had been. I told her about the business of the lost cross and chain. Who had they belonged to?

'The custodian of the society,' she said. 'Carreras was furious that José had simply given them away.'

'Did it have special powers? The cross?'

She gave a strange answer. 'Well, yes, if he gave it to you.'

Our conversation turned to the church we sat in. Pre-Roman, it was dedicated to St Martin, the patron saint of soldiers, knights, and tailors. It was mentioned in 1016 as 'Romanicino'. The area we were in had been and was still known as 'Las Gavarres'; it had been the *Domaine* of landowners and frequented by people buying and selling the land. In 1076, the site came under the Church of St Feliu.

'This place is peaceful,' I said.

'It is safe,' she corrected. 'A place to rest up outside the magic square. What the initiates were doing on the journey in those days was heresy. Here there was a refuge, which became a restaurant, San Roque, in 1898. There was a church, a few houses, a fountain, but no resident priest, because the priest would have had other small parishes to attend. To walk up here would have taken six hours; with a horse and cart, maybe two. So no one could take the initiates by surprise.'

'So they had a lookout?'

'Or dogs.'

The church was simple and cared for. After a while Liliane stopped putting euros in the box, and we sat in a shaft of sunlight from the open door. I asked if there had been spiritual appearances here, but she hadn't heard of any. Again, it was a question of the energy.

What did it actually give to me, this place? It seemed my turn to ask myself the questions. The place was nice enough. Was it mystical? Where was the proof? I turned to Liliane for that.

'Oh, so you want proof? I can give you that.' She laughed. 'But first we have a good tea and then you do the Renunciation affirmations and we discuss a little about thought.'

I felt comfortable in Romanya, and the restaurant served good homemade tart with berries. Vacant rooms en suite were available. All I had to do was persuade Liliane away from the evolvement of another night under the stars with fountain water, blessed or not. Naturally, I would pay the hotel and all expenses.

'I release my hold on material things.'

'I release my hold on those I love.'

As I repeated these renunciations several times, she asked if I could see myself in bright white light. I could not. What she meant to ask was whether I could create it myself in my mind. For perhaps a few moments I was successful. She asked me to add to the list of renunciations, and for a terrible moment I was going to add the hotel and good food. She said I could release my hold on some quality within me. I chose negative thought. What purpose did it serve? It was an easy one to let go of.

'Thoughts are habits. You change them. When something you have chosen to renounce occurs, you simply replace it with another thought. For example: an affirmation. Let's take one José chose in 1954. "I am gaining strength from breathing through this exhaustion. I am filled with light from God, so no harm can come from me."' She paused. 'Notice he said "from", not "to".'

I said I had. I could also see I would have to let go of José and the thoughts about him.

'But of course you think of him. He is a finely attuned man, spiritual on a high level. It would be crazy not to think of him.'

We walked away from the hamlet and started downhill. She was going to show me the mystical proof she had hinted at earlier. First she asked what *mystical* meant. I said something that is yet unknown. She agreed but added that it would have stronger and different energy and resonance than everyday things and happenings that might in themselves once have been 'unknown' but yet were not mystical, like the antibiotic penicillin. The mystical was not bounded by gravity.

Through the trees I could see a cross. Nearer, it became a large stone, bronze monument. Its inscription: 'LOVE, GLORY, and REPARATION to the KING of SIGLES, 1904. YOUR KING-DOM COMES TO US.' That it was here in the middle of the countryside, unseen, was a mystery. 'Is this it—the mystical proof?' I asked. She watched me examine it. I asked what it was and why it was here.

'It's a monument to King Sigles,' she replied, merely stating the obvious. She walked on, and already I had to hurry to keep up with her.

The proof was half an hour away in another part of the forest. Liliane pointed to trees with some inches of their bark removed, their slender trunks like shaved legs.

'*Alzina*, or cork trees. It's from here they get cork for bottles. It's the local industry.'

We were in the hour before twilight, the blue hour. Through the trees I could see an arrangement of huge stones surrounded by a wire fence. I remembered them from years past—these unexplained stones of Romanya, which I'd visited with a group. In those days, they had just been there with no fence or commentary on a board in several languages. This time they seemed a little more arranged, cleaned up. The stones were considered on a level with Stonehenge.

Figure 10.2. The megalithic stones of Romanya.

'The Dolmen de la Cova,' Liliane said. 'A *dolmen* is a collective megalithic burial enclosure made up of several burial chambers.' She led me up to the first stone so I could see what she was going to explain. There was an entrance through which an uncovered passage made of stone led to a covered enclosure. In front of the entrance stood large stones in a circle. She pointed to the passage. 'The access corridor to the burial chamber is covered by that mound of earth and stone. This was constructed by a human group, possibly Druids. But how?'

'Like Stonehenge?'

'At least equally mysterious. The slabs are granite, but from where did they get them? How did they bring them here? They are huge and heavy. This is built with skill. The circle of stones is for the ritual ceremony. The entrance faces southeast so that sunlight can reach the funeral chamber at the exact moments of the summer and winter solstices, which shows that these people followed a religious practice.'

I asked when the dolmen was built.

'2200 BC.'

'So they were intelligent beings?'

'Certainly they were intelligent. They were *initiated* beings. In the funeral chamber the excavation group, led by a local Catalan historian, found a necklace, flint arrowheads, beads, human bones, teeth, a knife, fragments of pottery, and a bowl made of stretched animal skin and bone. The bowl was interesting because when struck it sounded the note F-sharp, with which we are already familiar.'

Liliane said the excavation of the area began in the fifties but really got going in the seventies. I asked if she knew the excavator. She did—the original one. Several thoughts claimed attention. Was he in the society? Had he gotten here first and chose the bowl as 'interesting'? Did it form part of later society rituals? Why the twenty-year gap between the start and the more intense period of the excavation?

'The covering mound served as a buttress,' Liliane went on. 'The cromlech is still visible.'

I wasn't sure what I was looking at. I found the arrangement of stones moving, sweet, sad. They were pure.

Figure 10.3. Entrance to the Balneari Prats, Caldes.

We did spend the night in a hotel but not the way I'd chosen. She drove to the spa at Caldes de Malavella, and we stayed at the Balneari Prats. I asked if the Dolmen de la Cova was part of the journey and she said it had never been. Why? It didn't have the energy pulse, the resonance. Why not? Who chose these points? I personally preferred the dolmen over much else I'd seen. She said again I went for the drama. I asked what the preferred opposite was, and for once she answered me, rather than my having to find the experience and work it out: 'For instance, the space north of the church at Romanya. It is a space, seemingly nothing else, but there is energy there. Modern people have not chosen such points, which were discovered centuries ago. But we can try to resonate with them. They can be found in the most undramatic, even tawdry, places.'

I'd known the Balneari Prats spa for thirty or more years; it felt like the home I should have had. Not even this journey would disturb my relationship with the place and the owners and my sense of well-being here. I'd spent Christmases, New Years, fiestas, celebrations, and heartbreaks in a room with a terrace overlooking the glorious gardens and hot springs. My commitment to and love of this spa made me feel invincible. I would try and share my enthusiasm

Figure 10.4. Dining room at the Balneari Prats.

with her. I expected she could see my relationship with the place; she could see everything else. Magnanimously, I looked forward to discussing it with her. I arrived at the dining room before she did and sat down anticipating the delicious four-course dinner.

In fact, my stay in Caldes was to be unlike anything I'd ever known. Reality was turned on its head. For a start, Liliane didn't come to the dining room at the correct hour. The first I learned of her arrival were two hands around my soup bowl moving it swiftly away. The speed was frightening. Was it poisoned? Had she asked the cook to add hallucinatory drugs to speed up my resonance and then thought better of it? I thought the worst or the best and then she said, 'Hot water with lemon.' She gave the soup bowl to the waiter and sat opposite me. I asked what was wrong with the soup.

'You having it at all. Your fasting begins now and takes–'

'No to the fasting.'

'You drink hot water with lemon throughout.'

'Can't be done.'

'Dry toast at–'

'I want my soup back. I will eat my dinner.'

She was quiet for the shortest time and then asked for the menu. 'Purification includes what you put into your body. There is the quick way and the slow.'

I chose the slow. For a moment, she had the ironical expression I'd seen once in Girona when I'd overstepped my shopping impulse. She ordered a meat-free meal for two.

'You will eat a healthy diet without meat or sweets, and no coffee or alcohol or white sugar. And you will drink the hot water with lemon. I see you've ordered a series of treatments and massage.'

'Naturally I'll pay for them.'

143

'You seem quite at home here.'

'They say it's my second home. Maybe it's my first.'

'At home enough to forget that you're treading the seven stars, walking with the Great Bear, on a privileged journey of initiation? I've cancelled the treatments. You have one massage each day.'

Before I could protest, she announced my routine: up at 6 a.m. with the hot water and lemon drink; a cold shower and one hour's walk, at first with short stops and then continuously—a lot of the walking would be uphill; morning practice in the garden; writing what was asked of me.

'You will make your admissions and confessions to God through another person.' She offered me a baked apple.

'You?'

'Not necessarily. You will do the psychic baptism, which will be explained to you. You will sit in silence for two sessions before nightfall. I have also arranged for you to have yoga classes.'

'There will be no time for meals.'

'On the night of the full moon we'll drive to S'agaro.'

I knew S'agaro. It was a beautiful, mostly unspoiled resort on the nearby coast.

'When thoughts arise that we have agreed are not beneficial, write them down and we will discuss it during our final talk last thing at night.'

I actually laughed. I did think it was a joke or a test, one where she would find out if I had a resonance with humour.

'You drink only water.'

Referencing our agreement to reject the unacceptable, I said I couldn't just drink water lying in a room.

'Oh, there's no lying anywhere. You have work to do.'

'So, all this is real. You're not having me on, Liliane?'

'What have you got against water?'

'It'll come from some fountain that has a myth attached to it, but it will still be water.'

'When a spirit on a high level approaches this earth, actual changes occur. Charred markings appear on the ground, left by the passage caused by the electric current as the spirit becomes manifest. Some people explain them away as lightning striking. Yet why are they always the same pattern and one that has a cabalistic significance? Portal. Doorway. Often when the spirit is present, water appears either as a spring or a fountain. This is blessed. Healing. Think of Lourdes and the vision that came to Bernadette Soubirous and the sudden spring of water that still heals today. In the eighteenth century, the Magdalene had appeared by the barraca, and the fountain had gushed up in that dry place. So visions bring change to the environment, and the water that accompanies them is alive, not dead, and healing, not polluted. You will change your thinking. Some thoughts are merely habits. All the initiates had to forego recurring thoughts, which took over from the skilful and the essential. The initiate is introduced to this change during the Purification practice.'

The waiter brought me coffee as always, a small, black espresso with a little hot milk, and Liliane waited for me to turn it away. I did hesitate before lifting the cup. Her presence there, her disapproval, ruined the coffee experience.

I defended myself. 'You see, I know this place and I like it. That's why it would have been better to go to the other spa.' I meant the Hotel Vichy, which had a cold, formal atmosphere.

'I think we can manage here,' my guide said, dryly.

I looked at the clock because the card game would start at ten.

'I wouldn't concern myself with time.' She'd already established that I shouldn't wear a watch. 'And the portable phone has to go. No contact with the outside world for now.'

If I was going to continue the journey, I had to do it her way. This place couldn't be more *my* way, and I felt that was why she'd brought me here. This was my territory; it was where I was strong. But a decision had to be made and she knew it, as did I; there was no need for more discussion.

The owner, Rosa Quintana, expected I'd sit and talk with her family and later go to the card room, but I was whisked out into the cool garden like a wayward child.

'Did the others fast when they came here?' I tried to sound friendly.

'The others did not come here. The early ones went to Besalú. This spa didn't open until the 1860s.'

That was a surprise.

'But the water is here.'

'The water has always been here and used since antiquity. Girona is over four thousand years old. The Romans built spa baths here, but after they left, the baths weren't used.' She pointed to the Roman ruins at the top of the hill that people took for granted. It was just there, the old bath. Didn't I, too, take a lot for granted?

I asked where Saunière and José had done the Purification practice.

'In a house in the forest near here. They used these waters. When your body starts to ache, you go into the hot pool. It has always been good for joint pain. And you use herb compresses.' And then she said Maria Tourdes used to come to Caldes, and I remembered that she had had leg problems.

'A heart problem,' Liliane corrected.

'A bad heart?'

'A broken heart.'

And that truth reverberated deep inside me until it reached the image of the young, dark-haired girl weeping convulsively on the bed in the house with the tower, holding tight to a scroll or parchment. Was it because Saunière had loved the singer? Had he forbidden Maria to appear at the recital? Shown no respect, she was shut away. It was obvious he preferred Emma Calvé.

'No,' said Liliane. 'He opposed the good; the parchment told her that.'

I asked about the mystical influences in Girona, and she said to comprehend them it was necessary to understand the beheaded pyramid. The top piece with the number 1 was the Tear of Isis. Had José talked of the Passage of Light? Number 1 was also Aleph. The beheaded pyramid included Seth, Isis, Osiris, and Nephthys; these were the four elements to pass through the light. Together they made the unity.

She looked at me and understood once and for all that I was not in resonance with esoteric thinking. 'It's all about unity—unifying the energies. Girona, square number 34, is ruled by the moon. It is water, the cup, the Ark of Noah, Isis. There are the influences. Just hear it. You won't understand it.'

She'd got that right.

'Much of the journey is not verbal,' Liliane continued. 'The different sites and their numbers are not transferable. You have to experience them. The underlying indications assigned to each site were never spoken. They remain underneath the surface of our communication.'

'So is it a code?'

'It's a process of evolvement.'

'What are the numbers?'

'The resonance, the key, the stepping stones to evolvement. The mystical language that could never be spoken.'

All I understood was that the magic square was composed of numbers and that the signature of the journey was made up of certain of these numbers that were relevant. The eleven sites made up the signature of the Great Bear. The numbers were never said aloud but received by a state of understanding that was divine.

Liliane asked me to write what I remembered of the journey so far in the new notebook. I was tired and aching, ankles swollen from the heat. She said Girona was swirling with unconnected mysteries. To know more I would have to know the Active Principle of Isis. She didn't think at this time sacred geometry was my priority. As we came to each site she would list the influences and ruling signs. She was very calm about my lack of esoteric knowledge and treated it quite simply. 'You have had other things to do.' Again she said the journey followed the constellation of the Great Bear.

'What is *shin*?' I asked. Saunière had mentioned that word in his account.

She explained that the following description came from her work in the esoteric, the Theosophical, and the material held by the society, all of which I should simply know in passing.

'*Shin* is the mother letter symbol. It makes up the number 360, which is known as the perfect year. The year used to be 360 days long until the orbit of the earth was disrupted by a catastrophe, after which five days were added.' She indicated that this occurrence had happened before time, as I would understand it, and that both Pythagoras and Plato had referred to it. Saunière was interested in shin and its relation to the Ray of Lightning, Thunder, Fire, and Pyramid Stones. The French priest was eager to master all mystical references to fire, power, force. 'That says something about him,' Liliane concluded with a laugh, but not with humour.

I slept lightly and didn't feel as though I was in my beloved Caldes at all. As always, the bells stopped after midnight; they always rang twice on the hour, which always raised thoughts of José, who was only a short distance away down the narrow road made silver by moonlight.

The garbage trucks came at 7 a.m. That was always a time for earplugs, but Liliane had beaten them to it, bidding me to rise and carrying in the hot water with lemon. She waited while I took the cold shower that she suggested I alternate with hot. This routine, so different from my usual life, was obviously going to finish me off. Maybe she wasn't José's friend at all, but his wife's. Had he ever *said* she was a friend? All he'd volunteered was that she lived in the mountains.

After a brief stretching and breathing exercise in the deserted garden, we were then off on this discordant morning, along the road where the chemist shop used to be and into the country where Canigou in all its various moods was always visible. Today there was snow on its summit, and I felt it was too powerful. The mountain's image, too acute, seemed to sear my mind. Little sleep, no coffee, no hot bath or breakfast—it was all definitely a mistake.

'Would you say you rely on food and stimulating drinks to keep you going?' Liliane asked.

'No, I would not.' Defensive now, stung with fury, I sat on the nearest wall. 'I deserve them. I've had a hard life, and if those things make it better, so be it. I'll go on ordering what makes me feel good.'

'Is it the taste, the look of the food, or the expectation? Or the fullness afterward?'

I didn't give the rather tart answer that came to mind. I should have, but I calmed myself and started walking ahead.

She didn't move, waiting for the answer.

'All of them.' I said. At least it was an honest answer.

I was out of breath long before thirty minutes were up. She sat in a field while I did the required leg stretches. She asked me to shake out my feet, arms, hands, and then to stand on one foot, hands joined above my head, and focus on a still object, eyes closed. This was a yoga practice with which I was familiar. But it was not familiar with me this morning, and I fell sideways. I tried again with the same result. I hated to fail. I hung down over my knees. This journey or whatever it was had of course become impossible. I told her I couldn't bear to have someone close all the time watching me.

'Do you have any questions?' she asked, unexpectedly.

'What business is it of yours what I think about food?'

'Because you're going to start doing without.' Liliane sounded firm.

I waited in vain for an explanation so had to ask what she meant.

'You're going on a fast.'

We had quite a discussion about that. I lay down across the grass but couldn't relax. I told her if I saw José I'd kill him.

From her rucksack she took two things: a sealed bottle of sparkling water from Caldes that she opened and gave to me, and an object wrapped in silk. I sat up, drank the water, and then heard a most incredible chime that seemed to go on beyond its time. I waited in some trepidation for it to end because I couldn't bear for it to end. In one hand she held a small bowl; in the other a metal stick. Before

150

the chime faded, she again struck the side of the bowl and again the sound filled the air, the woods, my mind. Immediately my restless agitation was quite gone. I lay back on the grass and realised that the chime made thought impossible. It claimed all existence.

When the chime finally did come to an end, I didn't feel loss or want to hear it again. It was as it should be. She ran the metal stick around the inside of the bowl and it stirred up a quite different, even hypnotic sound; then she placed the bowl above my solar plexus until the intonation ceased. I did feel sweetly healed and not in need. She was no longer the antagonist.

The return to Caldes took twice as long as the walk out had, and I sat on two benches and three walls. When we finally arrived, the breakfast waiter, seeing me, was amused. 'You're early. Or have you been out all night?'

If only! I ordered the full breakfast, planning all the time how to get the forbidden coffee without Liliane knowing, even though I did realise it was crazy. But she was there too soon, disgracefully intruding by cutting my order in half. Instead of orange juice, fresh pineapple. The other changes were far worse. Throughout the mean breakfast with various green leaves and herbs, I did not say one word.

As soon as I saw her going toward the village, I was up at the bar demanding a jug of coffee with hot milk. After I'd drunk it I did wonder why it was so important. I decided I would take the next coffee relaxed in the village bar. At eleven o'clock precisely, I actually ran, off behind the church, without obstruction, all the way to the bar. My gaoler caught me as I was reaching in between the beaded curtains of the doorway to make a gap through which I'd disappear.

'You can run! That's a surprise. So some good comes from so much obstruction.'

I said we would have to talk. I even took her arm to lead her to the church bench. Being close to that edifice might give extra strength to my words.

'Why should a cup of coffee be so necessary, so all-absorbing?' She seemed interested in the answer.

Not wanting to justify anything, I countered, 'Is it necessary for you to set these little rules? What has it to do with the journey of the Great Bear and Seven Stars?'

'Everything. If you don't follow my instructions and trust their purpose, it will certainly matter later on.'

So we went to and fro the subject of coffee. She explained it was not acceptable on the fast that came next, and, as I was attached to coffee drinking, I had to deal with it.

'What does coffee stir up in you? What past experience of deprivation has made you feel so strongly about it? Taste, expectation, stimulation denied?'

I said nothing.

She shrugged. 'Well, whatever it is, you've gotten over it, put it behind you. I don't think going without coffee is such a big deal.'

Going without. That could be an immense deal, but it was none of her business.

'Were you in a place where there was no choice about getting whatever it was you wanted?'

'Never.'

'Where people stopped you from getting what you so needed?'

I looked her full in the eyes and said that for now I'd go on drinking coffee, so we must stop talking about it. In fact, this confrontation brought up pain that I didn't expect, that had no place here, and I felt humiliated. It was the pain of being denied what you wanted.

'I hope your Purification practice will be honest,' she said. 'Otherwise, the consequence will come, but later, and on this journey "later" is too late.'

I went into the bar and drank a large milk coffee and examined the experience, took note of the taste. The first sip, the last mouthful. I then realised the problem wasn't about coffee at all but about being controlled and denied and so made helpless.

During the salad lunch I demanded to know what else was in store at these eleven sites. She said that knowing now would not help me.

In the afternoon she read me some of the Purification experiences of the fellow travellers, and I began now to have a link with them. Saunière had been terrified not so much that he would have nothing to eat but that there would be no wine. That was unacceptable and, like me, he had made for the nearest bar. In the forest there were no bars. He suffered. He disliked intensely being dominated for no good reason and said he would forego the whole journey if he couldn't get a drink. They gave him herbs and honey in hot water and it stopped the craving but not his arrogance. The books I'd read about Rennes-le-Château said that Saunière had had the grand life and that his food and alcohol bills were extravagant. Reports were that he liked to drink and that his brother Alfred had died an alcoholic death. I'd also understood that the French priest did not take criticism or orders from the local bishop too well. It seemed he did not like orders except when he gave them. He'd felt ill during the journey, but Liliane did not go into the details.

Verdaguer had accepted the whole process. He had felt so free, and then the need to dance, to fly, overcame him. He had collapsed from exhaustion and was put to bed for some hours.

The law student had terrible headaches and then felt overheated. He'd been wrapped in cold, wet sheets and then covered with heavy blankets and hot water bottles made of stone. This procedure had sweated out all toxins.

José had had the same treatment, with caster oil patches placed over his liver. His mind had raced and he'd been without sleep, but he had understood the process.

'So they were all laid up for some days?' I felt . . . was it smug?

'Three.'

'Weeks?'

No, Liliane meant days. 'They did it the quick way.' She read how light and alive they'd felt when letting go of their resentments. 'Let's start on yours.'

When I didn't locate any resentments, she mentioned the business of the coffee. I understood that coffee wasn't such a big thing. It was when you couldn't get it that it became important, and your mind wouldn't get off it.

'Exactly,' she said. 'We will look at attachments and freedom.'

When I asked how long I'd be on the hot lemon water and small meals, she gave no answer.

'So now you start your writing: resentments. Put them down.'

I said I didn't have any.

'Then start with me. You've got a few against me, for sure,' and she went out of room laughing.

I immediately phoned José from the hotel phone in the room. He sounded as always charming but also serious. 'Ask her for herbs.' He paused. 'My arms are around you. Remember that.' It felt better than a thousand journeys.

My resentment list became composed of occasions and acts during which I should have gotten the better of the situation but lost. Shamefaced, I wrote these first. Unresolved conflicts, the occasional hatred; they all had a go, at least on paper. Liliane had asked me to include what my part in them was. I defended my right to be angry with unjust treatment to the death.

I went onto the terrace to sit in silence. She hadn't given me any instruction about what I was to think or which position I had to adopt. To still my mind, I tried to recall the sound of the chime as the bowl was struck. I tried to find help from the woman of smoke. I could recall her instantly; she was indelibly there, but the warm, loved feeling did not accompany her arrival.

Dutifully, I did the series of exercises we had been building since the journey started. The problem was that I couldn't remember when the journey *had* started. For a moment, time was a problem. I was happy to go back to the sound of the chime.

After an early dinner of thin soup and fresh leaves, we sat by the small fountain and she asked how my experiences had been. I wasn't forthcoming enough. I did ask about the woman of smoke. Was she a spirit? My spirit guide? Or an apparition that hung around the debris of the Frenchwoman's garden? I believed Liliane had activated the warm, blessed feeling and asked if she would assist me again. She would not. She would not be tested. She was clear on that.

'The effect of your guides and the spirits around you varies, as does everything else. Your receptivity, the ease of the connection, and their strength of presence to some extent make the link successful or not. You are not being trained and developed to be a medium or clairvoyant but to get the most from this journey.'

She said I should now write a letter to each of the people toward whom I felt negative, putting in only the bad things, the accusations: you did this or that; you hurt me. 'Keep it short, sign it, and don't reread it. Do it tonight.'

I said I couldn't do all this. It was too much. What sense did it make?

Out came the account of José's revolt. Liliane read from her notes. He'd felt so tired—his eyes red-rimmed and un-focused—and poisoned by his own freed-up toxins that he wanted to throw up. He saw the Purification as a cruel and unnecessary act and would return to Girona as soon as he had the strength.

'Did he mention in his list of reviled persons Quim Carreras?'

She laughed. 'I am not allowed to pass on his private thoughts anymore than I would yours. And we are talking about the mid-fifties. I was not there.'

I asked if he'd gone back to Girona. She said he trusted his master from Ripoll and kept the faith.

I wrote the letters in my room, put them in envelopes, and sealed them. If I'd had scotch tape I'd have added that. She was not going to read one line. My beloved José might have trusted his master. My situation was different. I thought of my daughters, my grandchildren. They seemed a long way away. I missed my granddaughter, missed my life. I picked up the mobile and started to dial a friend in London.

At that moment Liliane came into the room with a tray of tea, some honey and lemon, and a flower in a thin, glass vase. I switched off the mobile, telling her that I had to make a phone call but would do it later.

'Not during these days. There will be a good time for phone calls when we go back onto the magic square and rejoin the path of the eleven sites.'

I wanted to know when that would be and for once she could deal with the future. 'In three or four days.'

I could phone my friend in three or four minutes, but I didn't tell her so. She gave me a few affirmations and closed the shutters.

'You'll sleep well.'

Then, at last, she was gone. I lay on the bed and thought, 'Out there is the mountain,' and it scared me. It seemed too near. I hadn't thought about the mountain in that way before. It was as though it had a personality.

Figure 11.1. Canigou, the sacred mountain.

CHAPTER 11

Abeautiful morning; everything was well and always
would be. Verdaguer had said something similar.
The birds, the trees, the grass: all putting out their
best. It was like the first day that had ever been.

'You're happy to be out of Girona,' said Liliane.

'Happier, perhaps.'

'To get away from what had been so glorious. As she
had been, too—Maria Tourdes.'

And then this glorious moment was gone.

I asked questions as we walked, but my guide didn't
give answers. Had she known Maria? How well? What
about Lucia?

'This journey is yours. It is not about me.'

'But you've done the journey?' Just to be sure.

'Many times.'

'Why so many?'

'Once for me. The rest for the initiates.'

'In this Venus Magic Square, what number is Caldes?'

'It isn't one. It's not a site. Like Romanya, it is a resting
point, out of the magnetic pull of the journey.'

'Why work on purification here then?'

'It will be easier for you here than it would be at Be-salú, which is Purification, square number 33. This is more Renunciation.'

I asked in what way Besalú 33 was harder, and she said because it, unlike Caldes, *was* in the dynamic and pull of the journey, so each experience there would be more intense.

We strode across the fields of Caldes on this exquisite morning, and I did feel moments of freedom. We sat by the pond with the best view of Canigou, and I remembered the splinter of fear of the previous night; it was no more than that. The beauty of the day burned out that image. Memory did not have to hold one hostage.

She said, 'What do you remember about the French-woman's garden?'

'The sound of the organ, the imprint of the tower on the wall.'

'What else?'

'Else? The gravel and tired tufts of grass.' I'd spent enough hours sleeping on it.

'What was its colour?'

'Oh, dear! Green.'

It was yellow. The green was farther away where the garden was in the shade. I did remember the atmosphere and the events, like the one when the man suddenly arrived to take photographs where the tower had been and interrupted the flow of our conversation. She said I always chose drama, and I wondered what was wrong with that.

'Nothing in terms of life. But everything when you approach the mountain. You have to absorb and so fill yourself with energy. Your lusting for information about the place is not helpful. You have to *be* the place. Attunement is your best ally. Why do you eat so much?' she asked abruptly.

Such a question, fast and intrusive, did not suit me.

'I feel too sheer for this.'

'Sheer. That's exactly what you have to be. Does food comfort you?'

I anticipated correctly a ravaging fast somewhere along the real route, of which we were still on the periphery. 'I eat to keep alive and healthy, and I *need* to eat.'

'Does it comfort you?'

I said I didn't know. It made me feel better. Was that comfort?

'Does it stop states of being from becoming sheer? Prevent a speeding up of ideas?'

'It keeps everything rosy. There's a sense of well-being, which is as it should be.'

'Don't be defensive. You stop the adventure of rising into other realms and dimensions by taking food and drink. It keeps you grounded. Those realms are uncomfortable, so keep your feet on the ground. Feel it. Use your feet. Not food. Food is your shield.'

I took off my shoes and did as she asked.

'The initiates go without food, drinking only water for many days. It speeds up their link with what they need to know. It would be impossible to experience what they do on a three-course meal. You eat to block your progress. You will have to face the certainty that in the end food will not do it for you.'

She gave me a bar made of herbs and fresh apple juice in a container. I tried not to eat like a pig. Going without breakfast made me feel weak.

'Go back to the French garden. What do you see there? Be there.'

I started once again with the mustard yellow—not green– grass.

'No, no. Go back to the garden in the 1890s.'

I saw simply the woman of smoke. She coiled around the dusty bushes, the littered gravel, her eyes full of love for this tawdry ground.

'Go past her. Go back. As it was in your dream.'

That was easier. I remembered even more. I could smell perfume, and I knew it was called Chantilly, by Houbigant. I could see the flat, curving scent bottle. My mind raced like a trapped burglar through a house. 'Stop!' I cried, and beat my feet on the ground.

Liliane's hands were warm and pulsing electrically as she placed them on my chest. The images faded and I could breathe properly. As she continued healing me, I remembered something about José and the Jewish Centre, how he had put on a concert of Sephardic songs in the 1970s. He had placed an upright piano in the courtyard, which I recognised as the one from Maria's house. The singer was Spanish, from Barcelona, and the courtyard was full. As always, there were masses of birds in the trees. The singer started toward a top note, but the piano keys didn't follow.

The piano was out of tune. There had been no money or time to get a piano tuner. A note was struck flatly, and a bird gave a jarring laugh and started to mock the singer. The audience in the courtyard started shaking, weeping with unacceptable laughter. The singer from Barcelona sang, the bird laughed, the piano key fell flat, and the audience held their mouths. Afterward a man said, 'It would have been better if the bird had shat on her,' echoing precisely what had happened when Emma Calvé sang in the Frenchwoman's garden in the 1890s. But why?

Liliane said, 'That's for you to decide. That's your work.'

On the way back to the spa, I said, 'They didn't all make it, did they? The law student, Saunière, Verdaguer, José, and their guides.'

162

'Why do you say that?' Liliane was on her guard.

'It just occurred to me. Was it . . .' I nearly said José, but knew it wouldn't be him. 'One of them didn't.'

'It doesn't matter. By this stage they were all going towards Cap de Creus and the devil's cave. You'll like that, as you like drama.' The Cap is the furthest east one can get in Spain.

'Don't you like drama?'

'I prefer unity.'

I wasn't sure what that meant, in her case.

On the last walk that day we turned towards a hamlet with a church and cemetery lined with cypress trees. We had to wait for a shepherd and bleating sheep to pass. I confessed to Liliane that the previous week I had left the Frenchwoman's garden to go to the Savoy Bar. I said I didn't follow her instructions because I never followed instructions, except possibly to save my life.

Why did I even tell her? That had been a week ago or maybe more. Was it because the day felt so good, and therefore I felt better than I had for months? Was it the cleansing foods or the clearing letters, the walking, the natural tiredness?

'There is no reason why you shouldn't have gone to the Savoy Bar,' declared Liliane. 'I listed eight things you should do, but sitting in the garden all day and night was not one of them. I think it's good that you used initiative and didn't stay stuck in indecision.'

Initiative? I should tell her my flight from the garden had been an urgent, impulsive, reckless need to see my lover. Yes, that's who he was. I couldn't say 'ex'. He'd never be an 'ex'.

As we walked towards the steep incline and the church of Llagostera, which never seemed to get nearer, I realised that Liliane had become a person, a protagonist, in my life. She wasn't just someone José had chosen whom I could follow for a few days through experiences that might resemble Disneyland or Dante's *Inferno*.

And then the mountain was there, hovering at the edge of my thoughts, all too important. Mt Canigou. Suddenly I understood why I'd confessed my duplicity. I might need Liliane. The mountain's presence made it essential that she know me.

The third day and I couldn't do it—the day. It was 6 a.m., the hot water and lemon cooling beside me. I could not move. Everything ached; I was a sack of exhaustion. Throughout the morning, Liliane brought hot herbal essences to drink and herbal compresses for my swollen legs. I had done too much. I had trusted her and was near collapse. I found speaking too much. I needed sugar, tranquilizers. Better yet, a visit from José might fix me up.

Liliane said my condition was normal and sat reading extracts from the law student's notes. He had written of how a scrupulous fast combined with a searching look at his life had him facing events in his past he'd assumed were well buried. He blamed the cleansing herbs, which had made him break until only his will had saved him. And then his will had snapped, too, and he was left as though shipwrecked in his own life. From that moment of surrender, he had built a new way of being.

'Why clear up the past?' I managed to ask.

'It is said that if you approach the end of the journey—which is really a beginning—and you have even a trace left of spiritual flaws or hidden bad deeds, then pity on you. You will be in great peril when you come into the presence of this end power. Pray for mercy, because it is many times worse than the fires of hell.'

164

'Who said that?'

'Someone who did not clean up.'

I deliberately did not look at my sealed letters, but I felt I should reconsider them. Feeling very low, I asked, 'What will I get out of this if I stick with it?'

'An experience you will never forget that will change you for all time.'

Señor Mons had said, 'The ones who came back.' What happened to the others?

She healed and massaged my knees and ankles, my fluttering heart, my burning eyes. Then she sat banging the bowl and the chime again took away all thought. It made my chest shake and body vibrate, as if I were engaged in a spiritual sexual act without drugs. I hung onto that chime as though it were the last intelligible thing in my world. I asked about the sound.

'F-sharp sustained, of course. It transforms matter.'

And I remembered that F-sharp had been the note made by the 'interesting bowl' found in the megalithic Dolmen de la Cova. I was hearing sounds from before known time, now forgotten.

The sound brought to my attention other matters I had glimpsed and then suppressed. Of course, the members of the society disliked me for writing the book; for knowing not enough but still too much; for being too in touch with, and maybe diverting, José. I still had more to find out, but they had found me first: I would be disposed of. And then came the mountain—more and more a presence on this journey. It was worse somehow than the society. It conjured up a huge image from my childhood that caused instant fear and was hard to describe. It was another matter on this journey that was not transferable.

Liliane took me to S'agaro that night, and we sat on the beach listening to soft waves and watching the huge, soulful moon reflected on the water. She began a chanting meditation, its sound singing out to sea to join the glory of the moon. It was a magnificent experience.

Others suddenly around us joined in, and we sat rocking backward and forward in various cross-legged positions: eyes closed, keeping the image of the moon on the water; eyes open, taking in the silver light. Who were these others? When I asked her she said, simply, 'Moon meditaters like you.'

It was then I admitted to myself that I rarely received answers, a truth that applied not just to Liliane but to Girona itself. Although my questions were simple and sometimes direct, they were usually rerouted into another consideration altogether. I suddenly wondered why the city—resourceful and rich with history, much still remaining—did not question and make more of the visions of the Lady of the Cup. Why did so few know of Saunière's visits, and why weren't these people even interested? Most of the inhabitants I knew from all classes and occupations didn't have time for the subject. I was reminded of something the nineteenth-century English writer George Borrow had written about Cordoba, a city in southern Spain. When I returned to Caldes, I found a note I'd made from Borrow's book, *The Bible in Spain*, written in 1836: 'Cordoba has no remarkable edifices save its cathedral, a magnificent and glorious edifice and well calculated to execute feelings of awe and veneration in the bosoms of those who enter it.'

The local people Borrow encountered 'cared little for the exploits of their ancestors'. Their minds were centred on the concerns of the present day, and they only noticed the splendour of the surroundings left by the Moors when they felt some connection between those surroundings and themselves individually.

Barrow goes on, 'Disinterested enthusiasm—that truly distinguish[es] the mark of a noble mind and admiration for what is great, good and grand—they [the people in Cordova] appear to be totally incapable of feeling. It is astonishing with what indifference they stray amongst the relics of ancient Moorish grandeur in Spain.' More interesting to them, I gathered, were the small concerns of the moment.

I thought how similar the Catalans in Girona were to the people of Cordoba: how they, too, lived in their present, many totally unconscious of the splendour of the street, the history, or indeed the secrets of the city. So many barely remembered the house with the tower, incongruous in its medieval or Roman setting. Or the fact that a foreigner, a young woman, had lived alone there for years, inviting cultured outsiders to musical evenings and social events. Not even the historians had questioned it. They did say that such a circumstance was not usual, not heard of. The only memory of Maria Tourdes left in the city was housed in the plaque in the garden entrance.

No wonder the Frenchwoman's garden was a good place to hide what should not be known. Surrounded by the self-concerned attitude of the citizenry, the private society must have had little problem.

Figure 12.1. Logo of the Balneari Prats.

CHAPTER 12

My recovery seemed slow. I stayed three extra days in Caldes and wondered if I had been actually ill.

Liliane said, 'But you have to remember you chose this. When I asked whether you wanted the Purification to be quick or slow, you chose the slow.' I did remember the sardonic expression she had had at the time, which I could have done without. I would have preferred more explanation. I may have chosen slow, but it was still too quick for me. When I tried to discuss it, she said, 'Do not quarrel with me.' I tried again after the short walk around the garden. Why did I feel this bad? I'd heard of toxins exiting unpleasantly, but this unpleasantness was worthy of discussion. Was my life festering inside me?

'Good. You are beginning to face what is happening to you. To force the issue, instead of hiding in dreams.' And she left the room.

What did *that* mean? I didn't like it. I sensed that somewhere in her short statement was a criticism of my affair with José. I went after her.

'Even better!' she cried. 'Now you are coming out of illusion and facing it.'

'It?'

'Your life.'

A young man joined us in the corridor at that moment, saving her—or perhaps me. I was hostile, she too sure. I realised I hated criticism. Maybe I should write another quick letter.

The young man was Juan Serrat. He spoke good English, had studied physics, and had taken a further degree at an English university. That was all I was going to know about him. Liliane told me that I was to take my letters on the next walk and that Juan would conduct my psychic baptism. 'And then we will be free and will start the walk to Palera,' she concluded.

I understood Palera was in the forest near Besalú, a small town known for its Jewish history and its broken bridge thirty minutes by car west of Girona. I didn't know how the minutes would add up if we started this craziness she called 'a walk'.

In the hotel garden, I did the exercises and affirmations on my own. I meditated on the house with the tower, but too many images intervened. I could balance on one leg, arms above my head, eyes closed. Once I thought I could discern an energy in the atmosphere. It was simply a matter of moving a mere two steps at a particular place by the pool. When I moved one way, I experienced a sense of weight in front of me; and then when I moved slightly back, the opposite. Was it an air current? Some effect from the water? It was certainly coming from the outside. I stayed in the place where I sensed the weight, and it didn't change. It was very slight, and to experience it at all took total concentration and, I supposed, attunement.

Liliane had gone; the car was not there. Juan Serrat came over to the hot pool and invited me to walk and see Caldes. When he mentioned coffee, I knew she had set a trap. Now, allowed to eat soup as well as salad, I could increase my walking, and we went towards the railway station in a marvellous sunset. Juan was calm and easy to be with and said he wanted me to understand who he was. If I chose, he would do the psychic baptism.

'I thought it inappropriate to join you suddenly, hear your innermost secrets . . .'

No one ever heard my innermost secrets, I thought to myself.

'. . . and conduct the small ritual of this psychic baptism without you having some idea of who I am,' he said delicately.

'Do you have to hear my secrets, innermost or not? Can't we just burn them?'

He suggested we have a coffee on the terrace of the second spa hotel, the Catalan Vichy with its neo-Gothic construction and towers. I chose mint tea and decided to try and phone my family again. For me, this was part of any square, magic or not. It was necessary. But what could I say I was doing? Juan laughed at that. 'You're playing with numbers. Tell them that. Your next one will be 33 Besalú.'

Did he work with Liliane? He was her student. His subject was quantum physics and biology, and he had a top job for a company in Barcelona. He worked with Liliane on precise matters concerning time and sacred geometry when he could. I asked how long it had taken him to tread the seven stars and walk with the Great Bear. He had not been asked to do the journey.

'So it comes by invitation?'

'Definitely.'

He told me the spa suited me.

'It always did. This time I don't know where I am. I feel I've been made ill.' I described the challenging days in the room and he listened actively. I liked him and wished he could guide my journey instead of Liliane.

'Being ill can be a useful process, as the effort to recover raises your subtle energies. Combat and overcome the illness and you become more evolved in this process. It raises you faster spiritually.'

I said I hoped so and asked if he knew José. Yes, he had heard of him. I tried to ask more, especially about the society, but he said that was within Liliane's province, so I tried to question him about the numbers of the journey. In his view it was better to be in the present one, the one I was in at that moment; there was already enough to do. Why look for a future one I wouldn't understand anyway? I tried him on what the 33 meant. Again he avoided replying. It was clear he wouldn't answer any questions. This was not a person who'd be hearing my innermost thoughts, let alone anything else.

Juan described the process of psychic baptism: I would read to him each letter I had written describing my pain as a result of the recipient's behaviour, injustice, betrayal—all of it. He would then burn the letters at a sink, run cold water over the ash, and throw salt on the plughole. At the end we would say a prayer and go outside for a walk. I might feel emotional performing this ritual, but in a day or so I'd feel free. All the stuff I'd been carrying, although held down and not acknowledged, would be gone.

Juan had lovely hands, and I trusted their definite, elegant gestures. I liked his eyes, his warmth, his small smile, dry and ironic. I didn't mind his curly hair or hooked nose. His walk was free and uninhibited. But I didn't trust him, or rather, those guiding him. He'd hear secrets, but not those in the letters.

He was continuing his description of our ritual. 'It's like an operation. You remember how you felt before, but the emotional charge is gone. Your memory does not go. It is not a lobotomy.' He also said a prayer asking to be simply a channel for this process. He'd performed the baptism many times, and the recipients found it worked.

'Why didn't you become a priest?' I asked.

'It wouldn't make this process any better.'

He wanted to know if I had any questions. I told him about the coffee, how Liliane had controlled me and I didn't like it.

'Perhaps she had to find a way into you, past your defences, so your relationship would become more dynamic. You seem an original person, and you've worked on those qualities that keep the originality. You don't want to be changed, and you don't welcome intrusion. You've had to look after yourself.'

He'd got that right.

'Be proud you're on this ritual path. After having walked it, Jacint Verdaguer wrote his masterpiece, the epic poem, "Canigou". When do you want to do the psychic baptism?'

'Let's do it now, get it over with.'

I wrote each letter quickly, emphasising the most potent resentments, and signed my name at the bottom of the page. I was surprised there were so few—only five. To Juan I read bits of the first and second and edited and reinvented the rest. He burned them as agreed and, when he'd thrown salt in the plug, asked how I felt. I was shaky. Tears, unaccustomed tears, would be next. When I said I wanted to be alone, he hugged me and left.

That night at the dinner table, there were surprises. The four courses were back and I could choose what I ate. Liliane even ordered coffee. She asked what I knew about Caldes, and I related some hopefully amusing stories about the spa and gossip from the past.

'You see,' she said, 'I am not your analyst, or your critic, or your girlfriend, or your audience. I am here to pass on the preparation for the journey. If you have a certain way of seeing your environment that is different from mine, I wouldn't think of changing it. But because we're on this journey, the subject matter has to be less dramatic and more basic. When I ask what you know about Caldes, I mean, not gossip, but its purpose, its energy, its resonance.'

I explained that when I had been in Caldes I had stayed at the spa. I knew little about the village.

'How many letters did you read?' The question was sudden, and I couldn't look her in the eyes. Of course, that gave me away.

'If you didn't pass on the full text, it's your loss,' she said.

'Don't worry; it's all on paper.' I still couldn't meet her eyes. 'I don't see why it's necessary to read it at all.' I didn't bother to add that I was sure Juan had read as much as he could while burning it.

'It has to pass through an initiate to be cleansed. And for you to be healed. How did Caldes get its name?'

I didn't know, but I had always found *Caldes de Malavella* a lovely name.

'It is not lovely. You don't even know its source.'

I did not.

'Translated, it means "hot waters of the bad old woman". Three kilometres from here is a castle in which an old woman lived, maybe two centuries ago. She sent her servant out into the village to kidnap a child. The servant took this infant to the cook, who ripped off its skin and threw the skin into a well. He took out the child's heart and cooked it, and the old woman ate it. The servant was then sent out again, numerous times, and noticeably the children of the village started to disappear.'

'Is that story true?'

'Before the time of the story, the name of the spa used to be Caldes de Joncar, so something must have happened to change it.'

The coffee arrived and tasted better than I remembered. I could see that taking a pause from something you liked made it more appreciated.

Liliane asked if I knew how Caldes began. I did not. She told me that the water had always been known for its curative powers and that the local people had used it for their ailments. The advent of the train in the 1850s had expanded Caldes's popularity. The middle class from Barcelona travelling on weekends to enjoy the countryside and fresh air had discovered these waters. They started noticing the benefits, and spa facilities were quickly put up. At that time, visitors drank the waters from the different springs and bathed in the pools. More people came from Barcelona and, as there were no hotels, they stayed in the houses of local people. Very quickly, these two hotels—the hotels Prats and Vichy— were built. The water started to be bottled. There were various small family-run lodgings at a cheaper price. Doctors came to set up practice. The locals stopped working on the land and served in the hotels. The girls were chambermaids and waitresses, and then massage was introduced. The locals turned their hand to that and to making compresses and giving sitz-baths. This all happened before the First World War. The super-rich of Barcelona were copying the European aristocracy's practice of visiting spas. They visited Caldes and made this their Baden Baden. They brought their families, servants, chefs, and stayed several months at a time. There was a striking distinction between the Barcelona curists and the locals, and considerable rivalry arose. There were entertainments, dances, cards, a real spa life. And to this spectacle, Maria Tourdes used to come after the priest's death in 1917.

'It's just a myth, the old woman eating the hearts of children,' I said. 'It has no point. Unless it's the first transplant case in history. She took these new hearts to restore hers, old and clapped out.' I'd always thought the name *Caldes de Malavella* referred to something marvellous—I loved saying it. Another unasked-for moment of reality.

The following morning, I had breakfast downstairs at the wonderful hour of 8 a.m. and Rosa Quintana, the proprietor, said, 'So, you're leaving today.' It was the first I knew of it. 'We've hardly seen you.'

I didn't want to leave. I told Liliane I wanted to stay longer because I felt a sense of well-being in Caldes that I hadn't found much in my life recently. She must have assessed this information as serious because she got out of the car and said we'd go for a walk.

To be walking in the Caldes countryside once again gave me a sense of well-being. Again I admitted I had not felt really alive for some time.

'So you need a fix,' she said.

Not of substances, but of high love that pulsated from one to the other, blessed. She wouldn't like that idea, but I told her anyway.

'Can you get that from people?' Her question was too innocent.

'Yes.'

'You are certain?'

'Oh, yes.'

176

'You like the high, but you can't take the drop. Love isn't always as you describe. There are quite a lot of drops. How does that feel?'

To me, the answer was obvious.

'So you try and keep the high feeling?'

'Who doesn't?'

Her eyebrows lifted a sarcastic touch, reminding me of Lluís of the Arc Bar.

'I suggest you start looking in the realm of spirit for what you occasionally reach with a lover. It belongs there. Ecstatic contact.'

'So this journey is about getting over love?'

'Today, yes. But it's about getting over the state of being "in love". Not of getting over love itself. Eight days ago it was about getting over fear of rodents. The day before that, escaping rapists, intruders, germs, the unknown. Here it's been about surviving in spite of being denied what you want. Tomorrow, we shall see.'

So she would still be there tomorrow. Why did I doubt that? Did I need her approval? That irritated me. I was who I was and had a right to be that person.

She wasn't even subtle with the next question. 'How did you get on with your mother?'

Oh God. I wasn't going into that.

'To cut to the chase, I got out early.'

We arrived at the pond with the best view of Canigou five minutes faster than we had the previous day. She moved in front of me, blocking any view I might enjoy. Her eyes were fearless. I knew I was going to hear something I could not avoid.

'Those with a hole in the soul have something in common. They seek the high and cannot tolerate the drop and will do anything to avoid it and go high again. Yet the drop is part of our circumstances. Most people go through the drop and accept it.'

'Good for them, Liliane. I've been through plenty of low times, don't doubt it.'

'What comes after Renunciation and Purification?' she asked.

'I wish I knew.'

'Forgiveness and Acceptance. We have to make a start now on forgiveness. Then, when we reach Palera, which is a forty-minute drive from here, we can do the ceremony of Forgiveness. Those who have caused you pain—can you actively forgive them?'

'Of course not.'

'Even those who have a right to oppose you? Or distrust you?'

I wasn't thinking straight. I said yes, I couldn't forgive even them. I thought she meant José's wife—for whom I had felt distrust at first sight. Who else in Girona needed my forgiveness? And why was I restricting my resentment to the Iberian peninsula? Was I mad? What about the rest of the world? What about that global abundance of unresolved conflicts?

'What about your family?' she said, smoothly.

Of course, I thought of my first son-in-law. There were no words to describe my hatred for him. I'd go to my death unchanged on that. And I had no intention ever of discussing it, changing it, or forgiving. No human alive had the power to make me do that.

'Can you say a prayer for him?'

Was Liliane mad as well? After what he'd done to my daughter and my grandchildren? 'Let's drop that one. I'd sooner forgive my mother. Yes, I'll do that.'

My mother was in spirit and probably changed anyway.

'Did you have a part in your son-in-law's actions?'

'Never.' I closed my eyes. Had Juan Serrat quickly, with his scientist's mind, scanned the letter as the match touched one corner? He had a good memory. Unfortunately, so did I.

'I had to hear and see what that greedy, revengeful bastard did to my daughter and the children,' I raged. 'I went through it blow by blow and didn't care at the end if I just ended up—'

'Dead?' she asked.

'Of course not. I had to pick up the wreckage.'

She still didn't understand. I asked if she had children.

'It isn't my problem, nor yours, if I have or not. This is about you. After the forgiveness comes a state of acceptance. I promise you it's worth it.'

She hadn't had children. She didn't know that terrible bond that is activated like a heart in agony when your child is in pain unjustly, hurt unjustly. You'd do anything to stop that suffering, even take it into yourself.

'So much of her life was stolen from her, distorted, deformed. I can never forgive. It will be the last thing I think of when I lie dying. It's not about loving a child. It's about the child being brutalised and hurt over and over again. That's what I'm talking about. It's "no" to Palera.'

'We come into this life with a blueprint of our journey, which has to be gone through whatever the pain.'

'So you're trying to say it is destiny?'

'However bad, you learn from it.'

'I don't think I want to take that part, which is after all my business, through this magic square. Forgive him? Hell would freeze over first.'

'So what are you going to do with it?'

'Live with it. Isn't that what I've been doing?'

'It's in your life. But "live"? I question that.'

'I won't discuss it again.'

She nodded once, and we walked back to Caldes without speaking.

I was mindful of what Liliane had said concerning evil and the harbouring of bad thoughts and spiritual flaws when arriving at the destination—she'd called it a fate 'worse than the fires of hell'. Should I simply go back to London? If the society had placed me here, they presumably had an intent concerning my outcome. I realised that suddenly taking off to the airport was probably not the one they'd had in mind. I'd stay on till the next square number—33, the town of Besalú—and then slip away. I no longer trusted Liliane.

She opened her mouth and words were on their way.

'Please don't speak,' I interrupted. 'As you said, you are not my analyst. My actual life does not concern you. Your only interest is in my practical relationship with the space around me.'

She nodded. 'So you have understood.'

'I can get out of this, can't I? This journey?'

She opened the document case that seemed thinner now, the pages changing probably every day. She flicked through to 1954. 'After the purification practice, José started to walk back to Girona and was angry at being prevented. He, too, felt he was being enticed to do acts that would become more unpleasant and not of his choosing and over which he'd have no free will.'

I noticed the 'too'.

'The Abbé Saunière refused to complete the Purification practice. He tried only the lightest matters. So he did it again later. Fully.'

I understood the significance of 'fully'. Unpleasant.

'Why do you insist I continue?'

'Because, like those before you and their guides, I realise that you, too, will be deprived of an experience that is immortal.' She closed the document case. 'Surrender before forgiveness.'

When I had a moment away from her, I phoned my children and wished I hadn't. The journey had no place in this conversation, and I felt estranged, suddenly too different. My youngest son said, 'Where exactly are you, Mum?'

Figure 13.1. Crucifixion tree at the Church of St Sepulchre, Palera.

CHAPTER 13

The church of St Sepulchre in the middle of the thick woods of Palera was bleak. At the top of the steps stood a young, naked tree with a crown of barbed wire. I had not seen a picture of the Crucifixion so punishing—the slim, stripped trunk, its two branches flung up like arms, the crown of wire digging in at the top. I expected to see a head, a face. I wanted to run. I said, 'Who did that?'

'No one comes here.'

Liliane had acquired the church key. There was no electricity, but through a slit of window we could see something of this austere place.

'This church is one of the oldest in Catalunya. From the tenth century.' Even her voice was subdued.

I pointed to a white shape in front of the altar. 'Is that a ritual stone?'

'Count Bernat Talleferro brought it back from Jerusalem.' In the twelfth century, he had been one of many Talleferro descendants and had a great name for courage.

I was sure someone would walk in: a presence disguised in a normal human body, probably smiling, with nothing—absolutely nothing—good about it. In the corner stood a wooden cross, rough and almost pagan, cut from a tree in the forest. On this you would suffer.

'Count Talleferro brought back a piece of the Cross of Jesus. The pieces of the Cross, the relics that are sold just in Europe, would fill an entire forest.'

'Fake?'

'But of course. They used to hide priests from France here during and after the French Revolution.'

I couldn't wait to get outside. We looked through the window of the house adjoining the church, which did seem pleasant, even lived in. 'The French priest Antoine Bigou from Rennes-le-Château hid here,' Liliane said. And then we saw a fire still smoking. 'Probably a shepherd lives here now.'

'So this is one of the sites of the journey?' I wasn't looking forward to the answer. What would I have to do here?

'Of course. It used to be called Redemption.'

She led me back into the dark church and I said I didn't want to do it, whatever it might be.

'Surrender.'

'How?'

'Give your life and power over.'

I didn't like that. 'But I'm in a church.'

'It is never used. Not for centuries. Kneel down and surrender.'

'To what?'

'The highest presence you can think of. I would suggest you surrender to that.'

On knees painful to the cold, rough stone, I knelt and said words of surrender to God. I added that I would do whatever was asked of me. I had to stay there in silence for the longest time. I started to feel a warmth, an energy, on my head and back and realised Liliane was sending a healing force so that I could bear this process. The silence was so complete it filled the church with sound.

'Just give up,' she said.

'What?' I whispered.

'All of it.'

I tried to look as though I was at least in the position of submission ready to surrender, but all I felt was the increasing discomfort and the fear.

Driving on, we came to Besalú. The Jews had lived there in medieval times, and recently uncovered finds, including

Figure 13.2. Besalú.

a mikvah, a synagogue, and a mortuary, had opened up a strong tourist interest. I thought Liliane wasn't going to stop there, and all I saw from the car was the river and arches of the old sector. Then suddenly she turned around by a broken bridge and pulled up against the riverbank, but didn't get out. Although I supposed we were now exceeding the planned time of the journey, she didn't seem in a hurry.

'Besalú, site 2, square 33, is symbolized by the wave, the fountain, and purification, which is why the initiates originally came here for renunciation and fasting. It is both the fishing rod and the caught fish, which is the first Christian symbol. So what did you discover by the pool in Caldes?'

Her question took me by surprise, which was of course her intention. I realised I had not mentioned the slight change of sensation occurring when I had moved a step one way and then another at the side of the pool in Caldes. Moving forward, I had felt a weight before me; moving precisely back, a definite sense of lightness. I believed it was an air current.

'It is a doorway closed.'

I had intended to take her to the spot itself, but other things got in the way. Was she offended?

'I wanted to be sure,' I explained.

'You will experience it again, so it's good you already have a slight sense of "the doorway", Daleth 4.'

Maybe she wasn't offended. She was intent on keeping me on the journey. Who was behind that intention?

'Another important element here is hope—to hope, to confide. This you have just done at Caldes. For the more intrepid initiate, Besalú instead is a place for the psychic baptism and to get rid of your secrets. But carefully, because another meaning of 33 is "Eye of a Door Lock".'

I agreed that the image was extraordinary and supposed it referred to being watched, not beneficially.

'Yes, I thought you'd like it. So what does it suggest? "Eye of a Door Lock"?'

'Eavesdroppers, spies, prison. Nothing good.' I asked where these images came from, but she wasn't going into that.

At the outset, we had agreed that she would tell me the influences and symbols of each place. I started to understand that they were signs underlying reality, a formation in code that to the initiates might make sense of the everyday and link with other spheres.

She turned onto the main road for Ripoll and increased speed, her driving easeful, skilful, her reflexes and judgments aimed at preserving life. I did ask why we were going so fast. She replied that we had a lot to do.

Pointing to the forest that for miles lined either side of the road, she said, 'That's the Garrotxa. We'll walk there on the way back. What effect is building up so far on this journey?'

I didn't have an answer. I thought of the initiates who'd gone before me. They were miles, light years ahead. I felt left behind, stuck in modern comfort. Had it happened during the Purification as I clung to the coffee, the mobile phone, my rights, my identity? Was that why I now felt so empty? The others, after a bowl of soup and bread smeared with olive oil and tomato, had been up and off. But where had they eaten their main meal? In small refuges, a lakeside tavern?

'In the woods,' Liliane said.

'What did they eat?'

'Berries, mushrooms in season. What they killed themselves. Fish, fowl, cooked on a wood fire.'

Right, then left, the road changed direction, fast as a switchback, and we were in the centre of a small, forgotten village with one road and a church. She stopped at a bar and was greeted by a dozen locals sitting in a semicircle around a stove. The counter was of old, scarred wood, the wall behind patterned with beautiful tiles. She told me it hadn't been changed for a hundred years. On the wall was a small version of the chocolate poster that had been painted in the Girona alley in the fifties. We drank glasses of coffee with hot milk and ate *lenguas des gatos*, 'cats' tongues' biscuits. The stove had a pipe going up into the ceiling and it rumbled and smoked, belonging to another time altogether.

The men worked in the mountains and knew Liliane well. One of them talked in dialect about a monastery. He was most attractive, one of the calmest men I'd ever encountered, which was a big surprise in that small, forgotten place. He said there was a change of weather coming and I should wear more clothes. He recited Verdaguer, some verses he'd known for years. I was sorry Liliane insisted on leaving so quickly.

Back in the car, I finally answered her question. Yes, something was building up during this journey. I had started to think more about 'the mountain'.

She asked in what way.

'It's impending.'

'But you used to live beneath it.'

That was true enough, but now Canigou didn't feel like the same mountain. I'd always said I thought it was glorious. Did I? When I'd lived in Ceret in the 1990s, a town frequented by artists and intellectuals in the foothills of the Pyrénées, the locals, having listened to so many tourists, repeated them in saying that Rennes-le-Château's treasure was an equation providing the arch-plan of human life in the future. It had been placed on this planet by extraterrestrial beings, the discovery of which would make the finder master of this world. It was stated by more than one French scholar, priest, journalist, and scientist that this arch-plan showed how to transcend death before your death, to become invisible, to link with past and future, and to see the blueprint of your life purpose. Knowledge of this material was hidden because in the wrong hands it would be lethal. It was said generally that the Vatican had always known of its existence. Even the French president, François Mitterand, during his visit to Ceret in the nineties, had been interested in the influx of travellers on their way north to the now-infamous parish.

'Considering what I've heard over the years, that sounds quite sensible,' Liliane said.

'People came to the mountain to claim energy. It recharges everything. It's a savage mountain, I remember my neighbour telling me that. She also said it will claim its sacrifice.' I thought of Lucia and shivered. Then I asked why we hadn't done any absorption or exercise of any kind in Besalú.

'Some places on the journey are neutral. We stop at those sites that pick up resonance. That's where absorption has a point.'

We passed through St Joan de les Abadesses, then Ripoll, next to the Pyrénées near the French border, its train station old and unchanged. There was the seminary and the Benedictine monastery. Surely she'd stop here, but without explanation she swung out of Ripoll and the mountains were suddenly above us.

Soon we arrived in Gombren, a tiny, pleasing village, soft and clean, its bells light and optimistic. The hotel where Liliane stopped was a traditional *auberge*—inn—and probably expensive. She got out of the car and lifted a small suitcase from the boot. Directly above, the sheer mountain seemed to begin at the roadside.

The hotel was simple, scrupulously ordered, and with excellent food. It was known for its kitchen as far as Barcelona. It never had unoccupied rooms. Liliane booked two, and I felt they were expecting her. She gave me the bedroom with the mountain against the window. The shutters, the wood, the stone, the textures, the floor—all authentic—gave a rich feeling to this simple place. I could hear the tinkling bell of a colourful, delightful shop opposite and the sound of pleasant voices and laughter. The bed was large enough, with a firm mattress and a white duvet exquisitely clean. The only adornment was a bunch of mountain flowers. I lay down and thought of the others before me, catching fish in the river, the occasional rabbit, a bird. They had succeeded. The duvet was delicious to the touch.

When I woke up, Liliane was in my room, having showered and washed her hair. She had brought me a tray of tea and said she'd reserved a table for dinner. I wondered, looking as we did, how we'd be admitted to the dining room in the first place. She said it didn't matter how we looked, as this was mountain country and the style practical.

'Tomorrow we climb to the site,' she said. 'The poet Verdaguer knew this area well and walked here, farther toward the Garrotxa, the forests. He stayed in a room in the sanctuary *La Mare de Deu del Mont*, "Our Lady of the Mount", with his window looking directly onto the mountain. That's where he wrote his epic poem, "Canigou", in 1896.'

I asked if this was one of the eleven sites, and she pointed to the mountain. 'Up there, toward Ribes.'

At least it wasn't Canigou.

The food was exquisite to the point that we didn't speak. Each dish was a work of culinary art, light and designed to blend in with the rest of the meal. After five courses, we were satisfied but not heavy. We walked out into the village, into the icy air.

'So what have we done so far? List your tests.'

'Reflect, enquire, renounce, purify, maintain silence, surrender. Absorb the atmosphere. Test the energy of a particular place, as I did in Romanya. Meditate on the dream of Saunière and the French garden.' She asked what I thought of the journey. It all seemed to be about me, too personal.

'Oh, you'll shed that. I said at the beginning that you'll have to lose a few things to become teachable. This village of Gombren and the path above it is number 39 in the Venus Square. It means "to accept".'

We went back to the hotel and sat by the log fire. I asked if she'd been here at other times, and she said we didn't have time for casual conversation. There was work to do.

'We've got to do the balance sheet.'

I thought here it comes, the price. That was fine with me. Suddenly, the journey was worth more than money.

'In your letters to those for whom you feel resentment—even hatred, sometimes—and the desire to take revenge, what was the common theme?'

'*Justified* hatred,' I corrected her. 'And I won't discuss my family.'

She didn't want me to answer immediately but to revisit what I'd written. After a while she said, 'Criticism. They of you, you of them.'

I didn't think so. I'd realised what it was: 'Settled people had what I often so needed and did not have. I've paid a high price for my freedom.'

My guide tapped the bowl with the metal stick. 'F-sharp sustained, resounding directly with your heart chakra. This brings you what you need. Nothing compares with what the spirit world can give.'

She struck the bowl louder, and a cat came into the room and lay in front of her.

'I was happy with him.'

She knew whom I meant. 'Yet you did not stay with José.'

'I didn't trust him.'

'At some point you will have to question whether your daughter had any part in it—in what happened. Do you want to speak of what did happen?'

'No. My son-in-law hurt and damaged the people I love too much for me to talk about it.'

'But this is not a journey of escape.'

I didn't want to hear it and asked how many magic square numbers we still had to visit.

'There's not one you can hide in. Best hide in sleep.'

That night in Gombren, in my sleep, I could hear digging, the shovelling of earth, over and over, and I understood it was coming from the Frenchwoman's garden. I woke, sat up, and put on the light. In the dream, it had seemed to be night and I was walking towards the deep digging, the shovel held by a strong man. I told myself I must remember to tell Liliane the next morning.

Figure 14.1. The Benedictine monastery at Ripoll.

CHAPTER 14

Liliane had awakened before dawn and gone out to look at the night sky. Did she say Orion was visible? It was still icy cold; I had a wonderful breakfast and was in no hurry to leave. Why move on? I would stay a few days and then take a taxi to Ripoll, a train to Barcelona via the town of Vic. I no longer felt the value of the journey as I had yesterday. Now I believed that high feeling had been the result of days with little food.

'Describe the French garden. What's there?' She took me by surprise. I remembered that the grass was yellow but green in tufts where the ground got shade. The garden was on different levels, with stairs up the wall, which was part of the original city wall with slits for defence and offence. There were other trees and a space where the palm tree had stood. There were steps down from the garden to the arched entrance. I remembered that the house door opened directly onto the track and was painted brown. And that there was a tower and the place always looked empty. Now I was describing how it had been when I'd first seen it in the fifties. José hadn't wanted me to meet Maria Tourdes; he tried to say I should never go there because she was a prostitute and the house was cursed. Surely he wouldn't be so inventive with his argument to dissuade me from something so innocuous. After all, I'd been in Paris around people more volatile than the Frenchwoman. Sarcastically, I'd asked him if I'd misunderstood what he'd said. Did I suddenly have a problem understanding the Catalan language?

Liliane laughed when I said that. 'No,' she said. 'José has a problem with control.'

And of course, I'd defied him and got inside the house, and there had been the freshly dug hole in the living room with the evil smelling earth and dung. What were they looking for, or burying? And then Beryl was outside, calling for me.

'Now you have to climb,' said Liliane, echoing Beryl's words from the past. But Liliane meant the mountain, not the broken city wall, with its loosened stone.

I suggested keeping the rooms in the hotel. Not a chance. Following square number 39—the ruined chapel—we were leaving for the next site, the town of Figueras. Besides, the hotel was full.

The steep, stony path upward into the mountains was impossible, and Liliane carried on talking about the French garden. What else had I seen? The memory had diminished since my last description. Speechless, breathless, I had to go up on all fours. Then came the crossing of boulders, using balance I didn't think I had. The wind had its turn and blew icy particles into my face.

'Have you done your work on the two recitals? Why did the birds interrupt?'

Why did she question me now when climbing took everything I had? Must be to get my mind off the hazardous journey.

'What is this about? Really?' I asked.

196

She did pause. 'Finding solutions to the problems.' The wind was now blowing up against everything, and I said I couldn't go farther. She managed to get ahead, find a path, and tug me onto it. The sudden fall of sleet took away all sense of direction.

'Could it be the note the singer made that excited the birds? F-sharp sustained?'

I was angry and demanded to go back. How could I trust this person?

'But of course you want to go back. This small plateau before the next ascent is the site of Acceptance. Of course from that you would run. But whether you like it or not, you have to experience acceptance here on this plateau.'

Whether or not this plateau was the site of Acceptance, it was surely a place of destruction, which wasn't immediately apparent. A dismal chapel there that had been quite savagely destroyed gave no shelter. That seemed apt. Why had I thought acceptance would be pleasant? In some places all that was left of this building were stones along the ground where the walls had been.

'It was here the master from Ripoll discovered that originally there were 360 days in the year, and this number became known as the Perfect Year. At least from ancient Egypt forward, this has been common knowledge for adepts and students of metaphysical strains. Now it is obvious that he was not the first to discover this fact, but discover it he did. Do you want to know how?' Her words were blown away and brought back.

I did not. I covered my ears.

'From ancient texts he discovered a polarity we no longer have. He understood a calamity had happened. The earth had moved. We were given as a result of this catastrophe another five days a year. Just now I asked about the birds because an eagle has been present since we left the hotel.

It doesn't move.' She pointed up through the arrows of ice. 'You are not listening to me.'

'I am cold and don't give a shit.'

Worse, I was helpless. How could I get down, get back? The remains of this chapel carried its tragedy. Liliane wouldn't give me any story or legend; she would only say that the place had been hacked to pieces, its people passing through unimaginable deaths. Even a sun-filled day couldn't improve that history, much less the ice storm we were in now. Why hadn't I simply left Liliane as I'd planned at number 33 in Besalú?

'But that is the point of Acceptance: accept the conditions, the eagle, even my words and the way you feel. Experience it, please.'

'What happened to the others who didn't make it back from this journey? Even Señor Lara of the Peninsular Hotel mentioned pointedly the ones who did come back, as if in opposition to those who didn't. Where are the others?' I knew the answer.

'Maybe they didn't want to come back.'

'Is this how Lucia died? Up here? She hated mountains.' My teeth knocked together in the icy wind. I realised this was not some sweet, alternative-treatment ramble in the countryside.

'Accept. Say after me: "I accept that I am in this moment and it is cold and I don't like it. I accept that I want to know there is something better coming to me. That whatever happens, I am safe."'

'How do I accept?'

'Let go and let be. Don't fight.' Almost hypnotically she spoke, her voice coming smoothly through buffeting wind. 'Who are you?'

'Patrice Chaplin, writer.'

'What part of you is Patrice Chaplin, writer?'

I shook my hands, one leg; I touched my head, my heart chakra, all parts of what could be me. Wearily, I listed my works.

Just then, I thought she mentioned change: 'What of this identity can you keep? Even since you made the statement, everything has been changing. Even your books are wearing out, yellowing with age, forgotten. Your life on the bookshelves is passing fast. Your clothes are wearing out. Your blood cells dance a different dance. You feel you own your legs that you've just shaken. Do they really belong to you? Did you create them? Get inside yourself and tell me what is yours. Go into a bookshop and pick up one of your books. Is it yours? Did you produce it? Where do your words come from?'

'From me. Obviously. I work at it.'

'What is "you"?'

'My memory.'

'Not too good. The Frenchwoman's garden didn't do well out of that.'

I didn't remember enough for her. 'What is it about that place you so want me to remember?' The words were lifted and flung around by the gale.

Again she asked, 'You, what is "you"?'

'My personality.' I shouted through the wind.

'Can you keep it?'

'Of course. And my soul.'

'Better.'

'My experiences. My spirit. My etheric body that I take on to the next realm to be presented without spot.'

I'd go mad if she didn't get me back down the mountain, the impossible tracks now slippery.

'Show me acceptance,' she said.

I asked how.

She shrugged. It was my call.

199

'I accept,' I said.

'Now allow a silence while that statement reverberates around you and in you.'

I looked up. The eagle had flown away. Did that mean something? How I hoped not. My acceptance was false, pulled out of me by the unbearable mess of my situation.

'What do you need?' she said.

'Help.'

'Will you accept it?'

I would.

Liliane held out her hand, strong and warm, and led me on a ragged journey back down to the car. I was saturated with water running and splashing beneath my clothes as though I'd been rescued from a near drowning. She gave me a towel. Actually, I was desperate. My teeth knocked together as if they were tapping out a mystic code. She drove to Ripoll, her hair dripping into her eyes, the car slipping in the sudden unacceptable deluge, and stopped at a café in the square. 'Let's get warm. They said yesterday the weather would be rough.'

I couldn't speak to her. How could she be so irresponsible? I knew I'd get ill and dreaded it.

'It's only cold and wet. You've known that before.' The way she said 'you've known that before' had its reverberation, alright.

'You have a lot to accept. You will get old, you will leave this place, you will take a passage to the next existence. To accept, you don't have to be passive or docile. You don't have to accept everything, but you do have to know the state of and the change in your body. Accept with grace. Just for a few minutes while we sit here. It can be affirmative.'

Accept? Did it mean giving in? To danger? To extinction? That didn't feel right. I'd fight to the last breath. I could accept good things—a prize, love, encouragement. Maybe you had to be choosy about this acceptance business. There was good, but there was also bad. Maybe she'd got it wrong.

She hadn't. 'It's not about being fortunate or unfortunate. You were just in the site where acceptance is most possible. The pulse of that place resonates with acceptance whether the climate is wonderful or unpleasant. You accept how it is.'

I told her the destroyed church was hardly symbolic of acceptance.

'But it is. What else could happen there? Everything else had obviously failed. At the last, you have to accept.'

I asked if the ones inside—the priests, the nuns—had had a terrible death. She said that was not part of what I must understand.

'Don't get sidetracked.' She paused and looked at me. I felt I was changing, but in what way I didn't know. I could relate much more to the previous initiates' experiences than my own.

'Saunière had to accept that there were things in his life he could not likely reverse.'

'Which things?'

'Probably the money he'd accepted, which meant that he'd have to work for the paymaster for the rest of his life, that he'd be stopped from leaving Rennes-le-Château. The brutal murder of his neighbouring priest Gelis made him think twice about departure, as it was most likely supposed to do.

'So the nature of Saunière's acceptance was practical. Verdaguer, on the other hand, had to accept that he was ill. He accepted that he was human and would die. He had a lot still to do. He accepted that evil existed. José accepted his human condition in every part of his body; he accepted that he was in nature and a part of it. It couldn't be starved out of him. He was a man of the earth. The law student felt his experience change from fear of the mountain to a feeling of resignation that he had to change. So he accepted the mountain and stayed there for some hours.'

She ordered more hot chocolate for herself and lemon tea for me. 'Now you have to go into silence and be silent; then you will receive. And then you will have the second part of Renunciation on the seven steps of the temple, which have nothing to do with the eleven journey sites.'

'Actual steps?'

'Steps at the monastery of St Pedro.'

We went outside to look at Ripoll. First Liliane showed me the Benedictine monastery, built in 879. Then the 'mite', the sanctuary for writers and poets, including Verdaguer. Finally, a large, closed house, the place where José and many others received their instruction and elevation into the mysteries. She did not stop there but talked of the sheep-shearing festival the following month. I asked about the large creature I'd seen on the rocks. Was it an eagle?

'A yellow eagle,' she said. 'Did you think it was a bad omen?'

Why on earth wouldn't it be? I wondered how to get her away from imposing these perilous and deeply upsetting experiences.

Quickly, she changed to the symbols of this site. 'Ripoll is 39. I will list its influences, so listen to the sound of the words: redeem, cure, save, take water out of the well, the eternal is 1, secret gallery, passage, the fallen angel. What do you choose from these?'

'The Fallen Angel.'

'The Fallen Angel fell into the well.' She kept it filled with her tears.'

'What well?'

'The one over there.' She pointed to a quite nondescript stone sign and iron tap by the wall of the civic building. 'It's not used now; people are afraid to go near it.'

I asked, 'So what is this angel, and from where did she fall?'

'The angel by divine law was supposed for one lifetime to be incarnate in a human body. The angel continually resisted this rebirth as a human being and finally was plunged here with little form. But the body chosen for it was now dead and decaying. The angel had to stay out its time here, and the only choice was to take on some of the undecayed characteristics of the dead female body that it should have inhabited.'

I asked if she believed this story.

She answered, 'They say here, in Ripoll, that if you go to the well and you see her around it, it's a sign of bad luck. If you look down into the well and you see her reflection, it's a sign of death.'

'What is she like?'

'They say her hair is like moonlight, her staring eyes are round, and you can see her breasts under a thin, silk slip. So why was this angel fallen? Because she didn't want to be a human being. You can learn a lot from such a spirit.'

I asked how long she'd be there, trapped.

'Remember the word *redeem*? You can ask for redemption.' Liliane's expression gave nothing away. 'We are all fallen angels sometimes.'

Did she really believe the angel was by the well?

She paused. 'It is part of the symbol and influence of this site, so there must be something in it.'

The sleet was hard, but one hour after we reached the Garrotxa the sun was shining, and it was a different climate altogether. We ate a late lunch at a modest restaurant on the roadside with many small rooms full of truck drivers and farm workers. The food was good and cheap. We didn't speak, ate quickly, and took the road for Figueras, the first town after the French border known for its one-star Michelin restaurant, the 'motel Ampurdan', and the Salvador Dali Museum. Liliane asked me from now on to be silent. She said the best approach was to use reflection and meditation.

Figure 14.2. The Salvadore Dali Museum at Figueras.

Figueras was a busy and noisy town, identified by Liliane as 'journey site 4, Daleth 4–Doorway, Portal; number 44.' She stopped in a main square by a fountain, and we sat on a stone bench in the late afternoon, pleasant and warm. How was I supposed to be silent in this place of horrendous noise: traffic, music, television, shouting, splashing water?

My guide took me to the Dali Museum and sent me in alone. I'd seen it many times and in the mid-sixties had stayed briefly with the painter and his entourage at his house in Port Ligat near Cadaqués. Coming out of the museum after a short time, I forgot about the instruction to be silent and told Liliane about my stay with him.

'That won't help you.' Then she asked if I'd seen Dali's painting on the entry ceiling of the museum. It is of the train station in Perpignan. I'd seen a foot coming down from the ceiling as though to crush me.

'Think back to your entry into that museum and try to recall the painting in detail.'

While I did as directed, Liliane waited by the fountain in the square. Then we sat in silence, listening to the sound of the water for some minutes, after which we got back in the car and she drove to Empúries on the coast. There was just enough light to see the sculptures along the shore. They were supposed to be authentic works of the ancient Greeks, although now restored. I remembered them before their restoration; they had seemed more genuine then.

Empúries was where both the Phoenicians and the Greeks had landed in 2000 BC. The cult of Isis had been brought to Girona from this coast. Girona had housed many religions and beliefs without objection. It was welcoming to all, even though it was a bureaucratic town after the eighteenth century. 'They found a rattle of Isis in the Frenchwoman's garden,' Liliane said.

I didn't know what that was.

'A ritual artefact.'

Empúries was now a tourist attraction.

'Is this a portal?' I asked.

'Portal, site 5, number 45 on the magic square. The site of Receiving.'

We sat in the twilight, and she asked me to close my eyes and open my hands; this I did, as I had as a child. An object was placed on my right palm. It felt light and about to fly off and away. I opened my eyes and, completely

Figure 14.3. The coast of Empúries, where ancient
Greek and Roman columns and statues still stand.

surprised, saw it was a small snapshot. In it, José stood beside me, arm over my shoulders, against a low stone wall.
It must have been taken in the mid-fifties. I was moved and
sad. A sudden wind tried to snatch the photo away, and
I closed my hand as though to keep a precious insect. The
wind tried again. How beautiful he had been. I looked as
though I was in another world. I told her I had never seen
the snapshot before and asked where she'd found it.

'From him, of course.'

I asked what she thought of it.

'That you had been together previously and were obviously meant to meet again, for better or worse. Your choice.
And his. We all have free will. It is a dual world. Good,
bad.'

Figure 14.4. The snapshot.

I thought that was a lot of words for a simple snapshot taken a long time ago. It revived too much in me, tugged at my heart, and I sat in silence trying to concentrate on the sound of the sea, a happy sea on this warm night. I knew José's views on reincarnation and didn't feel able to discuss them now with her. What was I supposed to receive? Searing nostalgia? Or was it a question of whether I could receive? It would happen in this place, number 45. Was I supposed to thank her? To receive, you had to be open to the offer. It didn't mean that once you had the object you kept it. I tried to give the snapshot back.

'Keep it for tonight and then see. It could be your talisman.'

I stood up and looked out to sea. Very slowly, Liliane guided me with small, side-to-side movements. I wasn't making an effort. I'd used up all efforts at the Acceptance site with the eagle that morning. So I received whatever it was that would happen. I expected, as in Romanya, that the purpose was to detect a change of energy. She led me nearer to the sea, and the moon was on the water, still full.

'In your mind, move to your brow chakra and let your consciousness remain there. The brow chakra is between the eyebrows, just above them. See purple light on that place.'

I could feel the light quite acutely, as though a purple bulb had been switched on.

'What is it you sense from the atmosphere?'

And then I understood. I was supposed to tune in with some current that was already there. Or that my presence activated. I asked her if that was right. For once she answered, 'In part.'

We spent the night in a small hotel on the coast at Puerta de la Selva. I couldn't look at the snapshot and placed it face down in my bag.

Empúries was filled with symbols and numbers and another angel. Liliane asked if I'd heard mention of the angel of the spirit of Old Saturn, the angel of Saturnian intelligence. I had not. I *had* heard of the Tree of Life and thankfully now learned that Empúries was also the name of the Temple of the Fourth Sky, which was one of the titles of Tifteret, a Cabalistic aspect of the Tree of Life. Empúries also had references to Adam, the First Man. She showed me exactly how he fit into Empuriés. Adam was made up of the numbers 1 and 4 and 40, equalling the Empúries square number 45. She sped through references to Red, Ruby, and Genesis, including Lot and his wife being turned to salt. She wanted me to hear this litany but did not expect me to understand it. I understood that it all symbolised a way of knowing, as we'd discussed earlier about the other sites.

She noticed that the snapshot was not evident. I had put it away. 'When you can look at and accept it, even love those two people, you are ready for the Great Bear and all it offers.'

When I opened the shutters eight hours later and saw the beach, not for the first time but the hundredth, I understood she knew that this place was where I'd stayed with José and my small children after I had left my husband to be with him. This was where my goose had been cooked, where I had met the inevitable, where there was no turning back. Was this memory yet another part of the practice of receiving linked to the old snapshot?

Across the bay in the village of Llanca, Maria Tourdes had spent time with her eventual husband—not the French priest, of course, but elderly Roger Mathieu, who also worked for the Vatican but in a slightly different way from the obvious priests, frocked and devout. Did she think of Saunière when she stared upon the water?

I wanted to get out of there. I did not want to see anything, feel one pang of nostalgia, experience one memory. I was quite clear on that. Receiving had many facets. I hurried unusually, got into the car, and so caught her attention.

'Where do you think you've just run from?' she asked.

'Once I would have said I've just left paradise,' I replied. She laughed.

After I'd gone through the daily ritual of exercises and meditation, Liliane asked me to go back to my vision of the Frenchwoman's garden with Emma Calvé singing and the bird laughing and to describe that place.

'Ought I to see it clearer?'

'There is no "ought" on this journey.'

I told her I was like a balloon going from the garden to the house, up to the bedroom. I seemed to bounce or float. But my consciousness was acute.

She said that when a person leaves his or her body to pass over to the next realm, they can spend some time visiting a particular place or person. They are then in their etheric body, which is the vehicle that takes the entire personality, with its memory and actions, over to that next existence. The etheric body is attached by a long cord to the top chakra at the crown of the head—as a baby is attached by the umbilical cord—and the sensation is as though bouncing slightly out of control. Frequently in that state, the thought arises, 'Why can't they see me?'

'So what do you make of all this?' she asked.

I couldn't make anything of it. Except one thing: the sound of a spade shovelling earth. I remembered thinking that there was something in that house I had not understood.

I spoke about the process of dying; I wouldn't want to get that wrong. At death, every part of us goes to another realm in what is called the etheric body, which has been joined to our physical body inside us since birth. And this physical, earthly body, spotted with decay, is just an envelope that we crumple and leave behind so that we can be free.

Liliane promised me that if after her demise I should sit beside her grave, she would not be in it.

Figure 14.5. The monastery at the top of St Pere de Rodes.

We climbed St Pere de Rodes, the almost perpendicular mountain at the top of which was a monastery. I was surprised I could approach it at all. The climb on rough terrain used to take forty minutes. It had been abandoned for years. It was said the bones of St Peter had been kept there. The saint's remains had been carried by boat towards France, but a storm pushed the boat onto the coast of Empúries. A legend? I didn't know. I said I thought there must be something behind the story for it to be a legend at all, and Liliane agreed, for once.

Near the mountaintop, at the monastery, she stopped and said we were at the place with seven steps she'd mentioned the day before. Here I was to perform the second part of Renunciation. She asked me how I felt, and I said that something had changed in me the night before and I did feel lighter. I believed it was to do with the amazing sense of well-being this journey had given me.

'This is site 6, number 20 on the magic square. Renunciation.' I was to ascend the seven stone steps of this monastery slowly and on each one of them make an act of renunciation. She asked if I could first encourage an inner state of calm and reflection.

'With each step you will be letting go of something you need to release. After each step you rest, drawing in the light, with its strength and support. The light shines down upon you with a loving feeling of protection. Close your eyes. See it now. See it in your mind. It is most powerful.'

She led me to the first step, and I repeated the statement after her. 'First: I release all my criticism and judgment of others.'

She said, 'The light is all around you.'

'Second: I release all my pain and confusion.'

She said, 'You begin to feel the light within as glowing and comforting.' Her tone was encouraging.

'Third: I release all my rigid attitudes.

'Fourth: I release my hold on material needs.

'Fifth: I release all my fears and doubts and negativity.'

She said, 'You are surrounded by light.'

'Sixth: I release my hold on the people I love.

'Seventh: I stand before you, God, totally empty, free. I pray I may enter your temple.'

'Keep your eyes closed.' She took my hand. 'The door opens, and you enter this spiritual sanctuary.' We moved forward slowly into darkness. It was peaceful, smelling of

must and incense. She asked me to say a prayer of gratitude.
I opened my eyes and could feel a shaft of light covering
me, brighter than anything around. I was certain something
out of the ordinary had happened. It seemed, however, that
I was standing in a patch of sunlight from the open monastery door.

'Down the steps in the pathway of light. Brow centre
closed. Purple light fading. Retain bright light within.'

I followed her words. I was now refreshed, renewed,
enlightened, and something told me I'd better believe it!
We started down the mountain, and she told me I was an
ungrateful pupil. I was getting used to hearing just about
anything now.

'Close your eyes. In front of you are seven white marble
steps. The entrance to the temple is closed; a white dove
circles its dome. See this in your mind.'

I did the seven steps again, moving only in my thoughts.
The words were slightly different.

'One: I release all negative thought.

Two: I release all fear.

Three: I release my hold on material things.

Four: I release my hold on those I love.

Five: I am clear and free for God's light to fill me.'

She told me to see the light bright and new. Pale yellow,
like the first spring day ever.

'Six: May I receive your light and be made of light.

Seven: May I now enter your temple.'

Liliane held my arm and we stayed still. People trudged
on the path beside us.

'Stay in the light and see it in your mind, covering
you in all colours.' I still saw pale yellow. Some unusual
impulse made me squeeze her hand, and I said, 'Thank
you.'

We sat near the monastery of St Pedro de Roda for a whole hour in silence. It had been abandoned for many years even by the fifties, and I then remembered the night when José had impulsively got a taxi to bring us here. The Arc Bar had been full, and the taxi driver, called Malaga, said he'd do it for nothing if Lucia in her gold dress was on the ride. Half the bar tried to squeeze into that taxi, some holding on to the sides. Lucia, Umberto Eco, Lluís, Paco the actor. We climbed the mountain in total darkness and the going was rough, not how it is now with its newly laid track.

Something incredible happened that night. Although I was there, I never found out exactly what it was. José and Lluís carried blankets and wine. A baker was already up and working in a nearby village, and he'd prepared rolls and coffee. I was with José, and he with me. I was ecstatically complete. I knew Umberto loved Lucia. Whom did Lucia love?

Jordi Solar, the cartoonist, and the old gardener from the house with the tower were there. José made a circle of lighted candles around us. We lit a bonfire and danced to a gramophone you had to wind up. It played 78s, and the favourites were Earl Bostick's 'Smoke Gets in Your Eyes' and the Platters's 'Only You'. A certain amount of drinking was done and the laughter was loud, blown by the wind. José gave each one of us a lighted candle, and we improvised a Catalan play about the monastery based on a legend. José brought the night sky and the distant sea and the wind into the story, and I kept thinking, 'He's mine. Mine.'

Jordi climbed up to the monastery and rapped on the door with a roasting fork. He shouted for those inside to come out. Not long afterward, Lluís saw a stranger walk towards them. 'We have an extra guest!' he said. Or was it an apparition? Lucia danced around from the other side barefoot, playing a ghost. The figure seemed to pass through

214

the partygoers and stopped in front of her. Later, I saw Lú-
cia sobbing and comforted by Jordi. Yes, Jordi loved her,
too. After we'd roasted sausages and toasted bread, we sat
around the dying fire and watched the breaking of dawn,
all good friends, looking forward to a beautiful future.

I turned to Liliane, who sat looking out towards the coast,
and thanked her for the gift of the snapshot. I was feeling
frightened. The event of that long-gone night on the mountain was still too powerful, far too present. It was supposed
to be in the past. Liliane pointed to the town of Puerta de
la Selva, which we could see in the distance. 'You lived
there in a fisherman's cottage with José and your children.
It must have been in part a happy time.'

'Why in part?'

'Because I don't think that anyone is happy constantly.
It would be unusual.'

I didn't want to remember the time in the cottage,
'happy' or otherwise.

'Yet, even though you had been happy then, you just ran
away from the memory.' She spoke thoughtfully, picking
up, as usual, on my feelings.

'I think I've got enough to do just with this journey.'

'So you're now leaving things behind. That is interesting. Nostalgia has to go.'

I needed to be honest because I didn't know what was
ahead, but I felt somehow it would take everything I had.
Therefore, I needed for her to know me properly so she
could, if necessary, protect me. 'Yes, I ran because I couldn't
bear the memory. That time was—it makes everything else
kind of dull.'

'How sad,' she said.

I told her I did not want to go into it and hoped to distract
her with my next question. I asked about the extraordinary

215

event that had occurred on this mountain the night in the fifties when we had come in a group and made the bonfire. What exactly *had* happened?

'Maybe it was another fallen angel,' she said.

'How do you know?'

'José mentioned it when he got to this point on the journey.'

'I wish I knew what he'd said about me.'

'Ask him.'

'Did Lucia do this journey?'

'No.'

'Maria Tourdes?'

'No.' Liliane got up.

'Why did you do it?'

'When we come to the end of our time on this earth, we will take no material thing with us. We will not take one cent in our cold, dead hands. The only things that we may take perhaps are our few good deeds helping others. These are what really matter in the long run. The good actions. What will I take with me when I go?'

I assumed she was reciting these lines for the purpose of making me aware of and maybe confess my 'love' and 'needs' so that I could be free.

Figure 15.1. The Devil's Cave, near Cadaqués.

CHAPTER 15

Liliane made me walk across to Cap de Creus, the farthest point east in Spain, the beginning of the energy line to Santiago de Compostela that ended at Finisterre on the Atlantic coast. She said this was the true pilgrim route of St James. She told me the exact numbers I was supposed to remember, but I became too concerned with not falling on the rocks and stones, which were slippery with green mould and with husks that she said were covered in lava from volcanic eruptions. We were in a conservation area that stretched for miles; I was to walk to the coast, and we were back to drinking only water and lemon.

'Why must we walk again?'

'There is no other way.' She wasn't worried how long it took—one hour, one day. Clocks had no place here.

As I crunched and slithered on this strange territory, I started asking more questions. I needed to get my mind off this experience. It had been pleasant for the first forty minutes—to be honest, thirty—and then impossible, a condition she said had to be overcome. I told her I didn't love everyone; many I didn't even like and some I couldn't stand to be with at all. Was she becoming one of them?

'Why should you like everyone?' Liliane asked. 'Why feel the necessity to be comfortable with those you don't like? Move away. We don't all come from the same soul state.'

'What are we all doing together then? Don't tell me it's a cosmic mistake.'

That made her scoff. 'This earth existence is the marketplace. This is where we meet spirits of all levels and origins. There is nowhere else we can have this experience, rubbing shoulders with those from distant hierarchies, high and low. You don't have to like everyone; you need merely to recognise God's spirit within them.'

'But they might be evil.'

'Then ask for the evil to be dissolved in God's light and that they, too, become children of God.'

'Evil exists. People write it off as sickness and forgive anything. They can't wait to excuse it. Evil makes me cold. I can feel it.'

'I believe you.'

'It exists,' I insisted.

'Of course.' For once in agreement, we got up and walked towards the Devil's Cave, also 20 on the magic square. Rebirth.

'This part of the journey is about going inside, facing your fear. You connect to nature. You lose all your supporting structure. Then you either have faith in the universe, or not. Shut off exterior influences so that your inner resources can surge up. Fears? Why are they present?'

I could think of a hundred reasons.

'Fears are present because things have not digested.' She emphasised 'things'.

I relied for survival on what I knew. Past experiences had taught me what to repeat and what to avoid. Now she was asking me to jettison my survival practices and enter into uncertain experiences that I would never normally meet. And to do so without the natural defences I seemed to have missed at birth. We had quite a discussion about that. I said that some defences I would never let go of. She asked why. I couldn't see the point of it—of dropping these hard-won effective practices that in the past had kept me intact.

'How many days does this part of the journey take?' I asked.

She didn't answer. Instead, she recited the signs of the Devil's Cave, a mixture of nouns and verbs: 'Visit, interior, earth, rectify, find, fraternity, friendship. Here you create. You do. It is also a place of hiding.'

'Like the barraca?'

'Yes, but of a different intensity.' She asked if I had any other questions.

I asked what was supposed to happen when I moved from side to side then forward and backward in a precise place—feeling with my body, its senses, the energies around me.

'When you have the experience, you will have the answer.' She spoke as if she meant to say no more.

'But I need to have an idea of what I'm working towards. I'm consumed with half-answered questions, not knowing what I'm supposed to be doing. What was I supposed to identify in the Frenchwoman's garden, either in actual memory or in a dream state?'

'That you have to find out. You have asked the question: what have I not understood about this house? You need to continue to seek the answer.'

'Ascending the seven steps, I noticed you used the name *God*. Does everyone relate to God?'

'It depends on their spiritual resonance. God as we know him has a hundred names. There are also in this universe other deities, an ascending scale of deities.'

221

My legs burned with tiredness, but I tried to continue walking on this uneven, slippery ground. I started questioning the behaviour of the previous initiates.

'It's a good question, but according to ritual it is asked at journey site 11, Portal—the pillars of the temple, the cup, the chalice.'

I was now boiling, sweating, my legs pricked with pins and needles.

'Yesterday your skin was running with melting sleet and raw from icy winds. This must be better.'

Exhausted, I flopped down on the stones. She told me to stretch, and then she beat and pressed my legs and feet. I was angry and breathless. She moved to the shade of the nearest tree, which I saw with horror was the only tree ahead of us. After it, there were no trees, only tough roots and withered bushes of who knows what origin.

'You can walk for miles here,' she said, pointing to huge rectangular stone slabs scattered across the ground for as far as I could see. 'You can use those like stepping stones. They're graphite. They used it in the construction of Cadaques. You must have noticed it.'

I was looking into a treeless distance with no respite. The sun blazed too hot for April. I suggested going to Devil's Cave by car.

'But there is no road.' She gave me her scarf to cover my head. 'I am taking the quickest route. So just keep going.' She set a pace and said to keep to it and it wouldn't be so tiring as giving in and dawdling. Up rocks, down crags. Across horizontal slabs. She was thrilled by the graphite, jumping from one to the next. I expected I would arrive with nothing left of me except a stalk of bone and a heart at the top. Shrivelled like a dying red flower pumping to the last—something Dali might have painted. She had a stab

222

at cheering me up by pointing to a lighthouse. 'The cave's below that.' Who knew how far 'that' was?

She talked all the time. 'The Devil's Cave is related to the planet Venus. Its date is the 15th of Ave.' I was too tired to ask what that meant. 'The cave was the site of the Ancient Feast of Dance and Joy,' she went on. 'Its letter is *Kaf*, which symbolises the cup or chalice and reigns over life. You could have a lot of work to do here.'

Before we got to 'here' she tied her scarf around my forehead, covering my eyes. Surely this was a mistake. I was blindfolded.

'Who are you?' she said.

I nearly answered, 'The same as yesterday.' If I wanted the blindfold off, my answer had better satisfy her. I could say 'grandmother', 'mother', 'once a wife'. Stay in the present, counselled my wise mind.

'Traveller.'

She took my arm and led me forward. This exercise was to help me rediscover trust. We sat on a low stone with a vertical slab behind it, which gave some small shade.

'This is Rebirth. Next comes Freedom.'

I could hear water, the swish of oars. A bird screeched; the flap of heavy wings cooled the air.

'What is this journey about?' she asked.

I wanted to say 'finding solutions'. I said something about experience and growth.

'You may be a traveller. What you are is a seeker.'

I felt she was right. Was that why I could never stay in one place, always having to move on? I started to tell her about the past.

'This journey is not about you and your experiences in life. It is about your passing through and mingling with different energies in this Venus Magic Square. And what you experience at each site. What you take in. What you discern when you use your body as an instrument of attunement. You are in preparation. Do you know truly what a magic square is?'

Truly? I had some idea. I wanted to know for what exactly I was in preparation.

'You are here at the entrance to the cave of hell, and here rebirth is offered to you.'

'Is *that* all it is?'

She didn't laugh. I did. I kept it short. My guess was that preparation happened later. After all, we would emerge from this cave whatever its legends or names. I did feel a slight panic that my lack of feeling connected with today's intention would cause me to miss Rebirth, which sounded pleasant and positive.

'Maybe you can lose more before the exit of this journey.' Liliane made it sound like a fairground ride.

'But I have lost many things.' I hated the blindfold. 'My resentment, contact with my outer world, not to mention several kilos.'

'Oh, to arrive at this summit you will lose everything.'

I didn't like that prediction, but the worst part of it was the word *summit*. It made me think of Lucia. Then my guide said she would leave me and I should stay where I was, blindfolded. She would come for me after a period of time.

'But what shall I do?'

'Do? Absorb the atmosphere. As at every other site. Just absorb.'

'What if I panic?'

'Then think of the woman of smoke. Ask her to be present. Only yesterday you experienced receiving. That will help you. Receive this place.' She put the water bottle into my hand. The sound of her feet crunching away into the long distance was not pleasant. I actually started to pray.

I dreaded people passing by—they would think I was a beggar—or, even worse, the passing of one person. A rapist? A thief? Was Liliane watching me from a distance?

Blindfolded at the cave's entrance, I didn't absorb anything. I remembered Lucia in the 1980s, knocking on the door of my room in the old Hotel Centro. The furniture shook with the sound of it, but then every sound in that place was dramatic. She told me they'd put the building up for sale and I sank, horrified, onto the bed, wishing I could buy it. But would owning the old hotel help me reclaim the old happiness? She talked of how she'd stayed in Maria Tourdes's garden as a child, with the view of the mountain always there. I invited her to my apartment in Ceret at the foot of the mountain.

'I'll say I will come, but I won't,' Lucia said.

'It's closer to Canigou.'

'Oh, but I don't like mountains.' She said it as though she was frightened of them.

'A bad experience?'

'Definitely. I wouldn't be caught dead on one.'

She said she'd see me the next time I came. But I didn't see her again.

Lucia had always warned me to stay away from anything having to do with the workings of the private society. 'Too dangerous', she had called it. Whatever she meant, something had frightened her, leading this beautiful, luminous person, sheer to the point of transparency and who was afraid of mountains, to make the ascent to the top of Mt Canigou, and her experience at the peak had been so perilous that it overwhelmed her. José and a priest had brought her dead body back down the mountain, accompanied by priests ringing bells the whole way.

It was Lluís who told me the news of Lucia's passing. He assumed it was because of a health problem but also said the mountain was too much for her. The mountain? Like an ailing animal that senses death and needs to find a place to die alone, she had gone to the emptiness of Canigou. But her operation and treatment for cancer had been successful. I knew Lucia had revolted against the custodians because she wanted the secrets they held to be made prudently more accessible and so benefit the future. But in the end she knew she would never prevail against the society members, so she finally returned the material she had to the mountain.

Lluís and I had sat in silence in the Arc Bar, drinking whatever he'd put into our glasses.

'She always said she'd have a wild death,' he said.

I asked when she'd been buried. Her husband had come from Italy and taken her home. For a moment, I didn't believe it—that she'd died on Canigou. 'She hated mountains.'

'You should ask José,' said Lluís. 'She had to go back up there. That's what she'd said.'

When I had found José, he said Lucia had climbed up with artefacts, some of which belonged to the society. One of them was a document, pages long, recording the transformation ritual for the initiates, which took between two and four hours to complete. He also said that she had taken the sacred cup, supposedly the Grail vessel, but that it had been retrieved. I understood that she had taken three items, the third being an amulet, to a sacred place at the peak of Canigou.

He added, 'The ritual document was one of many copies. That's what she was doing—returning them. Returning the ritual objects because, like Saunière, we'd failed in our purpose to perfect the ritual.'

'And the shock of what is there killed her,' someone else had then said. Of course, it would turn out to be Quim Carreras. He was always precise, whatever the cost. I wasn't given time to ask what *that* meant. I was thinking of her last words to me about mountains.

'Lucia always said she was terrified of mountains. She must have been shocked by something she already knew about,' I said.

José didn't disagree.

Figure 15.2. Lucia, who didn't like secrets.

Liliane scraped off the blindfold. I wiped my eyes to reconnect with light. Devil's Cave was beside me, its entrance a doorway of rock sloping to the left, behind it a world of stone and water flowing past as far into the rocks as I could see. I refused to show her I was impressed. But I was impressed. The cave had a magnificence, a luminosity, beyond human endeavour to create. This place would not be easy to enter. It would demand a price, and, I thought, in my case some experience of change too heroic and awesome for me.

Beside me now—how had she got there so silently?—Liliane said, 'Verdaguer said this place was where he defied gravity. He lifted out of the site's weight into a higher state of being, which we as humans had once known.' She lifted me from behind and got me up solidly on my feet. I had to admit I was sunk in gravity; I was its victim, its creature.

Now that I was standing, the cave appeared even more splendid, more magnificent in its vastness and high roof than any castle or palace. No human being could ever make an impact on this site or be even acknowledged there. It was the antechamber between this world and the next, and I had to admit that the devil chose well.

I noticed that the stones of the cave were of a uniformly dark green. 'The stones have holes inside,' Liliane said. They're called magic stones. Some of the rocks are older than the pyramids. Huge waves carried them to this place. There are two important influences here. *Yod*, name of the tenth letter of the Creator. It is never pronounced. It represents the eyes of God. And *Kaf*, the eleventh letter, which symbolises the open hand and also the cup or chalice. Kaf reigns over life and is related to the planet Venus.' She drew a circle over a cross. 'So much that is here relates to Girona.' I asked her how, but she was moving on.

We were walking again now through the cave entrance, my legs numb, which had something to be said for it. We walked over the curving ridges of this stone empire and arrived at a small gap in the rocks leading to the sea. The view reminded me of the Hanged Man card in the *Golden Dawn* Tarot deck. The lighthouse was above us. There were no beaches, no people. The inner cave continued to the side, dark and mean and well named. In contrast to the outer vestibule, the inside of this chamber was hell.

Liliane sang, chanting Yod. Her voice echoed, coming back as a choir of voices, some deep, even gruff. She sang out to the darkness, and it answered as we walked one behind the other into blackness of the cave. Her voice had a lovely sound, and she got me to join in and the effort of singing became hypnotic. She made many incantations and I heard a higher sound, not possibly hers, whirling around in this huge place without end. I'd never heard a sound like it. If I had to describe it, I would say that it ranged from howling up to angelic cadences, but it truly was beyond description. A note was running through this chorale that I recognised as F-sharp, and I did reverberate with the sound. My physical body was now forgotten. I was outside of my bones and flesh, existing only in consciousness. In that state I had no possibility of choice, and there was no question of leaving. Time didn't pass. There was no time.

When we exited the cave, the sky was black. Had we been there all day? Was it night now? Impossible. The song of the cave was louder now and all around us. Even the stones were singing. There was a simple explanation: 'It's the mistral,' Liliane said, 'from Canigou, blowing through the holes in these stones.' It was an almighty sound, and the sea reared up and sped into the cave, splashing, finally, a long way off.

I think I said I was hungry. She pulled my cheeks and held their flesh in her strong hands, warming them. 'You, my dear friend, you will have lunch. We will go somewhere very nice. We will get away now because the noise of the stones can be like sirens calling.'

Liliane knew the lighthouse keeper and got a small boat in which we rocked hellishly in the tumult of sound and wind to Port Ligat. And she said, 'Lunch?' Had we missed a whole twenty-four hours?

'It is now two o'clock. You were in the cave a short while. We walked a maximum of one-and-a-half hours. You have been through the process of a rebirth.'

Had I? My breathing was different, as if there was more space in my chest. That was all. Perhaps my effort just to survive had kept me from sensing more. Liliane said it might take a while before I knew further about it. 'Even the stones agree with you, and we will now eat.'

Near the village of Cadaques, Liliane stopped by Dali's old home, Port Ligat, now a tourist attraction. 'You know this place?'

'In another lifetime, another destiny.' I said. Don't think about that time, I told myself. Definitely don't surrender to the past; only the unknown seemed safe. I deliberately concentrated on the things that had not made sense and needed answers. I realised we had not met one person on the walk to the cave. And I wondered if she, by chanting the sacred word *Yod*, might have called up the wind—the wind that was so much a part of the Catalans' lives; the wind that they loved or dreaded, that became part of their songs. This wind, called the *tramontana*, lasted nine days.

The Motel Ampurdan in Figueras was one of the best restaurants in Catalunya that served the dishes of the province plentifully and reasonably priced. It had been in business for years and succeeded by an excellence that was not pretentious or exclusive. Dali had eaten there. Josép Pla, the Catalan writer, had his table. It catered to the well known, the artists, the politicians, and just those who appreciated good food.

After four courses in the comforting room, I was quite recovered. The stiff-legged stalk with a beating heart that

I had just been, crossing a relentless territory of stones, was smothered in well-being. I did ask my guide if the cave was a portal.

'But of course,' she said. Not for me, I thought. I hadn't experienced any kind of subtle energy there.

She asked if I wanted to go as far as Collioure in France, the next step on the magic square. I said I was surprised to have a choice.

'But you are free. Remember? Rebirth. Freedom.'

She sat in the square by the fountain. 'To repeat, in Figueras we have Daleth 4, symbol doorway. Water. Also Dam 44, the mother letter relating to the Tree of Yezirah, the preformative world of Patriarchs. Influences and symbols are blood, giving birth, burning, inflaming, enthusiasm, magic, the sign of Aries, the Phoenix bird, and the ruling angel of II Gemini.' I asked for more explanation, but she just looked at me, her eyes a clear and quite lovely blue.

'It suited Saunière here. He was under the sun sign Aries and sought fire and resurrection. Figueras is also represented by table, calendar, measurement, diagram; these he also sought when crossing the border into Spain. Another important influence is silence, to be in silence. Figueras is likewise the place of crystal.' Then I did demand an explanation, at least of crystal.

'I have agreed with you that I will recite the underlying symbols of each site, but we will not examine them. That is another journey altogether. These symbols form a timeless, universal language that you have to allow yourself to experience.'

'All this for quite an ordinary place.'

'It's not the refurbishments and modernisation, the new look of the thing, that we relate to. You should know that.'

She took the motorway into France and turned right to the coast. It was five in the afternoon, and Collioure was crowded with tourists and artists exhibiting their work, mostly commercial and not good.

Collioure used to be an exquisite fishing village with a Templar castle, a port, and colourful cafés along the walk to the harbour. I'd gone there with José on my sixteenth birthday. We'd come a short distance, but the journey was long because in those days trains were inexplicably slow and we had some trouble with the frontier police. Franco didn't like his countrymen running around too much. The soft, crystalline atmosphere of Collioure, the extraordinary light, was still there. Even the smell. Forty years earlier it had had a small, friendly population, fishing nets spread between the boats, artists painting around the harbour. We'd sat with them on the beach and eaten bread smeared with oil and tomato. Everything, every drop of moisture in the air, had been heightened as though made of light. It was no

Figure 15.3. Collioure, a place of extraordinary light.

surprise that Collioure had attracted Picasso, Matisse, and many others.

I pushed through the almost static groups of sightseers, all looking for the same thing that had inspired the artists. There was too much trading on a time that was gone. All these seekers got was the effort of getting through the crowd to the harbour, where overdone painters in 1920s Montmartre costumes flaunted their produce. No more bread with tomato but enormous, complicated ice creams adorned with strawberries, chocolate confetti, tiny tinsel windmills. Why had Liliane brought me here?

'To absorb the site.'

I thought she was joking, but that she never did. I complained about the crowds and said it was impossible.

'Get to the source. Forget about them.'

By chance, we were standing by one of the old places, the Hotel des Templiers. I remembered the owner with the grand moustache. I couldn't focus on anything. 'Help me,' I said.

'Site 7, Portal, square number 19; Transformation; Eva, the first mother of everything living; to make clean. The Templar rituals transforming matter into light.' Liliane spoke quickly, not expecting any questions, and something about the words, the rhythm, the way she recited them did have an effect. What it was I couldn't clarify, but I did feel different, as though I were listening to a poem being read. The effect had something to do with the rise and fall of the cadences. Perhaps, as she said, the sense of the words themselves was not understandable; they could only be experienced.

I closed my eyes and recalled that first day when José and I had been in Collioure when I was sixteen. Its soft colours and translucent, crystalline atmosphere had made it seem as though the town were made up of a different

233

fabric; and I felt we could walk right through the skin of the place and out the other side, as though it were a stage set. The place belonged to an illustration in a children's fairy story, the first one that a child would see and never really forget.

Liliane took my arm and we walked with purpose to a waste bin. She kicked dropped litter. 'Look there.' And I saw on the wall the black cabalistic sign for doorway. 'Most people would think it's a lightning mark. All the important information is hidden in signs and ritual. That's how it is carried down through the ages.'

She seemed now to be in a hurry, and we went directly to the car. It took a considerable time to move forward in the queue and leave the car park. Then she swung onto the road straight north to Perpignan. 'We will get there just in time before the light goes. Perillos, site 8, number 10 on the square.'

I could think of only one word for Perillos: *desolation*. The village was absolutely still, but there was the feeling of something having just happened, something momentous. It was completely and utterly empty. Old houses were in various states of dereliction, no sign of a road or track. The deserted church was locked, its cemetery with tombstones in the same state of deterioration as the houses. All around this forsaken hamlet was a stretch of innocent, green land for some reason historically known as the Valley of Death. I thought that in the distance I could see the ruins of a once-great house. There was no sign of human presence, and the broken, hollow doorways were too dark, too menacing. I expected something to arrive—but knew that, whatever it was, it would be unexpected. And then a church bell rang once and I started running.

'It's only the wind,' said Liliane. She questioned me about the strength of the impact of the place. After all, she'd rarely seen me run. What had I absorbed? For once, too much.

We walked to the mouth of a cave with grotesque, bewildering formations that Liliane said were stalagmites. 'Perillos, number 10,' she intoned, 'dominated by solitude and isolation. Influences: to fly, wolf. The word *Yod* represents the origin or the father and symbolises God as origin of everything that exists.' She again gave no explanation, and these symbolic words started to be self-sufficient in themselves—I started not to need explanation.

'Where are the people?'

'Over there in the village of Opoul. They left because they could hear chanting underground. And other unexplained things. Yet several renowned individuals wanted to live here in Perillos. Otto Rahn came here, as did Cassini, the famous Italian mapmaker. He delayed leaving for over two years. Why?'

I didn't have a clue and had not heard of either person. 'Perhaps he found the unexpected?' I said.

She laughed. 'Without knowing it, you are right.'

A sense of menace hung around Perillos that I thought too out of the ordinary. I hated its feeling of abandonment. In contrast Opoul, there in the distance with its mere two hundred residents, represented a hive of activity. How I would like to meet just one of them! Even a worker on the land. A gravedigger. A priest.

'It's deserted here,' I accused her.

'Only to the unseeing eye.'

For the first time, it was I who decided when to leave a site. Liliane got the car started with difficulty and then sped across the countryside to Rennes-le-Château.

'Is this still Freedom?' I asked.

'Preparation.'

For the first time, I felt able to see my guide as a person. During the journey, from the first day in the barraca, Liliane had been more a presence. Now she started to come forward, a strong woman of few attachments. Her features were well defined, her mouth full and uncompromising. Smiles and laughter, which she used frequently, made most things all right, except for someone like me who'd been nourished on rejection and half-truths and all the various deceptions of the metropolis.

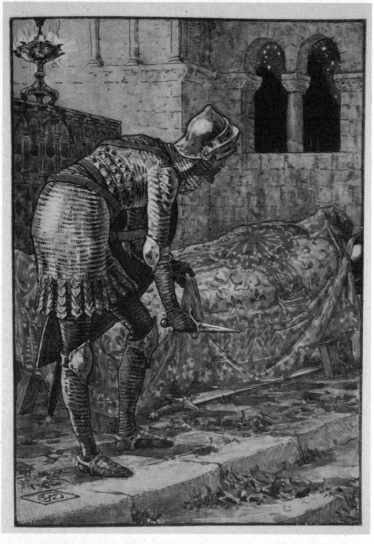

Figure 16.1. *The Chapel Perilous,* by Walter Crane,
based on Sir Thomas Malory's *Le Morte d'Arthur.*
Was Malory thinking of Perillos?

CHAPTER 16

We stayed the night in a simple hotel in the small town of Quillan, where Maria Tourdes had spent much of her childhood. Her parents came to the town to take the waters, the cure having been available in those days. Now, like the town's once-famous hat factory, the spa was closed down. Rennes-le-Château was a short drive away.

'Perillos is not a place,' Liliane said.

'What is it, then?'

'A state of being.'

I said it was filled with fear. Liliane shrugged. She'd risen above the cares of worldly life. Why dwell with fear and insignificance? Transcend your small vision and dwell in the light, which equally existed. She discovered and examined portals. A lifetime of spiritual practice had set her free.

We spent the evening on the subject of that abandoned village. I wondered if the chapel there was the Chapel Perilous in Malory's *Le Morte D'Arthur*, written in 1470. The day we were there, the chapel had been locked, but apparently inside was a crypt with an unknown tomb that no one would approach. They called it 'The Tomb of God'. Although the chapel was closed, passers-by heard angelic music coming from within, beyond anything heard in this world.

Liliane brought out the document case, which I hadn't seen for some days. 'Here is what the Master from Ripoll told José at magic square 10: "Perillos is an existence that still exists. It is brought into being by practising initiates."' José had asked where it was and was told it didn't matter. The important thing was the elevation, the level of evolvement, of the group of initiates. Perillos was considered completely impossible as a place for human beings to inhabit. Salvador Dali called Perillos a state of mind that could only be inhabited by the initiated.

'What did you feel there—by the chapel in Perillos?' she asked.

'In a quiet way, it was too much, too powerful for comfort.'

She asked how I was with 'too much'. I sensed we were getting near my journey's end and suddenly did not look forward to it. You don't have to do it, I told myself. I might need a day off, I told her. I could see *might* was the operative word in that sentence. She just laughed. I realised we'd been on the journey nearly two weeks.

'Dali was completely changed by Perillos. But we meet him on magic square number 42. Perillos has layers of realities and dimensions that he tried to wrestle with during the last forty years of his life.'

'Why did they leave? The inhabitants.'

'They all started dreaming, always the same dream. It was a terrible dream. They were afraid to sleep. They heard sounds they could not explain. In the eleventh century, the Lord of Perillos had sorted out and stabilised square number 10. It had been through an apocalyptical process. When

José complained that the lord of Perillos had not succeeded and that no one—not one person—was there, his master replied, "They say the devil lives there and God is buried there." So that's not bad for one abandoned village.'

Outside on the dark street of Quillan, Liliane said I should do the exercises: breathing, chanting, absorbing, balancing on one leg, eyes closed.

Standing there, my concern was now with the finale of the journey. Now, I increasingly viewed Liliane not just as an encouraging presence but as a fully fledged, separate human being. For guidance, now I turned more to the initiates of the past. I reached them in my thoughts, especially the poet Verdaguer, and felt his eloquence and occasional gentleness, his charisma, closer to me. In my thoughts, I asked him to help me locate the elusive energies I could not yet feel around me but was assured were there. Why did everything feel the same?

And then I got what might be either a message or the result of an exhausted body and overactive mind. Liliane was behind me as I moved slightly backward and then forward, focusing on an ordinary wall in front of me. From where could anything come if the space was so limited and bricked up by this unnecessary wall? Then what came was, 'Ask her about Ramon.' It was simply a thought, not a voice with an accent or an image like the woman of smoke.

I said nothing, but Liliane responded immediately. 'Ramon of Perillos in the fourteenth century was a diplomat interested in literature and a soldier and chamberlain to Juan the First, King of Aragon, whose passions were music, literature, and astrology. They became friends. At forty-six, the king died suddenly and probably unnaturally. Ramon, Lord of Perillos, set out on a pilgrimage to a sacred site in Ireland, St Patrick's Purgatory, to enquire of the condition of the soul of his friend, the king. St Patrick's was the only functioning purgatory in Europe at the time. First he was purified by fasting and prayer, and then he descended into the Netherworld, passing through the Land of the Lost, finding Paradise, and finally returning to earth. He certainly had some spiritual initiation in Ireland, and when he returned to France he said he now understood that at Perillos, his territory, there was a doorway to another world.'

I asked what she knew about Verdaguer.

'Why? Does moving in front of this wall bring him to you?'

That was a new possibility.

She kept me moving slightly, almost hypnotically forward, backward, my concentration lifting into the purple light of the brow chakra. The rocking was mindless and comforting, and the wall became not different but more detailed, as though it was the first wall I'd ever seen. I could take in the slight changes of pattern made by the street light. I could see the mountain and that it was waiting, yes, even more than the custodians were. Canigou was waiting, and it was worse than any human power. What had I got in me to go up against that? What visions had I experienced in the past fourteen days that could aid me? One woman of smoke, possibly. One dream. I wanted to get the experience over with. Was the mountain already magnetising me, as it reportedly now did planes, skiers, and tourists and had Phoenicians long ago? Had it done so all along from the very start, from my first agreement to do this journey?

Liliane was up having breakfast at 7 a.m. She told me to eat and drink all I wanted because it was going to be a long walk.

'To where?'

'Rennes-le-Château.'

'Is this yet another impossible exercise to test my commitment?'

'The car's broken down.'

I remembered the curving hill up from Couiza to Saunière's village from the early visits with José and later with friends from Ceret. Even in a taxi, it had felt effortful. I said I couldn't do it.

'I think you should. Portal 9, number 47 on the square. You have to deserve the approach to something as powerful as Saunière's village. Do you understand humility?'

I started to say what I thought it was, and she stopped me after the first sentence.

'Humility is a state of being that colours your actions. A state of grace.'

'Will I need humility up there?'

Liliane laughed. 'If you *are* humble, it will be the first time the place has seen that attitude. Humility gets a bad

Figure 16.2. From the top of Rennes-le-Château, on a clear day Spain is visible.

time. It's misconstrued, disliked. It's not about being humble, which is more a craven apology for being alive. A gracious, caring, spiritually evolved person is imbued with humility, which God loves. So let's walk.'

The view from the top of Rennes was worth the four hours it took to get there. From the Tour Magdala, I could see across endless space to the foothills of the Pyrénées and behind them, Girona. Below on the parched land were the remains of a broken mill and, farther on, the steep mount of Bugarach. Eternity, 'beyond space and time', is how this view has been described. In the village, a cool breeze sent a tree rustling, swell full of summer sound, across this strange territory that seemed simply to wait in the light, syrupy sun. Everything here was in various stages of decline. Since it had become famous, nobody was sure who had the responsibility for the village's upkeep.

'Saunière used to walk in those days up and down to the train station in Couiza. Sometimes he hired a *caleche* with a driver to take him to Perpignan. The villagers never knew what to make of all they heard. His life was a sermon into the unknown. It will never be understood, they said.'

My visit to the Church of the Magdalene at Rennes-le-Château was short, and I was glad there were groups of agitated seekers with so many flashing cameras; it was like a fireworks display. Not a sacred moment to be seen or felt. The church was smaller than I'd remembered and sinking into the ground crookedly. The paintings of the Stations of the Cross were too forceful, as though insisting on a meaning different from the expected. Their imagery was clear and disconcerting, and the devil by the door—Asmodeus, known as the demon of Lust—was hardly a figure of spiritual celebration. I did not even want to think of my first visit to this place, then empty and ignored, in the mid-sixties when I'd seen the hunched, bullish figure in priest's robes. The memory was enough to get me moving towards the church door.

'What?' Liliane asked. 'Walking out already?'

'Running,' I answered.

Outside, she pointed to the Tour Magdala, constructed on the very edge of the plateau. 'No one understood it,' she said. 'With all that money, why build something simply neo-Gothic? He could have done something superb.'

'Was Saunière good or bad?' I echoed Maria's question.

'Oh, he fell from grace. He got to like the power and the worldly pleasures. His cabalistic identity—Samael—he would have understood. What a fall! But he had work to do.'

'What is Samael?'

For once she answered. This would be something I could understand that would not interrupt the journey.

'*Samael* is the devil in the Cabala. *Sam* is the temptation of our ego. We want to do our will, not God's Will. The devil is ego. It is not connected to the divine tree of Aziluth. Man has free will. Choice. Sam rebels against the Divine. *El* means archangel.'

'So it is the fallen angel,' I said quickly. She didn't disagree.

'Did Saunière understand the Cabala?'

'To some extent. It carries the key. That's one reason he came to Girona. The Abbé Saunière had to follow his pay-master's instructions. He had to build this tower to match the one in Girona. One in the north, Aset (serpent) Isis; the other in the south, Nephthys (the vine). These form the golden cut or golden section, the magnetic path. The towers mark a central place that is hidden and known only to the initiated. Activate the towers, and you change the chemistry of that place, which then enables matter and spirit to

245

leave and also re-enter existence. It allows contact with the layers of existence beyond us, not normally in our reach. So this activation at the centerpoint can reclaim the past, existing on the etheric plane, although whatever comes through may not necessarily be what was called up by the initiates. In unwise hands, the power of this process would send the planet into unthinkable darkness. How does this transformation happen? Saunière had to complete the uncompleted. I asked why he was chosen, given that his hands were supposedly 'unwise'.

'Oh, he was powerful. He understood what passes between those who "know and have". He wasn't just chosen; he was in a position to find things for the Habsburgs. And he had to unite North and South. And he had to leave a message hidden in symbol for those yet to come. He certainly wasn't digging for gold bars in the Frenchwoman's garden.'

Liliane suddenly changed topics. 'What happened to you on your original arrival at square number 47 in the Church of the Magdalene, which just now you couldn't wait to leave? Don't just recount the memory. You will sit down in the church and relive the experience.'

She had allowed no time for surprise or protest. I managed to ask how I should do this act, which seemed impossible.

'By absorption, as you have been taught. Absorb that visit with José and Dr Arbós and the secret you experienced there that you think is safe. Not talking about something doesn't make it safe. Surely you remember Lucia's argument against secrets. That they are elusive, dangerous, and give the holder unwise power.' She knew more than I'd supposed.

'Be more practical. When did you last feel the well-worn gravel with your feet? Take off your shoes.'

246

'Do I have a choice?' I pointed to the church.

'Certainly. If you want to continue across the magic square to site 11 then do what is asked; otherwise, we stay here for a cup of tea and take trains for Quillan, as Saunière used to do.'

And then it occurred to me that of course not all of the past initiates would have made it to the summit, the exit, the end that is the beginning. Which one had dropped out?

I could see she didn't expect that question. 'It won't help you,' she replied.

It wouldn't be José. Or would it? He wouldn't succumb to endless intrusions, queries. He would just, as I'd heard him put it, *'Fou le camp'*—"get the hell out".

In the church now, she offered me a choice of seats. I was beyond choosing.

'Just sit in the middle pew and close your eyes and be there,' she said.

'What's the point?'

'It's useful for what comes next. Going back into your past is a valuable practice you'll do many times.'

I felt she was talking about the other side of everything when, after death, I would be facing my own day of judgment.

'Remember humility. That's why we tried to locate it this morning.'

'Do I have to be in the church?'

'Obviously.'

Of course, I thought suspiciously, the ones who wanted to know—the custodians—needed the whole story. I wondered again what had happened on that sweet, innocent, sunlit afternoon in this Catholic church all those years ago. Did it somehow leave them vulnerable? What did they need to do?

247

Obedient to the past, I was back in Girona, and remembered when, one day in the 1960s, José had stopped in grief by the space where the Frenchwoman's house and tower had been. 'One day it was just gone,' he said. 'Even the royal palm tree was cut down, its huge root lying there as though wounded, gaping to the sky. Why did they have to do that? The whole town was outraged. They looked, they searched, lifting stone by stone.'

'They?' I asked him.

'This is an unholy act. I am going to do something for her, for the Frenchwoman. I'll make sure there is nothing else for anyone to get.'

'Who are they?' I asked many times. This was the mid-sixties and Girona was changing. Tourism was already ruining the coast.

'A group that wants what is here.' He chose the words carefully.

I assumed he meant the Vatican.

'Too late, poor thieves, in the night. The treasure is long gone.'

Then I remembered my first visit to Rennes-le-Château. The journey by car had had to be the way it was. In spite of torturous turns through dramatic configurations of ancient rock, Arbós avoided oncoming cars with a magnificent arrogance. He handled hairpin bends with the finesse of a heart surgeon—which, it turned out, he was. He needed speed because he had an operation to perform back in Girona. He and José had to arrive in Quillan and search for Maria Tourdes's old house urgently. But they found little of interest. Coming back to the car, Arbós noticed that the light was still good and suggested spinning up the hill to Rennes-le-Château. 'You never know,' he said.

The car shook to a stop at the top of the hill, and we went straight into the church. José and Arbós searched methodically, even flicking through a torn hymn book. I sensed it was a treacherous yet beautiful church, somehow on the edge of something that was not safe or even divine.

And then I saw it, the thing that could not be there, not even in a nightmare, not even in the last, mad, hellish thought. In front of the Stations of the Cross was a dark, hunched being in priests' robes. His eyes like swords swung into mine, jet black, filled with power, built up from hundreds of years of unimaginable existence. And behind him, covering the Stations of the Cross, was the old poster from the alley in Girona, the one advertising Torres chocolate, which seemed to be made up of light. Was it the way the light struck that wall? In a rich and deep tone, the apparition had spoken the words, 'Only from a gold cup'. Yes, it must have been the way the light fell and the shadows lengthened, but the figure seemed more real than Arbós. It did not wish me well. I was there, seeing too much without understanding any of it, and shouldn't be involved in this conspiracy of darkness. If I told José about the apparition, I was sure he'd deny its possibility. Anyone would. The being's hands had held two swords crossing over his chest. As I ran wildly from that place, circling down the road back to civilisation, I knew I would never talk about what I'd seen.

Until then, I had believed that this world was basically a good place, complying with a reality that had always been understood. I was sure an explanation for what I had seen was beyond human power to give me. If I spoke about it, the happening would only become more powerful and perhaps attract more visitations of the same sort. What I'd witnessed was real but had no place in reality.

Now, back in the present in the same church, I told Liliane some of this experience. I wondered if the figure had been Saunière. He hadn't looked like the priest in the French garden. She was looking at me, and I kept my eyes towards the altar.

'How much have you left out?' Her voice was not without challenge. She, and/or they, were looking for something that I knew but they didn't, or that I knew and shouldn't. We still sat in the church as though protected by our own personal silence. All around were the tourists overturning everything, even sacred objects, looking for the secret of the universe.

'You are not in danger,' Liliane continued. 'You are sensitive and can sometimes make contact with those in spirit. I hope I've heard the whole story.'

I asked her to explain the Rennes-le-Château underlying symbols.

'It comes under the Angel of Virgo. Symbols—tiara, sanctuary, altar, hill, shepherd, tooth of the key, and baptism. This is what the initiated ones understand. It takes much work to get even this far.'

'Do they relate to what happens here?'

'Very much so. Also in Cabala, Yod 10 + VAV 6 + Alejah 1 + Lamed 30 = 47. So you again get a sense of other parts of this experience.'

I got again a sense of relating to the sounds and the rhythm as though it was a foreign language or not language at all.

She drew the Cabalistic signs for each one. I thought of all of them the tiara was most extraordinary. It indicated style and opulence. I knew from my research that the village had been the stronghold of the Visigoths and for a while held a royal status.

We started down the hill, and she thumbed a ride to Couiza. We got a train to Quillan, too late for lunch. She made a delicious picnic, which we ate on the hillside near Quillan in an unusual silence. Did she sense I had edited the visit to the church with José and the doctor? She offered me a time to ask questions. So I wasn't getting her instruction on a plate anymore. I had to prove myself.

'That church: its strangeness is what draws the attention, but it's a cover for something else,' I said.

'Why did you come to this conclusion?'

'It's meant to distract. It's very demanding, so you think only of that and nothing else.'

She seemed pleased. 'Now I will tell you what is really happening. The church is decorated in such a way for one reason: it leaves a message for those yet to come. And that message is hidden in symbol. Saunière had much to accomplish. He had considerable knowledge of the rituals necessary to enter other dimensions. He took the Cabalists' way.'

'So he wasn't grandiose, a man of pleasure?'

'He was also an initiate on a high level.'

'Did he finish the journey?'

'Maybe you will find that answer.'

Liliane got up, ready to take the car. Had it really broken down, or had she been determined to get me walking up that hill? No answer to that. I asked why in Rennes she hadn't asked me to absorb the atmosphere.

'You absorbed the past. How do you feel? As you expected? Or otherwise?'

I did feel lighter, different, less concerned with the usual habits. What I experienced now I had known only in brief snatches before. Freedom: I thanked her for this.

She drove to Perpignan and stopped at the station. 'Now we heal the past,' she said.

251

Figure 17.1. The railway station at Perpignan, Dali's painting of which is now in the Frankfurt Museum of Art.

CHAPTER 17

Liliane came out of the Perpignan railway station's buffet and pointed to Canigou. 'It's got its cap on today.'

The mountain seemed to be hanging over the station in its immensity and uncaring potential for destruction. They used to say about Canigou when I lived in its foothills, "It claims what it wants."

She asked if I knew the expression about the cap. I had heard it. 'It means its peak is covered in cloud.' She gave me a coffee and we shared an apple tart. 'Dali stood on this platform and saw Perpignan station as the unknown centre of the universe.' She waited for a response and we sat silently finishing the tart. She said, 'Dali knew in that moment and realised he was alone with the realisation.'

'Am I going to feel that way?' I asked, suddenly.

'It seemed that here Dali had experienced another place altogether. He had quite inadvertently stepped into another time and space, and it affected him profoundly, as one might expect. He spoke of an apocalyptic vision. So now I want you to remember the painting in Figueras, square number 44.'

I remembered a man falling down through space, feet first, and a train coming towards him from behind. On each side on the platform were lines of agricultural workers, some from existing, well-known art.

'What else?' she said.

'Yes, there was a cross.'

'Not just any cross. One that is square with four lines of equal length. A Celtic cross.'

The Celtic cross was bright light running from each corner of the picture and crossing over in the middle. I asked if she had known Dali. She had.

'He was a complicated, curious man, sensitive, not a showman only out for drama, as some believe. I used to visit his house in Port Ligat, near Cadaques, which we passed yesterday. I told him about Ramon of Perillos and his "other dimension", so Dali went up to the deserted village and understood many things about Daleth 4, Doorway. He felt the devil all around him. Even the post code being 666—supposedly the number of the devil—was not simply coincidence.'

I, too, had known Dali, but not to such a grand degree.

'He painted the picture in 1964 or 1965,' Liliane continued. He was mystical, esoteric, looking for what was beneath worldly reality, and he certainly found it. He traversed many spheres, little known, unseen. He was a seeker, a magician, and he wasn't afraid of the outcome. But what he experienced here at the Perpignan station was bigger than all that.'

'Have I got to experience what he did?' I'd heard Dali had gone to bed suffering with depression for quite a while towards the end of his life. If there was a choice, I'd rather not go through it. She said Dali put the experience into his work.

'I hope Dali did make that statement. Of course, this station is the centre of the world. It's where he sent off all his artwork to the States. He didn't trust the post, especially in Spain.'

And I used to see my ex-husband go with Dali from Port Ligat to Perpignan to send off a picture for New York. I asked her what she thought had happened to so change the artist. She pointed to Canigou.

'The Portal.'

Did she mean he had gone through a portal? She didn't answer my question but chose to change the subject.

'What is eleven?' she asked.

I knew that some people who were drawn to energies and ley lines found a special significance in the numbers 11:11. I said I was often aware of that time in the morning and would quite simply see it on my kitchen clock, staring at the two elevens until they changed to 11:12, which was something quite different.

'Eleven: Eleven. In sacred geometry, the two elevens are the columns of the temple. The doorposts of the portal. Perpignan. The dark and sterile mother. Binah, the third sefirot of the Tree of Life. World-universe. Earth. To excavate. To mine. To dig. Course of water. Flame. Perpignan falls on square 42. Forty-two degrees refers to the rainbow. The angle between the horizon and highest point formed in the eye of the observer.' She had understood these symbols from years of research and initiation.

She was about to leave the platform, car keys in hand. Quickly I asked about Dali. Did he go to the peak of the mountain? Did he go through a portal?

'He had to be prepared first. You can't just jump into it. You have to sit calmly attuned to one thought, allowing an opening of the portal to become visible. It takes a great deal of attention.'

'Did Dali see a vision? That's what it's all about, isn't it? Calling up the vision.'

'If only,' she said. 'If only it were that.'

And I felt we had come to a decisive moment. Leaving the subject of Dali's progress, I questioned my own. Would I be allowed to continue? So far I had managed meditation and increased the depth of that experience. I had no more information about the dream of the priest in the French garden. Physically, I was fitter, toned, lean, more flexible. I was less needful and didn't become desperate if food or drink were not there. The early fears had melted away. I probably could spend the night alone and told her so.

'Good,' she said.

I didn't like the sound of 'good'. She started walking along the platform, seeing Canigou from as many angles as possible, and I followed.

'We have to get shovels,' she said.

Naturally I thought I'd misheard. I asked what hotel we'd stay in. I quite liked the idea of one near Ceret and would invite her to be my guest for the night. After all, she'd done so much for me, even if she was the enemy. She did not reply to either my question or my invitation.

Still in the station, I again checked my progress and thought it positive. I could chant and feel a change in myself. My breathing was better, no longer the city breaths of a Londoner. The stretching had been wonderful for my legs and back, and I thought the arthritic knee was mercifully improved. I ate less and better and not for comfort. My thoughts were different, more concentrated on what was around me. I did not feel the change of energy when moving slightly in a precise place. But yes, I did feel freedom now and then. Overall, I was feeling good until she asked, 'When did you last look at the snapshot?' I hadn't. 'Until you can accept it you can't progress. So lift it up from under all those things and look at it. And keep doing it. The habit will reduce the intensity. You have to accept the past and all that has happened in it. You will learn to heal some of what has happened.'

She waited for me to get out the snapshot and do what she'd asked. There was no delay when she made a request. I did. Then she said, 'Now we go and get the shovels.'

'Why?'

'To dig our graves.'

Inland towards the mountains, the unexpected happened for Liliane because the usual place for the grave-digging process was swamped with unaccustomed rain water. I took it to be an omen. It meant we should not dig graves. What were we supposed to do with them? Die in them?

She moved higher up into the countryside somewhere behind Le Boulou. So far, I had not seen her engaged in anything she had not done a dozen times. She had to test the ground as well as the area for safety, including the contingencies of people, snakes, adverse weather, animals.

When we'd dug our graves, could we then go to a hotel? I mentioned the one near Ceret. She walked higher and found shelter in the rocks. It was almost alright, and then she saw the field. She took out a pendulum and dowsed each place.

'We take the field. We mark the outline of each grave and then you start digging the earth and put it to one side. It must face north.'

'Why?'

'We came from the North and must never forget it.' She said she'd go to Le Boulou and get water and fruit before the shops closed. It was getting dark. I asked for more food and offered her money. It didn't take long for my fears to be back.

She went off in the car and I watched its tail lights into the distance. All around me was the unknown, the advancing darkness soon making it dangerous. It would be filled with some of the things I dreaded and introduce a few more. I put down the shovel. Had I come nowhere in these two weeks? Was it all back—the fear, the needs, the disappointments? I did the chanting, my voice reedy with nerves. Why attract the injurious, the rodent, the criminal, the chance killer on his way home, almost giving up for the day? I didn't trust meditation. I needed to be acutely present. I wished I could hide. I had to make friends with the environment, be part of it, have it on my side. It was just a field, and I could not get any sense of connection with it. What would José have done? He would've enjoyed the oncoming night. The streak of light on the horizon, the distant sound of a train. He'd find peace. I discovered I was not José.

I tried prayer. I could feel Canigou behind me. What did they used to say? Skiers don't go there anymore. If you ski on its body, it takes its payment. Planes don't go near it. It magnetises to destruction. In the early days, several planes had crashed there. Yet Verdaguer wrote the magnificent poem in Canigou's honour. Perhaps the mountain liked that.

I started digging. Then I took out the snapshot, and in the half-light I could see the figures. I hadn't been thinking with all the dots on my dice; the danger wasn't coming from the unexpected in my surroundings but from the only too expected in my heart.

My companion. I knew—how I did!—that Liliane worked for the private society, the custodians. The outcome in my case could not be good. As soon as they knew whatever it was I knew, I would be no more. Why else was I alone in the middle of nowhere? I was even digging my grave for them. The girl in the snapshot would have known that instantly. She would have done what she always did, which I would now do—run for it.

It took seconds to pick up my things, put the bag on my back, and start running in the direction Liliane had taken. When I heard the car returning, I'd get out of the reach of the headlights. Le Boulou was possibly at most an hour away on foot. The running had to be given up; I started fast walking. What if 'they' were already present in the field? Of course, I should have asked José much more about this impulsive suggestion. Why go on the journey in the first place?

I was over the slope and could see the lights of the small town. I had to stop and bend over to get back my breath, and then I saw the three men standing by the road smoking. I saw them in the headlights of her approaching car. If she stopped and talked to them, my departure had to be better planned. I moved farther away where no possibility of light could reach me. The car slowed and I heard her voice. Even in these circumstances, her laugh sounded so attractive. Panic took me yet further into the night, and I decided to circle around the town and go towards Ceret.

When my grave was found undug, the pursuers would go to the railway station, the taxi company, the bus stop. Liliane was moving off past the men, and the car rattled as it hit a stone. I had five minutes, possibly.

What I expected did not happen. There was no hooting from the car, no alarmed calls to the men. I slithered and slipped down towards the road. Then I heard the men call goodnight, one to the other, as they went their separate ways. Beside me a dog barked. It was so near I could see its teeth. Held back by a chain in its owner's yard, it reared up in anger and frustration. I cried out, but the car was already coming towards me, headlights seeking traces of my flight.

Liliane had made a fire. By the time we returned to our place in the field, the sausages were already cooked. She had not asked why I'd been so far from my grave location or if I'd been planning to run away. Now I dug with my last strength but she still wasn't satisfied. The grave needed to be at least three feet deep.

'Why?'

'You wouldn't lie in a shallow grave, I hope.'

'But it will take hours.'

'You've got nowhere to go, so where is the problem?'

I now explained my departure as fear driven. I still had my ace: the information. Whatever came out of me would be as shallow as my grave. She attacked the ground with strength and measured movements, and her grave was finished before the fire burned down. Skilfully she roasted vegetables in the glowing wood. I crouched beside her and ate as though it was the first meal I'd ever had. The food was delicious. The fresh air, the wood smoke, the energy raised from digging—all were delicious. The freedom was back. She heated a pot of water and made tea.

I started a question, beginning with 'When . . . '

'Oh no,' Liliane said. She didn't like that word.

'What do I put in the grave?'

'Just yourself.'

I tried to laugh. She helped me dig and the hole took shape and the stars were full. She scraped out the loose earth and told me to lie in the hole. Then she covered me with a blanket and my coloured shawls. She, better dressed than I, lay in her grave with one covering.

At first she told me about the star systems directly above and then those farther away. After a pause, she started chanting and asked me to follow the sounds. I felt this took a long time, but for once I had no sense of time passing.

'Tell me the story about the visit to Rennes-le-Château with José and Dr Arbós. Just the bits you left out.'

There it was. There was no question of continuing this journey. How had she got me in my grave? I tried to sit up. It seemed impossible. She'd weighted my body with stones between the shawls and the coat. I asked about these.

'They are to keep you warm and the small animals out.'

My account of the afternoon visit to the church was the same as before.

'Is that the whole story?'

Of course not. I pretended to sleep.

'Just tell it as it was. All of it. Especially the chocolate ad from the Girona alley.'

So I told it as it was—the whole story, including the appearance of the hunched figure. Surprisingly, although the event had upturned my sense of reality, it did nothing much for her. I sensed the story was not what she had expected at

Figure 17.2. Poster featuring Emma Calvé.

all. The society members were looking for something else. I was sure of that.

'Why didn't you tell José?' she asked.

'Finally I did, but only much later.' Then I asked her how she'd heard about the story.

'From José.' She took me back to the chocolate poster, and I asked why it was apparent in the church. She said Emma Calvé used to advertise chocolate. Her face was everywhere.' She added that oddly, perhaps by chance, chocolate had played a small part in Saunière's story. She hadn't told me why the poster should be reproduced by light in a Catholic church. What was it that the society wanted? I decided to try and find out. Helpfully, I asked if there was anything more that she'd expected.

'The Cabalistic sign for *doorway*. The dark symbol. You must remember it.'

'Oh yes,' I assured her.

'Where was it in his church?'

I didn't know.

'Behind the apparition.'

I didn't know how to answer.

I supposed she sensed that there were parts missing from the story and they unsettled her. I asked if I was in danger.

'The priest needed to speak to you: "Only from a gold cup." Perhaps you will find out what that signifies.' She sounded reassuring.

'But why was the poster covering the Stations of the Cross. It's unholy.'

'Maybe he liked chocolate.'

And I could smell hot drinking chocolate. It seemed to have been there in my before-sleep experience of revisiting the past in the Frenchwoman's garden when Emma Calvé sang and the birds squawked.

Liliane said next I would learn about protection. She asked me to cover myself, first with pink light so that I was sealed completely as though in a sheath. The light must cover the soles of my feet. And then I should see the pink light encased with rich gold. 'Now all impulses and needs leave you. Give in. Let all tension drop. Look at the stars. Let go.'

I once asked José if he was afraid of dying. He said, 'We only have this moment, but we should go on as though life were eternal.'

Lying in my grave, it felt as though part of me asked José questions. Who is the Lady of the Cup? He answered that she could on occasion come back to this earth. The ritual could bring her—to heal, to save, to empower. He understood it was the Magdalene. I closed my eyes and could see large, white birds flying somewhere between me and the stars. They were free and joyous. Were they the spirits of the initiates who had gone before? Between them were spirals of gold light.

'You have to move your legs, arms, your whole body,' Liliane said. 'Tense, release. Keep it warm, the circulation strong.'

I could feel creatures crawling up my legs. From the weight of their legs I could not tell their size. She told me to cover myself again in gold light, especially the soles of my feet, and ask the questions, 'Where was I between my last death and this birth? What did I see?' I heard a rushing sound in my ears. I thought I heard her say, 'But you have to go through this. It's no good to keep running to him.' Again, I wondered if she was a mind reader.

When José had done the ritual in Girona in 1976, he told me that the Lady of the Cup had sent forth a stillness unlike anything he'd ever known. He told me he'd felt as though a door had opened and he was being pulled towards and through it; he sensed there was a passage of light and he so wanted to follow it. 'Why didn't you?' I had asked. He said it was because he didn't know if he'd come back. The pull had been so strong that he'd had a sense of holding on to the doorposts.

The ritual José had performed was similar to the one practised by the Cabalists in Girona in the Middle Ages. It was contained in an equation, pages long, taking between two and four hours to perform. It was an equation for the usual transformation.

Liliane was speaking again. It seemed I mustn't fall asleep. No chance of that. I asked if she had performed the ritual. She had and now took others through the process. How?

'The initiates do patterned, repetitive acts and manipulate their bodies, using the normal reactions of the nervous system to such stimuli to arrive at a state of ritual trance. The process was described in the "Sworn Book", of which there are few copies in existence.' I understood this book to be a medieval mystical manual of which she had a copy.

Then my memories returned. I could see the French-woman's garden as it had been in what I could now only describe as my vision. And there was a chocolate advertisement on the kitchen wall. It was in French and included a picture of Emma Calvé. The chocolate 'Guerin-Boutron' was of 'Qualité Superiéur'. The main office was '28 rue St-Sulpice, Paris'.

I could hear Saunière's voice, deep and rich. 'I want to complete the uncompleted. The towers mark the point.'

Liliane had mind-reading abilities, it seemed, because she commented on what I was thinking. 'But Saunière failed. Did he find the portal? He didn't complete what he'd started. He practised faith but knew evil, and his work was never finished. He never did unite North and South.

264

Once those realms are brought together, there is superconsciousness; a higher plane is within reach. Other realms can reach us.'

'He didn't finish the journey,' I said, aloud.

Liliane said, 'Just be still and let go. And let the experience of death take you. Don't fight.'

My chattering teeth woke me up. I was surprised I'd slept. Liliane was building a fire and making tea. There was a pale light from the east. She started singing and then dancing. 'Come and dance,' she said, and helped me up, and I seemed to become unstuck from my grave. I hoped it was for the last time.

Liliane began her typical rapid string of symbols and influences. 'Canigou, Portal, site 11, number 7 on the magic square. God. Initiates of Adonai-ha-aretz. A.H.A. My Lord of the earth. Tenth Sephirot of Azilith. World of God. Unmanifest Messiah. (Egypt-Horus.) To get lost, to die. Recollect, unite, or join; accumulate. Fish and to fish. *Zayr*, the seventh letter in the Hebrew alphabet, signifies centre, sword, seed.' I wondered if these powerful snatches of information usually helped those on the journey.

She waited for me to respond.

'What is the most powerful?' she asked.

I was thinking of 'to get lost', 'to die'. Also 'recollect', 'unite', or 'join'. That this site should be the World of God was not surprising. Was this where the Unmanifest Messiah became apparent?

I gave myself a new site all of my own, number Zero— End Up. Time for a decision: Did I leave now? Was it safe to leave? Or did I go to the end, which was also the beginning? Retreat or adventure? I automatically wanted to ask the one person who would help me, José, but these were my questions, not his.

'Did José go up?' I asked. Liliane nodded. Then I supposed I would, too, and we started walking to the car. On the seat I saw a description of a magic square: 'Magic square of order or an arrangement of n^2 numbers visibly distinct integers in a square that the n numbers in all rows, columns, and diagonals sum to the same constant.' The language was so garbled that I understood why there was so much I would not understand.

An hour later, we were sitting on a rock at Le Vernet, a French spa village at the beginning of the north ascent of Canigou. I knew it would come to this. After a night lying in an insect-filled hole of putrid earth, I felt reduced. This was my worst time so far. And then she said I must find my own words for atonement and ask forgiveness.

I could not believe this new demand and felt ready for the grave, any grave. I decided to take a room in one of the many pretty hotels and put off all other decisions until I was ready. She didn't like that, arguing that this unskinned state was precisely the right one for me to start climbing the mountain. Why else had I stripped my habits and defences? From acute awareness I would become free.

I wanted to creep off back home. We went to and fro the decision, I all the while feeling the old snapshot in my pocket. What would that girl have done?

'What's up on the mountain?' I asked.

'Find out.'

Saying I'd have lunch, I got to my feet and sat at a table in a restaurant filled with locals and curists at the required hour of 12:30 p.m. Liliane joined me and I said I'd take a train to Paris. First, though, I'd take a room in this hotel where the restaurant was, as I was exhausted beyond reason.

'I don't know anything,' I told her. 'I haven't uncovered anything. José has said only what I put in *City of Secrets*. Tell them that.' I was referring to the custodial group.

'Can't you envisage this journey being offered to you out of love, not threat? Why look for bad motives? You see you have to clear your early resentments. They inform your present responses and can make you miss a wonderful experience.'

'What do the custodians want?' I had nothing to lose, I thought. But I had. 'I'll tell you anything.' I opened my arms wide and couldn't have appeared more honest. Never show your cards to your opponent.

Of course, Liliane had reassuring answers. We'd go one level up the mountainside, spend the night in the monastery there, and then decide. 'And you don't have to go home by way of Paris. I'll drive you to Perpignan and you can take the plane to London from there.'

I felt better after eating, and I walked on my own through the peaceful streets. Liliane waited by the mountain path quite calm, even friendly. Perhaps she felt she'd failed.

'Now we climb,' she said, and walked slowly, easily, up through trees. The path was reasonable, the air pure and scented. At the first bench she stopped and we did the exercises.

Number 7. The initiate. First we do the healing.'

I listed the remaining resentments, hurts, and disappointments of my life and thought I was finished.

'Now get to the real matter. Your daughter. Why blame the whole problem, whatever it is, on your son-in-law?'

'Ex!'

'I want you to think and remember well her part in the trouble. Even small things. Especially small things.'

Unwillingly, I produced a few incidents. As I spoke I could feel warmth rising in my solar plexus, then my chest. Liliane's hands were lifted, and from them came this heat and energy.

What was my part in the family problem?

I didn't have one.

The next topic was José. Why should the man I had loved, and sometimes still thought of, not love someone else? I was too tired for all this.

'What you had with José is still there. In memory. Of that you can be sure. Accept both of these conditions—your past relationship and his marriage—and then forgive.'

'Forgive.' I would prefer a tree-load of vengeful custodians. 'Forgive yourself first and then the others, the causes of your pain, the carriers of injustice. Do it and you will be free.'

Some things I could never forgive. I stood up, prepared to go on walking.

'After you've done that, you heal your past, parents, childhood.'

I said I would return to the village below to spend the night in the hotel.

She questioned why. Was it to feel safe? I could sleep on the mountain. I asked why we'd had to spend a night in a grave.

'To come to accept death. To have a sense of giving in, of letting go.'

I would never give in. I'd fight to the last gasp.

'You have to leave this body to make space.'

I asked what for.

'The journey.'

That didn't sound too good, and I thought of my early conclusions that the custodians wanted me bundled off across these magic squares to be lost for eternity with whatever forbidden knowledge I'd picked up. Yet there *had* been magic moments in my life. Would they allow me those? Would I have occasion to recall them before my conclusion?

'Who told you to guide me?' I asked.

She did hesitate. 'It will be explained to you.'

'I would like to hear it now, at sea level. Mountains make me think of Lucia.'

She stood up and I didn't move. I was dishevelled, dirty, in shreds of tiredness. I wanted to go back down now. 'People don't want to sleep on mountains, Liliane. That's why they have hotels.'

Calmly she said I should ascend to the first refuge and then I could choose between climbing higher and going down, going home.

'I can't and won't climb to the top.' I stood my ground on that.

As we walked up, Liliane looked pleased. 'So you will stay a little longer?' I believed she thought I was suffering from some exhaustion-induced paranoia. Perhaps I was. I felt truly taken to my furthest point. She talked about magic squares as though that would help. 'They've been on this earth for over 4,120 years. Dating from the time of the prehistoric Chinese Emperor Yu, there is a famous Lo Shu square, which according to legend appeared imprinted on the back of a magical turtle.'

Fascinating, but what had this to do with me?

'Remember, magic squares were once used for the prevention of dizziness and also for longevity, which seems to concern you suddenly. A magic square is a talisman. You are crossing the Venus Square right now. It will protect you.'

She taught me some signs of protection that had come from ancient Egypt: Mentally over your enemy, place a green pyramid. You need only to see the outlines of the pyramid. A mid-green colour. If the enemy is particularly aggressive, see a figure 3 over the middle of his or her body on the solar plexus. A green 3 with a long tail. You can place a green triangle over those you fear. See your enemy in white light, and mentally push him or her back until the person becomes a white dot. Protect yourself by covering your whole body, from the top of your head down to the soles of the feet, with a pyramid of gold light. Paint this gold—bright gold. Use your imagination. Around your door, mentally paint blue light, a mid-blue from the Mediterranean. Sprinkle salt around the edges of the room. Cover your building with a green pyramid.

The path was still good, and ascending even that small distance blocked all thought and I became lighter, in a better mood. Here there were just thick trees, countryside, stones. The imperious mountain was far out of sight.

After fresh apple juice and tea in the first refuge, which was no more than a hut, we climbed narrow, rocky paths with extreme twists and turns. The view with each step up expanded, becoming more wide sweeping and soon magnificent. By the late afternoon Liliane asked again if I could experience some forgiveness on the two points of my son-in-law and José's marriage that could not be negotiated earlier. I answered that I'd say I could, but it would be untrue. Quite kindly she replied that it might affect my experience at the end of the journey. I noticed the word *might* and suspected that her tone would be harder the next time I gave a negative answer. I assured her that my traversing square 7 was unlikely. I had agreed to spend the night in the monastery of St Martin to give the journey a proper end.

We climbed in silence towards St Martin, and I again thought of the others before me. Verdaguer seemed so much further away than the rest, on the plane of another

s.Martin de Canigou ~ PORTAL #7

Figure 17.3. The monastery at St Martin de Canigou.

reality. He was the most evolved and finely attuned, filled with spirit and light, and he seemed to acknowledge me as I climbed his beloved mountain.

'He had the same difficulties as everyone else,' Liliane said. 'He raised conflict. What he said, people listened to. He was charismatic. The Church threw him out.'

I had no feeling about or sense of Quim Carreras's ancestor, the law student.

'He wanted the ritual, the doorway, the transformation, the leaving and arriving in heightened levels of space and time.'

I didn't understand.

'The ability to leave these five dimensions and so become invisible. He felt it often on this journey and said that, towards the end, his body was "simply not there". He was "without needs".'

'Did he get all those things?'

'Not at all. The law student went on the wrong road and believed the Grail ritual was in Arcadia, Greece. He stayed the rest of his life in Girona, forever seeking what the ancient texts he'd discovered in Paris had promised him. Before his death, he instructed a young student named Boche to go to Arcadia, and on the way up to this mournful place, where even animals didn't leave shadows, the student was murdered.'

She sat on a rock and took out the document case. It was filled with new pages, more than ever. 'You have heard of the Zohar, the book of Cabala. José quoted from these pages when he reached this square number 7. "The soul when sent to earth puts on an earthly garment in order to be able to look without injury into the mirror whose light proceeds from the Lord of Light."'

Verdaguer said upon arriving at this very spot, square 7, these words: "The air is full of souls. Those which are nearest to the earth descend to be tied to mortal bodies. They return quickly to claim bodies, being desirous to live in them."'

Saunière wrote: "Lord, I am happy in this world and do not wish to go into another realm where I shall be a handmaiden in an apron and exposed to all kinds of indignities."'

She closed the sheets back in the case. 'I wouldn't want you to think that your personal acts, which may sabotage your fulfilment on this journey if you climb farther, are the worst fault. Saunière, for instance, was involved in practices to raise the dead.'

Our discussion had taken quite another turn, and I was jolted out of my downcast mood. 'The dead? What did he do to them?'

'It is a dangerous practice to disturb the tranquillity of the souls; it interferes with their evolutionary development into higher states.'

'Did he do it?'

'It was said he had.'

'Why?'

'Power, knowledge. Perhaps he took money for it. You see, what he did had to come out and be known. This journey is called "Walking with the Great Bear; Treading the Seven Stars". You won't have this experience because you hang on to your hurts. Hand them over to God. Or to the woman of smoke.'

I wasn't sure about the second choice. The peace and love I had felt at that first moment of seeing the woman of smoke had come from my companion. Liliane was more powerful than I had first thought. She was, among other things, a magician.

'Think of the woman of smoke. Call her up.'

Together we sat, eyes closed. I could see a wraith of smoke curling and lifting around dustbins and trash cans, as though looking for small things of value. Her eyes were open and round and filled with an immense compassion. She was drawn again to rubbish and litter.

'Don't arouse the dead and try to bring them back. You interfere with the spirit making progress in the next realm. You hold the person back.'

Was Liliane talking to me? Her eyes were still closed, and it seemed she was passing through a message or repeating some text she suddenly remembered. She got up and said we should increase speed to arrive before dark at the monastery. She was again practical and fully in the moment, and I did wonder if she could channel those on the other side of life.

Was Quim Carreras part of the society? He, the religious scholar, was envious of José—of his courage, his past, the admiration he still received from the city. Cocteau had approved of José's uniqueness. Carreras accused José of doing what he believed in without due consideration. He chose to despise José for not taking a scholarly, rational approach. I asked Liliane if Carreras had been a member of the private society.

'Oh yes.' Firm answer.

'Is he alive?'

'Over there.' Firmer answer.

I took it he was dead.

'Did he do this journey?'

'No. He went to South America.'

'You do mean he is dead?'

I remembered the last time I had seen Carreras. He had looked well travelled, tanned, and slim, with the graceful movements of a cat. His hazel eyes held a challenge. Their beauty made me shy. He said Maria Tourdes had made a decision to hand her life to God.

'If you just leave yourself open, if you are casual, you don't have a spiritual direction and you can let in all sorts of things, especially darkness. Go towards the light and you are safe,' Carreras had said.

I had asked him if Saunière was good or bad. He replied he was not a judge of the clergy in France. He understood evil and its remedy, light. Perhaps in this magic square, number 7, I should be considering Carreras's advice. I felt darkness around me, both actual and outside of my existence.

I told Liliane I did not like the dark feeling. It was in fact black, opaque, as dark as wine gums. On the edge now, I could neither move forward nor take my preferred choice—downward.

'Accept. Ask for help. Receive. Heal.' She took my hand and tried to lead me.

I clung to the thought of Verdaguer and how out of every experience and mood on this mountain he could make a verse, a line, a sound. She was talking, explaining, making reasonable my predicament. I knew it was exhaustion, the altitude, the too-positive ions in the air. It was a classic panic attack. I stood still, trying to breathe, and then lay face down in the bracken. She pulled me up and made me sing. Together we did two verses of a Catalan traditional song I'd learned years ago. I let all the blackness pour out in the singing. I sang until I had nothing left and was lying again face down on the ground.

Liliane gave me a plastic cup of water to which she'd added drops from a bottle of herbal tincture. 'This sort of occurrence happens to some extent. The ritual produces a stimulus of the nervous system to such a degree that the normal defences of the brain are lowered. The range of perception is therefore much longer and too vivid.'

'So I won't be one of them. Only high initiates can be given the ritual process.' Not one of these, I still clung to the bracken.

'Let's not limit things.'

I still stayed with the panic-attack diagnosis. She sat beside me and did not seem concerned.

'Do you want to know where the ritual documents were kept?'

I sat up and brushed twigs from last night's grave dust in my hair.

'During the Napoleonic War in 1810, they were safe in the house next to the chapel in Palera, which you visited. After the war ended in 1820, they were moved to the house of the Frenchwoman in Girona. It was then inhabited by canons from the church. Many of the documents were in the family of José's great-grandfather.' She was trying to get my attention, trying to get me to follow her words.

Shakily I got up and heard a clinking sound going back down the track. I assumed it was a stone. We kept on up the twisting path, and the effort and freshness of the air brought back some energy. I thought no more about the hotel at the bottom. I thought of José digging and clearing the French garden. It would be a tribute to Maria's memory, and he'd already placed a plaque by the entrance: 'The Garden of the Frenchwoman'. José had talked about Verdaguer and of how he was involved to some degree in the private society and used mediums and occult practices to exorcise the powers of darkness. Verdaguer believed illness was caused by demonic intervention. The Church suspended him, and he was sent to a retreat near Ripoll. I thought it was where José himself had been initiated, but when I'd asked recently he had pointed to Canigou, saying, 'I was up there, on the mountain.' He had spoken from a serious place in his memory. I remember asking if he had wanted to be involved in all this.

'Never.' A bird had drawn close to him, settled on a branch, and made the calling, jarring sound of the one in the Jewish courtyard during the concert. 'It always comes to me and calls me to go away,' he'd said.

'To?'

'The mountain.' There was only one mountain for the Catalans.

And the bird had sung its heart out.

276

Now Liliane reintroduced the present and pointed up through the trees. 'The monastery of St Martin.'

It was only when I knew I must call my children that I discovered the mobile phone was lost. I looked not without desperation at my companion, but she never carried one. It occurred to me that she'd taken it. The thought didn't go away. I'd had it in the restaurant. And then I remembered the clinking sound of what I thought was a stone dropping down the mountain. My phone?

'Can I use one in the monastery?' The building seemed to get no nearer, like all objectives on this journey.

'They don't have one for guests. There is one in the office. You can ask.'

The phone had been securely fastened in my pocket. How had it fallen out?

'When you threw yourself face down on the ground,' she said.

'But I can't lose that. Should I go back?'

'I told you at the start on this journey you will lose everything.' And she carried on upward, struggling through her own exhaustion.

Liliane was known by the nuns and monks of the monastery. When I lived in Ceret the arrival of women in this male community had stirred up a protest, especially as the women were young. I didn't get a chance to see the nuns, as I was given a cell with a bed and washbasin and a window with a view of the sky. Liliane brought me a tray of hot food and said later I could take a shower and we could meditate and pray in the chapel.

I could see the premises had been recently refurbished, and I was right. 'Tourists now come around the year; they're brought up in jeeps, given a guided tour, and returned to base,' she said.

'So it's not like in Verdaguer's time?'

'But of course not.' Her vowels were elongated and her tone overloud through exhaustion. She sat cross-legged and said we should do breathing exercises, and a small meditation. Then I could ask questions.

Tomorrow I would return to London or continue the journey. She asked me again about José and I told her that, yes, I wanted him to love only me. I could see the folly of it, but I still did feel a sure sense of loss of that love I had once known.

'But of course we are all cut off from the love we have once known. That is the continuing problem.'

Was she talking about my time in my mother's body? I hoped not. I wasn't at all sure that my mother had wanted a pregnancy.

'Of course I'm not talking about your mother.' Her voice was louder and tiredness sent it forth without restraint. There was a tapping of protest on the wall, and we both quite unexpectedly started giggling like children. It was the best feeling that day.

At 10 p.m. the monastery was filled with exultant song, and amongst it I recognised the sound that lifted my spirits and made my heart dance: F-sharp sustained.

All this exercise had begun because the city of Girona housed secrets to which I was made privy when José had suffered a heart attack in 2003. Otherwise, I most probably would never have known of their existence. Did I really know anything about them, even now? I'd been told some and researched more. Others, who wanted different outcomes, either allowed me more information or wished me ill. I'd written the book *City of Secrets*. I'd also made use of the power of the establishments, which I'd better keep to myself. But still, Girona would have its secrets.

Some cities had areas where the mystical, the improbable, and the Divine converged. On our first visit to Paris in the mid-fifties, my friend Beryl and I had caught the attention of Jean-Paul Sartre and Simone de Beauvoir, whom we met as arranged each morning at 11 a.m. at the cafés of the Flore or Bonaparte. I remembered Sartre saying that he had found New York lacking and soulless on his first visit. He said, "The streets look so alike they've not been named, whereas our Paris streets are full of alleys and twisting bends and secrets. I was alone in a city—New York—that hugged its secrets." By that he meant that, unlike Paris, New York City held its secrets to itself. Sartre was excited by Maurice Barrès's belief that certain cities held secrets and signs not possible in small towns, the country, or the coast. Sartre could stand before an alleyway and sense that things were making signs to him and that it was necessary to decipher them. It was the secret meaning of objects that he wanted to capture.

When Beryl and I met Sartre and Beauvoir in the mornings, it was mainly for discussions on existentialism. At that time we were beyond doubt existentialists living in the moment, and so we had an identity at least. We wore very tight drainpipe trousers and rope sandals that you could buy on London's Charing Cross Road for three and sixpence. Our nails were painted black and we wore huge, Brigitte Bardot kiss curls over our ears, streaked with a gold dust that in certain climates turned green. We danced in the street just for the love of it and took the roads as they came as long as they were different. Jean-Paul Sartre and Beauvoir were probably the only two people who understood us. They could see through the makeup. We lived for now. *Tomorrow* we couldn't even spell.

Figure 18.1. The path to Mt Canigou.

CHAPTER 18

We made good time in the early light. Liliane pointed across the plain far below to Pech de Bugarach and behind Rennes-le-Château.

'So that over there is where this mystery all began and why we are on this mountain.' I said.

'Not a chance,' she replied.

'Then it began in Egypt.' I'd had enough sleep to be clever.

'The mystery began before the journey moved to the north. It started before Atlantis. The sacred mountain was then Mt Sin of the Sumerians.

I had to ask for clarification.

'After that, the sacred mountain became Sion in the Holy Land and then Canigou in the north. The journey belongs to others as well as to us.'

I definitely did not want to be on it. I wanted to go home and sit in the nonchallenging half-comfort of my life with the dogs and cats. Layers were being peeled from me and too much information placed on my thin surface. I didn't want to change. It was hard enough living with what

I knew. But it was a lovely, divine morning, and that would be my undoing.

As we'd agreed, Liliane stopped where the path forked, and I was to decide whether to continue the journey. Without pause she started talking.

'I didn't finish what I was telling you last night about the agonising sense of loss. We are cut off from what held us on the other side of this life. In coming to this earth plane, we left that love of our true companions to make this journey to loneliness with new, untried people. And these beloved ones in spirit can't help us.'

I asked why not.

'Because we have been pushed out to make the passage in this life in order to learn the lesson of separation and loss.'

'But I don't remember these beloved ones.'

'Your spirit does.'

I wouldn't have believed her except for the rising up of a far distant memory: When a very young child, I had been walking with my father, who was on leave from the Second World War. The day in the late afternoon was beautiful, overwhelmingly so in the colours, the sky; and I thought this beauty didn't belong to 'here'—where we were—but to over 'there', which was a place I knew but not of this world. That other place was always brilliant, vital, and so much more than this muted territory with its little streets and usually tamed colours. Where we were was a doll's house, and I was squeezed into it. But the beauty of the day, as I was holding my father's hand, had linked up with that other, more real place. The dazzling sky and magnificent sunset had stirred my memory perfectly, and I knew—how I did!—that I must not forget or lose the glory I had known and just come from. I was so small I was barely walking. I tried to say 'over there' to my father, but I had no words and he couldn't understand. He thought my finger pointing 'over there' meant I wanted to pick a flower. And he picked it for me, but that wasn't what I was meaning at all. It was my first encounter with misunderstanding.

Later in life, when I had spoken on occasion about that experience of another world, someone said, 'Read Wordsworth. He wrote about "trailing glory from where we've come".'

Now, standing with Liliane on this glorious morning, I could still see myself with my father looking at that bloodied sunset which led to the other realm; and memories stirred of how in childhood on beautiful days I had known that this existence isn't all that is.

How could I be frightened, remembering what could never be forgotten? Yes, I would go to the summit.

Liliane and I continued walking; there was no need for discussion. She sang the songs of the mountain, and for that time I felt exhilarated, joyous, and free. I had revisited a place that I'd lost; the mountain had given me that.

We ate the lunch the nuns had prepared for us on the next plateau, and she again asked my intention.

'For what?'

'This journey.' She ate calmly with big, strong white teeth, chewing enough and properly before swallowing. I told her I would like to go through a portal. She asked why. I didn't know, but I had a growing sense of adventure, something to do with the air and the sense of well-being I felt on the mountain.

'To get over a love affair,' I said, unexpectedly.

'Oh yes, I can see you would need to enter a portal for something like that.'

Was she being sarcastic? It would be the first time.

'Did the other initiates receive visions?'

'It takes great attention to one's practice for an initiate to invite and make manifest a being from the next sphere. Days—weeks—of prayer, fasting, chanting, meditation, breathing, exercises. Hours of incantation. The being called forth may appear as the Magdalene, the Lady with the Cup, or worse. The initiate has no control of the size or placement of the being that appears. In the case of Charlemagne, it filled the sky. In the 1976 ritual, it stood above the hill, obvious to everybody.'

'But that is what this is all about. Calling up spirits,' I said again.

'Not remotely.'

By the afternoon, I wasn't so confident. The exhilaration had evaporated, leaving me with more usual thoughts. Ahead of us was a river of swirling mud, and Liliane pointed to a rock on the other side onto which I would have to jump. To land on that sharp, loose-looking object with all the force I had was insanity. Her answer? She would go first. It was a question of attitude, she said. I asked for an alternative and looked at the tree next to me, checking to see if—although also insane—using it might be preferable.

She made me practise jumping from one rock to another on our side of the mud, and I started to feel perhaps a touch of confidence. She promised me I would free up and overcome fear. Together we ran on the spot, stretched, ran some more, and then she did the jump. I was right. The rock was as loose as an old person's tooth, and she clung at the last moment to a frail tree. Straightening up, she kicked and struggled the rock into position. I knew she would. And then she looked at me. She seemed to be waiting. At school, gym was never my subject. I remembered trying to vault the buck, the box, the horse, and I remembered the results. Pass on the leap across swirling mud.

'But now you have a choice,' she said.

Yes, I could pray.

'You are not fourteen.'

I did pray, and then Verdaguer's words seemed to sing in the trees: 'How powerful the awakening to see Canigou leaning with its forehead in the sky, its feet in the sea. The rise of our glory has passed on the wings of illusory dreams as the meteorites that dress the sky pass.'

The words splashed with the mud, swelled with the breeze. Although I didn't understand all of them, it was as though through Verdaguer the mountain spoke. And just the sound of his words comforted me. Maybe, like him, I belonged to this mountain.

I started a long way back and then ran and jumped with every bit of life the afternoon allowed me. Making it near the rock, I slithered and slid and would have fallen, but Liliane had hold of me, her giant's arms around my tiny earthly waist. One of my shoes came loose and was rushed off and away in the yellow-brown ooze. For a moment I thought I could hear chuckling, but it was only the mud pouring like thick soup over the rocks.

Liliane opened her rucksack and gave me a pair of her shoes, and we moved back from the edge. The shoes were too big. She took off thick socks and I put those on. The footwear was feasible. I thanked her and didn't comment on the loss of the shoe.

The next two or three hours were spent climbing, walking, stretching, resting; we didn't speak. I did not look forward to the climax of this journey. I had a sense that there would be a change over which I would have no control. During the last few days, I had sensed Canigou in my deepest self, and the feeling wasn't altogether pleasant. The mountain had seemed to get nearer even when I was going farther away from it, and now I was on it. Where did the journey go from here? 'Was there something after square 7?' I asked Liliane.

She didn't answer, so I asked if I could go to the middle of number 7 and then stop and return down the mountain. It seemed safer.

'I bet José didn't finish this,' I said. 'And Saunière didn't.'

She sighed. 'José finished it. Saunière left it. Verdaguer lived it.'

I didn't want to lose myself. It seemed to be all I had left.

'But loss is the price of being here. It is an existential fact,' said Liliane.

Up and farther up we went, I now on all fours. I repeated a few lines I'd learned from Verdaguer and hoped they would please the mountain: 'The throne of the Pyrénées is too small for you. To be great today you woke in the shadow of the cross.' Soon I could see the next refuge, and the sight of it encouraged me. Between that thought and the next a sharp bank was suddenly in my way. It was high, perpendicular, made up of earth, rock, and tree stumps. There was no way around it. Liliane said there was no option but to climb up. I sank down and simply gave up. I told her I couldn't.

'Charlemagne would,' she said.

Again, she'd go first.

I let go of the effort of pulling myself up on all fours and lay face down on the rocks while she behaved, I considered, unexpectedly. From memory she quoted a passage about the mountain.

'"The monks want to go to the northern part of Catalunia and crown the mountain in a secret sign, but there are pagans at the peak. Protect yourself in the name of God. Before the Count dies, let us go to the top of Canigou with the sacred symbol of victory to place the crown." Verdaguer here writes of sacred symbol. What is it, do you think?'

I didn't know. I didn't answer. I was still face down on the rocks. I asked her to recite more.

'I can only give you a rough translation. You have to read this in Catalan. "The dark clouds surround a dying giant already in the heights, turning off the stars one by one. But the cross that was guiding us is higher than them. In the name of God, let's go up." Some have died on the journey in the performance of the ritual preparation,' Liliane added.

'Why?' There seemed so many possibilities of death. I was very mindful of the perpendicular wall of earth and rocks. I said I'd rather find another path. She said there was no time. Time? What had that to do with anything? She pointed; the sky behind us was a weather warning. We had to get to the last refuge above the tree line before the storm broke. I could hear a vehicle in the distance. If I could I would have run to where it was and thumbed a lift up or down. She started climbing, all her muscles engaged in the job. 'Follow me,' she said. 'At the top you will have to push me up the last stretch.'

I copied her movements, concentrating so that no thoughts intruded to undermine this pitiful attempt with fear of consequences. Grit and shrubs fell on my head as she scuffled to the top. I couldn't look up, but I sensed she was leaning over, watching me. She wasn't there yet. A new horrific instruction: 'Hold on with your left hand and push my buttocks with your right.'

My feet had to be better placed. My left hand was holding a secure shrub, but letting go of the right hand made me gasp. I pushed one of her buttocks. She told me to keep my hand there until she reached the top. Then I got stuck. I was hanging by my left hand from a stubbly branch that would only take so much. I was going to fall and die. I didn't want to think about the pain. Thoughtfully, I assured her I must let go of her buttock and think only of myself. I grabbed at a protruding stone just as she heaved herself up and out of sight. She told me not to look down. No chance of that.

'Just reach up with one hand and grab that next branch. If you do this and get up here you'll have opened up a whole new life for yourself. You'll be able to achieve things unimaginable now. Just reach up and trust.'

It took minutes—lots of them—but finally I did, because I was so tired of being afraid. I shot up one hand and made contact with that rough branch, finally grasped it, and then scrabbled up with my toes digging into the earth like a desperate child. My other hand, the one that had been still clutching the loose, wayward branch from before, now let go and flung upward to grab Liliane's outstretched hand. And then suddenly, improbably, I was at the top, and we both yelled out in celebration. She pointed down at the gulch below.

'Look how far you've come!'

'I could have died doing this.'

'What a good place to die,' she said.

The next refuge was a simple hut in which travellers had left fruit and bottles of water. There was a kettle, clean cups, and, outside, a table and chairs. From her rucksack Liliane produced yet another welcome trick: sandwiches— bread, cheese, tomatoes, and ham delicately packed by the nuns of St Martin.

I could see the mountaintop from this plateau and asked how far we had to go to reach it. She had her first laugh that day. 'You know, my dear friend, we don't ask that question.'

'What is the whole journey really all about?'

'Solving problems.'

'This 7 square?'

'All of them.' She looked up at the sky and didn't like it. Perhaps she could see things I couldn't. Storms? A tornado? 'Finish the food; then we go to the track and hopefully get a ride to the last refuge.' She said it usually took an hour-and-a-half of walking, but she didn't think we'd get there ahead of the weather. I could see she knew the mountain. I asked if she sometimes went up to the peak.

'Many, many times. Summer, spring, early autumn. I've spent nights up there.'

I asked if her stays there were in the manner of a ritual.

'Not at all. I just lie there and look at the stars and watch the dawn. It is quite beyond words, so I won't try them.'

I realised Liliane loved the mountain. She knew it in all its moods: when to trust it, when to stay still. I helped her clear the table and wash the cups, and again she recited parts of Verdaguer's epic poem.

'"The dark clouds laid across the sky like the coat of a dead giant and by lightning flares a huge chariot is seen crossing the path and strange voices are resounding while ours dim. Who is coming up to take our palace? Must we leave our door? Who comes up? The sacred night coming with the cross. In the name of God let us go up."'

'Who is speaking in those lines?' I asked.

'It's Verdaguer, describing the pagans and spirits at the peak and the priests who are going up to replace them.'

The food had made me feel better and I could walk the rest of the way. I assured Liliane I wasn't tired at all.

'But you must stop before you're tired. You won't get ahead of what is coming from the west.'

I looked at the sky and it was blameless. There wasn't a gust of wind from an approaching storm, no distant thunder. But for some reason, Liliane insisted on going to the track, which was well made with enough space for vehicles in both directions. Eventually she got us a lift with a forestry worker, and within half an hour we were at the hotel refuge situated on a plateau with a magnificent view of the peak.

The sight was worth writing poems about. It was stark. It was awesome. The air was clear and cold. I wanted to be there for the rest of my life. It was unlike anything I had ever seen. I asked if we were still on magic square, number 7. She pointed to the peak.

'The Seven.'

And it became obvious that somehow—I didn't even dream how—I would be under the stars and 'beyond words' on that mountaintop.

Liliane explained that farther up she had a small cabin, which had once belonged to the rescue service. She also pointed out the lightness of being that I was experiencing in coming face-to-face with the mountain peak. This lightness could not have been possible, she said, had I not done the work of preparation and change during the last two weeks. Perhaps now I would comprehend change and know that I was a different person. Even my shape was altered, she told me.

The family-run refuge was old and filled with the atmosphere from a dozen decades. I didn't need my absorption skills here. Torn posters on the wall dated from the 1920s. The bar top belonged in another era. The dining room was large, with long tables and a wooden floor. The terrace faced the mountain and gave some shelter from all winds except the tramontana. The fireplace, large enough to warm the room, had two dozen comfortable seats drawn up around it. The family mixed with the guests and played cards and held evenings of French dance. There was room for a hundred clients a night, and some stayed full pension, meaning room and board, for several days. The bedrooms were small, plain, and scrupulously clean. The air, made up of elements other than those I was used to hundreds of metres down in a bad city injured with negative atmosphere, filled me with delight. The ground was hard and there were few trees, but my attention was drawn constantly to the mountain. Its ridges, its body, were so near, so available, and yet the peak seemed farther away up here than it did from the flat lands below. The woman behind the bar was soft and peaceful. The place claimed peace as its right.

'I wish I didn't have to leave here,' I said.

'Then why do you?' she said, her eyes wise. 'It would be good for you up here.'

'What about going down?'

'What about it?' She herself stayed in this refuge with its view of the beloved mountain for weeks at a time. It closed in early October and opened in April or May. The feeling of peace intensified as the hours passed. Later, I asked how long it took to get to the top, and she said she thought that someone used to mountains could do it in under an hour.

'Walking?'

There was no other way.

We talked about the ceremony of the longest day and about how Catalans on both sides of the border streamed up to the summit and celebrated the solstice, singing Catalan songs and holding high, flaming torches until the sunrise. Some ran down the mountain, through the villages of Catalunia, passing the lighted torches one to the other. It had taken the entire night.

Liliane, her hair washed and tied up, sat beside me at the bar drinking hot chocolate. 'So where are we with the French garden? What have you discovered in your meditations?' She intended to take me by surprise.

'Nothing. I remember it less well.'

'Go back to the dream.' She made me tell it as well as I could. 'Look at the colour of the diva Emma Calvé's dress. What is it?'

I could not remember. What had the priest talked about? I thought it was a vision that had appeared by a fountain.

Almost hypnotically, Liliane took me back into the garden, and what did I see? I could hear the whir of insects. The women cooled themselves with small embroidered fans and drank fresh lemon juice. The priest kicked the ground, scraped at it with his shoe.

'Why?' she asked, when I stopped speaking.

Why? It was as though he had seen something. Or had trodden in something unpleasant. Or his shoes weren't clean enough. I told her only that I thought he had a quick temper.

'Did you see it? What was it he scraped?'

'I wasn't in a position to see it.'

She moved to the business of the birds. What was beside the tree? I thought a ladder, but it was oddly shaped, like a staircase. How many steps? Seven. The more hypnotically affected I became, the more pronounced the images. A buxom, healthy woman stood on the top step offering an apple she'd picked from the tree.

'Why does the bird interrupt the concert?' Liliane waited. 'See the bird.'

'It didn't like Calvé's singing. Or she reached a note that set off the bird, just like what happened in the Jewish Centre.'

I was awake now. She'd lost me.

'Which note?'

I didn't know. I was irritated. I wanted to go out and see the mountain.

'High? Low?' She wasn't going to let me get away with approximations.

'High. It was a struggle to get to.' I remembered that.

'Sing it,' she ordered. 'You can sing.'

And I did, but whether it was the right note I couldn't tell.

'A top F-sharp.' Liliane was pleased.

She put on all her clothes and said we'd walk before the cold set in.

What was it about that house with the tower? What had I not understood? The question was becoming more important, even urgent.

Climbers came down from the mountain and went swiftly into the refuge. My guide asked another question but I couldn't hear because the wind had got up. A climber shouted a warning, and Liliane raised her hand in acceptance.

'Do you remember the black mark outside the village of Cassa and the one at the shrine in Girona? Or that one by the rubbish bin in Collioure?'

I did not. The wind took all my attention.

'It marked the place where a vision had been seen.'

I remembered that much, but not the shape or size of the marks.

'Have you seen the mark anywhere else?'

I had no idea and answered roughly. 'I can't remember everything. I have a selective memory. I can't fill my mind up with trivia. There'd be no room for real things.'

She actually laughed.

'The dark scorch mark, always the same, shows the place of an appearance from another dimension. It is a sign of protection, but mostly it is always and forever the sign of a portal, a doorway—Daleth, number 4.'

293

And then I realised something I should have known. The buxom woman on top of the ladder could not have offered an apple from that tree because it was a royal palm. Liliane suggested it was not an apple but something else. I thought of the typical distortions of a dream.

The storm from which she had run suddenly came on like gun fire. The frail trees shivered as though in pity. I told her she could add storms to my list of fears. Lightning brought guests who loved storms onto the terrace.

Liliane and I went to her room to share meditation and chanting and to experience the subtle changes, if any, of the space around us. Could I detect a difference in the atmosphere between the right and the left? I could not. It wasn't an idle question. She was looking for an experience I was going to need. The storm had my head in my lap, hands over my ears. I kept thinking of the words, 'A coward dies a thousand times, a hero only once.' Someone had told me that during the storms of the past.

'Aren't you tired of being afraid?' she said, gently.

'Would it make any difference?'

'We've only got the edge of the storm here. It'll be over soon.'

'And then will come another fear.'

She laughed and, giving me a glass of water, said now she would ask more questions. I was then sure that this was her job: she worked for that society in Girona and needed to know a particular thing they obviously thought I'd seen. I'd tell them and then they'd kill me. Did I have the answer they had always looked for and needed? Had I discerned a missing link they sought? Even so, they'd still kill me. I wouldn't go near that peak. The irony was that I hadn't the slightest idea of what they wanted to know. But I was sure that, even if I had, the best thing would be to stay silent.

The dinner was copious, the dining room full. A huge log fire roared, and the places around it were soon taken. The guests had eaten and drunk their fill and now told stories of the mountain. And then they were gone, and Liliane and I had the place to ourselves.

'We start at dawn,' she said.

I wanted to ask what she wanted from me but didn't dare. Before we went to bed, I asked again why we'd spent the night in a grave.

'I've told you. To make friends with death.'

'Is that the end or beginning of the journey?'

'For some people.' Was she intentionally ambiguous?

I felt increasingly uneasy.

She said, 'The priest from St Feliu didn't make it. We know Saunière didn't. He just wanted quick information and tried to buy it.'

Maybe I was alert to energy changes after all, because now I was sensing one in her. She was not calm in herself.

'What stage are we on now?'

'Redemption.'

I didn't like the sound of that.

'Tonight you make the act of surrender. You hand over your will, your life. It is an action.'

'To what? To whom?'

'To God, I would suggest.'

That night I dreamed I was in front of the old chocolate poster in the alley behind José's hotel in Girona, where no light could reach and even the old-fashioned lanterns clanking in the mountain wind did not infiltrate the blackness seething with staring cats. A new moon was trapped at the end of the alleyway, its silver essence shining on the eyes of those creatures, giving away their secrecy, and they started to howl and screech in obedience to this lunar influence. I seemed to be standing against the old stone wall, the poster from the forties peeling and torn. It was where I had used to meet José in the mid-fifties. A wind full of ice from Canigou rattled the bins and thumped the doors. Only black and silver existed here; no colour got through. The cathedral bell chimed midnight and was echoed by lesser clocks across the beloved city, and I knew he would come and that this was the only place in existence to which he could come. I waited for him by an alley next to the eating place, Chez Beatrice.

'But it's been closed for years.' The voice was not José's. Part of the dream, then.

And then I smelt the eau de Cologne he wore in his hair and ached for the touch that would follow. I ached for him, for this man who held, even now, all the memories of our lives; and his lips were against my ear even though of course I could never see him.

'*C'est le destin, peut-être,*' he said. 'It is destiny, perhaps.'

And then, in the storm's wake, I awoke to the radiant day. The light seemed to pour out of the mountain itself; yet that black and white place with its lunar light was still with me.

Figure 19.1. Site 11, Mt Canigou, Portal.

CHAPTER 19

The day after the storm was clear and blessed, its translucent air filled with tiny diamond drops of light. For the first time in weeks, I dared to enjoy simply being. This unexpected happiness allowed me to escape from the growing anxieties waiting like patient creditors needing to be reckoned with eventually. This journey was about survival, not surrender. To survive, I should spend all of my energy responsibly; and here I was, free as a bird, skimming across a stretch of lake at one with the bits and pieces of light, stunningly bright on the water. The unanticipated joy of the moment belonged in childhood from a time before anxiety and darkness. I wasn't sure if that time had ever really existed, but the innocence and joy of children was an idea onto which I lovingly held.

On this lake, an hour's walk down from the refuge, Liliane let the boat slow and then glide up against the opposite bank. Parts of the waterway were still iced up, thick enough to skate on. For once I clambered onto land unaided. She tied the boat to a tree and read from the sheets in the document case. There were few left.

As we walked down through the forest to a clearing she wanted to visit, the light made wonderful designs composed of sun, shadow, branches, frost. The sudden breeze brought into being the scene of a castle with dancing figures in lace and a troubadour with a tall hat. The troubadour fell to the ground, his hat of ice melting in the sun.

'At the end of magic square number 7, José said of himself that he was of the earth but had been momentarily lifted from the pull of gravity to a world created of light,' Liliane told me. 'The very structures in that world had seemed made of light, and it was a place where he had felt all that he should and more. But he could not stay there. He had to leave the crystalline figures of sun and ice and be on the earth.' She pointed to the empire all around us still made of frost and sun, white light through trees moving in a chilled breeze.

'And then where did he go?'

'Where he prepared himself to go.'

'Where do I go?'

'You have a choice.'

I liked it. I didn't like it. I bent to look at the fallen troubadour who was now simply a tiny pile of sticks. The castle with the dancing figures now took on a new cast—a smiling head wearing a crown that lifted and slid in the dangerous heat of the approaching sun, surrounded by animated figures of gold with pointed, nodding heads and crossed, thin legs, gossiping endlessly.

'We walk back over the ice.' Once again, Liliane's definite tolerance for danger was apparent. I said yes. Perhaps I was getting used to it all. We kept on walking downward and there on the path was a small, stone chapel. The door was held tight by a clasp. She unlocked it and opened the door wide, allowing light and air to enter.

'Go inside.' She was behind me.

Was this it? The end, the beginning? I hesitated.

She saw the point of going first. Once inside, she lit a candle.

'Come and look at this.' She pointed forward, and I poked my head around the door and could see nothing obviously dangerous. It did occur to me that she could, being stronger, push me to the ground, go out, and lock me inside. Who would hear my cries? The birds? What had happened to my trust in her?

Finally, the artefact on the chapel wall took my attention. Painted on wood, the colour was still vibrant, hardly flaking, even though the artefact had been painted in the seventeenth century. It was rectangular, with a top curved in a semicircle and no frame. 'Have you seen it before?' she asked.

Was she referring to the artefact? In it, a woman had climbed a ladder against a tree and stood on the seventh step picking a fruit from a branch. Two men waited below. The tree, circular like a ball, had thick foliage and a sturdy trunk. It was full of birds leaving and flying away. Layers of landscape were visible behind the tree, and a jewelled crown circled the bottom of the trunk. A basket hung next to the woman.

'She stands on step 7. That's significant. And the crown shows upliftment, power, honour. This is square number 7,' Liliane said.

'She's getting apples.'

'Oh no. Branches. They'll be whittled down and become staves.'

She waited, but I had nothing to say. Yes, the ladder was gold.

'A stave from this tree is given to the pilgrim on his journey through passage 7.' I asked if I got one. 'Not at this height.' At some point she did tell me the tree's name, but

I lost it in what followed and have not been able to find it since. It might have been *yew* or *juniper*.

I now looked at the landscape painted around the tree and in the distance recognised Canigou. I asked if the birds were part of the pilgrimage.

'But yes. They are symbols of enlightenment.'

We sat on the narrow, polished bench to examine further this rather ordinary work. I asked who looked after this chapel.

'I do. Is this painting what was in the garden in your dream?'

I said no. Suspicious now, I would have said no in any case. In my dream the woman had an apple not a branch, and the ladder was a staircase. I told her I never remembered dreams normally, which was true.

'We will have to get you a stave. For your pilgrimage. You take it with you.'

'So I can either go to the mountaintop, or what? What's the other part of the choice I have?'

'You can sit here and meditate.'

I was surprised. It sounded so simple.

'So I don't have to go to the end?'

'That will be your decision.'

'What will I miss?'

'Oh well, that's another thing altogether.'

An hour or so later, she took me back to the refuge and asked me seven questions. She said she would ask them again and then the choice would be made.

'Do you forgive your son-in-law?' she asked.

'No.'

'This would be a good time to let go of that resentment. It may cause you to miss splendour.'

'It will be there as I lie dying.'

302

Did I let go of my hold on José?

Never. Couldn't be done. I hoped the other five questions would be easier.

They only seemed easier: Did I hand my will over to the supreme spirit of the universe? Did I walk with my stave, untouched through evil? Was I prepared for whatever the guide felt I should be shown? Would I devote the rest of my earthly existence to helping others on their journey? Would I swear an oath not to reveal the contents of my journey?

I said yes, and the journey was now a pilgrimage.

We would now make the preparation. She burned oil and the chanting began. The chakra healing was strong, the fumes from the oil and the burning twigs making me light-headed. I could feel a slight shift throughout my nervous system. The movements I had to make were repetitive and took me beyond exhaustion.

When I finally got to my feet, I felt as if I'd grown in height. Ash from the burned twigs covered the floor. The smell of the burning oil stayed with me.

Outside, the mountaintop was pink with sunlight. I watched it, not even caring about the cold. All fear gone, I was ready for the journey. I understood that I knew very little about the bigger landscape, the immensity of life. Watching the mountain, I wondered why it was silent. What if it wasn't really silent but was making a huge sound, too huge for us to hear? If we did, our skulls would crack.

The trees by the refuge were dry and stunted and twisted by winds and storms. They weren't suitable for the meanest stave. Even I could see that. Liliane went back down into the forest and cut a thin, straight branch from a mountain pine, which she spent time whittling down to an admirable stick. The refuge owner swung it and admired its decided whip. He brought her a pot of varnish to seal the wood perfectly.

'It will do to ward off animals, but not the fallen angel.'
He laughed.

Why mention that? I thought of Lucia on this mountain, her dying. And I remembered the earlier mountain, St Pedro de Roda, less fearful when Lucia and I had gone there with the group of friends in the fifties. Something had happened there. I never understood what Lucia had seen. I thought it prudent to enquire a little more into the subject before climbing farther. What *had* happened on St Pedro the night when Jodi Soler had banged on the empty monastery door? Would Liliane add to the story? She swung the stave and gave it to me.

'What Lucia and the others saw—was it a vision?' I asked.

'I told you not.'

'What did it do?'

'It started to come down from the mountain and Lluís thought it was a woman. As it drew level, the group could see that it had Lucia's face, but older. It spoke to them. It spoke just as she did, yet Lucia herself was still there, standing beside them. It gave a warning: Lucia must return to the mountain what would otherwise inevitably fall into evil hands. Whatever it was terrified Lucia, but the others just thought they were drunk.'

'What was it she had to give back?'

'What you were working on in your research. The Grail ritual. The chalice.'

'You want me to go up?' I looked at the peak, ever more distant. 'And yet you tell me this now. Remember, please, that Lucia died in the process.'

'Lucia took off her gold dress and said she would never wear gold again,' Liliane concluded.

'Why?' I asked.

'She obviously didn't want to flaunt gold any more. After what she'd seen and heard that night on St Pedro, fortune became perhaps the enemy.'

We walked swiftly for the first time towards the steep slope now covered in frost. How could the summit be a simple hour away? I said something about distances being deceptive.

'And appearances.' Liliane was never lost for words. They poured out of her, exactly the ones she chose. Was this fluency a result of making the journey? Reaching the destination? 'It's the journey that counts,' she said. 'Not the destination. Saunière was a man of appearances, wouldn't you say? Think of your dream of the garden.'

Had it been a dream? I had definitely been back there in that house and garden on that day in the 1890s, but how could I have made such a visit? This mystery was more alarming than anything else. I tried to make her understand, but she responded with some placating remark to the effect that intuitive people could go back to and return from their past lives on occasion, especially if stirred up by a practice under the Great Bear. Under that influence, even an ordinary, closed person will see many things. The Akkadian name for the Great Bear was *Akanna,* and in Egypt the most prominent star in that constellation was called *Ak,* which means 'the eye'.

'The eye symbol was important to the Egyptians.' Liliane explained. 'The right eye depicted the sun, the left the moon. They were called 'the eyes of Horus'—the eyes of visionary seeing—so therefore is it a surprise that you see both the present and the past at a certain time in that garden? Your question should be: what is it about the garden?'

So we were there again.

'Was Saunière good? Bad?'

What a time for that question, stuck as we were over two thousand metres up a mountain.

'He had taken too much power for himself,' she went on. 'He felt pleased with his ego. He descended the ladder into greed and power and so darkness. We have a choice.'

I hoped so. I sensed she was warning me about Saunière, hoping I would reconsider my closed attitude about my dark side and share more. I had no opinion about him. He'd become inexplicably, suddenly wealthy beyond belief. He went to Paris, which led him directly to Spain, made a strange set of symbols in his church and a tower that no one understood, ate and drank well, and presumably had enemies. But he wanted something more. Otherwise, why bother with the house, the tower, and Maria Tourdes?

We had walked only some moments, and already the refuge was deep down the mountainside, almost hidden.

'It's a portal, isn't it? On this peak.'

'But of course. Journey site 11.'

I was alone here on the rocks, beyond human help. I no longer knew what to think about Liliane. The surroundings, the atmosphere, the sky filled me with a sense of awe I could only describe as biblical. Perhaps I should do what she said—about the forgiveness. I had vowed I'd never forgive, but that was down in Perpignan. Up here was quite another matter. I said I would lie dying, hating my son-in-law, but those were Perpignan thoughts. I was facing this huge landscape that had nothing to do with my past or even with me. I was an intruder. I'd better become a pilgrim.

I knelt on the white, gleaming surface of the mountain as the rim of moon came into sight and asked for forgiveness. I didn't think I could ever actually get on my knees; that was the first miracle. Liliane knelt beside me, said a prayer for me, and held me tight, loving, comforting. I had to fight hard not to cry. Yes, up here was not the same as down there. Not by a thousand lifetimes.

Liliane said we would now eat and not make any decisions. We walked back down to the refuge. Its windows were hung with fairy lights, and I walked towards it as the true home I had always sought and never found. Inside, I smelled life's abundance and goodness, not the ravages of nostalgia and loss. We sat by the fire, and she talked suddenly about her life.

'I came here in the sixties and put myself in the middle of a forest on a mountain. I lived in an abandoned shack. I had no phone, no water, no lavatory, no television, no radio, and had to get on with it. For days there was nobody. Just me and my thoughts. And I came from the centre of Manhattan.'

'So what happened?'

'I had to get to know myself. After a year I could make a link with anything far or near. After another ten, I could traverse the stratosphere.' She asked suddenly if I had any questions.

As the refuge owner had mentioned an angel, I asked what a fallen angel was, exactly. Was the one he mentioned the same as the one in the well at Ripoll?

'In spirit, everything has an ego until it passes into evolvement at another level of existence. All egos are thinking, rational entities that have lived in human or other forms in the preceding life cycle. If it is their karma to incarnate again, they have to abide by that karmic law. If they delay in complying or refuse, as did Archangel Michael, in due time the bodies predestined for them become defiled. Rebellious angels are then hurled down into hell with their pure spirits and egos imprisoned in bodies of unclean matter—in other words, flesh—only to return to this earth to sit out their karmic period of incarnation. But they are not of here. The one in Ripoll made of blue fog has no physical body. It is cast into the well to wait out its time.'

'For what?'

'To go back to spirit.'

'So how long do I have to wait to go to the peak?'

'We go now.'

I couldn't quite hear that. Surely she'd made a mistake. I asked again, and she put the stave and a thermos flask of tea on the table. 'Before dark.'

'The shepherd's staff, which becomes the circle and the serpent,' said the refuge owner. 'With this, Moses challenged the magicians. It's in the Bible. I'll go and get the covers you'll need.'

I jumped up, knocking the chair back. 'I've got to phone my children.' I ran to the bar to use the phone. The connection was too bad to know who was speaking. I went back to Liliane and picked up the flask, the stave. I put them down roughly. 'But I must phone José.'

'Let your next call be to God,' she said.

'So you are on the pilgrimage.' Liliane spoke calmly. 'It is arranged that you will be met at the doorway.'

That filled me with questions she chose not to answer.

'Who will I meet, and why?'

'Expectations will not help. Trust would be a far better ally.'

'And after the pilgrimage?'

'Rebirth.'

'Where?'

'Do you want an insurance policy? There are no insurance policies in love affairs or pilgrimages or any of the things in life that matter.'

308

'Did José do this? Tell me.'

She held my arm, comforting and calming, as I slid about on unexpected ice. I wished she would talk about what we would do *after* the portal. The sky was still blue. It got lighter as we climbed. I was nervous on the one hand, and on the other I felt it my right to fulfill this journey. I would go to the end and the beginning. Why should I always be the carrier, the chronicler of others' actions? This action would be mine. Why was I always in the fame-shine of others?

'You climb the mountain, and you will know freedom. And then healing. And then love.'

'What do I have to do? At the portal?'

'You attune as you have done these last weeks. And the space in front of you will change. It will slide open.'

I wanted to be sure of exactly what a portal was. I understood it was like a wormhole to other times, other places.

'Portals are in precise places at various locations on this planet. They can be approached by those sufficiently initiated to recognise the vibration and to match the resonance. A portal to the average eye is invisible. It is a passage beyond the five dimensions we know; some insist there are only four. The limit of each dimension is nine, and a new level begins at ten. Portals have a magnetism that can be immense. They are not all the same. Some are weaker; others carry negative desires and past, evil events. Some are so glorious that no approach can be made, so powerful that to draw near them would be to dematerialise. These portals are protected by an area of low energy around them; those entering that zone become depressed and unwell and go away. Portals contain all that has been and all that will be. You must resonate, have some ability to do so, even to talk about portals.'

'Have I so far on this journey?'

She didn't hesitate. 'No.'

'Why should I go near this one?'

'It relates to you.'

'How do I come back?'

'By polarity. You will go from the North towards the South and then back to North, which is where we all come from. And never forget that. To forget is dangerous for us. Do not lose your North. They say that in Spain.' From heart she recited phrases of Verdaguer translated for my benefit, and they matched the mountain perfectly. '"Oh, save Catalunia: the dark night moves away. The clouds are melting. The sun is shining on your pure tip. Goodbye, caves of Ribes. I'll never see you again. Cleansing fountain of live waters. Basket of flowers from Nuria and hips of green mist hanging from the sky. The wood bearers will never hear my singing as they go their way, and the shepherd who is watching the woods won't see our garments when the morning starts. No more Knights lightened up by love will come to the caves that were only opened by love. If somebody finds my nest once more he will find it without me. In these mountains to take away my fame clad in fire comes Count Arnau. The sun and the marias that the heart loves forever goodbye."'

'He talks of the portal that can only be opened by love. Remember those words,' she said.

I carried the stick and wondered if it would go with me.

'When you are in place, you do your calm breathing; you chant, meditate, absorb, attune. Let your body sense if there is a change in the space around you. Chant on F-sharp. You know how to reach that note. You have a good ear for music.'

'I just know it,' I said. 'I always have.'

She didn't answer.

The landscape changed and the sky took over. We were higher than anything around us. We sat down before the last approach to the summit. Was this the place number 7, the doorway? If José did it, I'd do it. Simple as that. The custodians? Did she work for them?

'Did Verdaguer do this?'

'Of course. He talks of the portal that can only be opened by love.'

'Do I simply walk through the doorway?'

'Your body is here. Your superconsciousness goes through. You travel with your etheric body on the astral plane.'

I asked about the stave.

'Drop it as you enter. You need nothing. Everything will be gone. I have told you.'

I remembered her talking about superconsciousness, so it would be like taking a heavy drug trip.

'Why keep asking questions? Every answer I give you only leads to another question. Just go into it with new eyes.'

I insisted on knowing something of the experience.

'But you have no control. You're there. You go with it. There is no choice. You never forget it.'

That remark comforted; it made me think I was coming back.

'How long am I there?'

'Not too long.' She laughed. 'Otherwise, you won't get back into your body.' Was that what happened to Lucia?

Who had really suggested I do this journey? It seemed to be José. Were the custodians behind that? Did he realize they were? Did I trust him? Until death.

I suggested to Liliane that instead of going through the portal I should do a simple test. I was sure the custodians' way was to get me to the summit and push me off. Wasn't that what had really happened to Lucia? So I preempted them by saying that I would drop off the mountain and fly. That was the test.

'If God needs for me to live, I'll stay up in the air. If not . . .' I shrugged. 'Then I wouldn't have deserved the journey.'

Liliane laughed. 'You have to have enemies.'

'Why?'

'It's what you're used to. What you're capable of dealing with, perhaps.'

No. The mountain itself had pressed me, pummelled me, forced me beyond my capacity. I felt dragged across this mountain, ravaged out of my senses. There wasn't a talisman or magic square on earth that could put me back together.

A bird skimmed across the rocks and landed beside us. Hopping from leg to leg, it reclaimed its balance. It watched with one eye all that was around, sensed no danger, and started to sing, the sound raw, jarring like the bird in the dream.

'It comes from far away,' she said, and gave it a name. It was white, grey, strong, huge.

I talked about a French composer, Olivier Messiaen, and his music celebrating birds, his understanding of their existence as being partly in the realm of spirit. I could talk forever to stay where I was.

She knew that Messiaen wrote exultant sacred music in F-sharp. 'He chose that key because it corresponds with what is beyond. You, too, will meet that sound again.'

Did she mean the portal?

She stood up, which was the last thing I wanted, and gave me my chill-proof, padded coats and thermos flask. 'What progress did you make with the snapshot? You don't mention it.'

'Oh, that did not get better.'

'Can you accept it, that time with José? Just see it as part of your life?'

'I looked at it repeatedly as you asked me to, but it couldn't be made ordinary. Mere habit couldn't do it.'

In truth, the snapshot was just as powerful as when she had handed it to me in Empúries. That moment in it was without end; it would reverberate forever. Nothing got better than that moment in the photograph, so I took it with me; it was my only object. I had it pressed close to my skin, but I didn't tell her that.

'Did Saunière in your dream scrabble with dirt in the garden to uncover the cabalistic sign for doorway? That dark mark indicating where a vision has been present?'

Her question did stir some memory of his angry foot and his shout of surprise. I wouldn't tell her about the garden. I'd take that with me, keep it safe. Had Saunière found that mystical sign? That must be what the custodians wanted to know. It was the third time she'd asked me. To delay the answer might be my insurance, after all.

She pointed upward. 'It will only take some minutes to get to the top. Charlemagne would do it to reach the portal.'

And a terrible thought occurred to me. 'You will be with me?'

'No, I stop before. I am not your guide at that point. Your guide is from another time.'

This betrayal was beyond anything I'd expected. Reckless now, I almost ran to the top, heart pounding, legs numb, knees in pain. I slowed only when I anticipated what might be waiting on the summit. 'They', the ones hired by the custodians, would hear my ragged approach.

But the territory here was not for humans, and somehow fear had no place. I climbed the last inches up into

313

the sky, ready for what I had to meet. I wasn't alone. With each step, I could feel the symbols and small descriptions of some of the sites we'd passed through. I could feel their sounds inside my head comforting me. It felt like a language of an unknown being, a motherly source, a big bear. Certainly not human. I didn't need to know the words' meanings or content, as I'd first thought I did. If I had understood them, I'd have lost this communication with the sound. 'Yod. Yaveh.'

The summit was empty. Surprisingly, it was as small as a dance floor, with patches of ice. Everything was beautiful but beyond expression. The summit was held in on all sides by a dark blue sky of twilight with stars huge as plates. I felt compressed, as though covered by an upside-down dish. José had done it. I'd do it. I'd spent days on the preparation, peeling the layers off the past. What has Liliane said? 'Don't pre-think. You'll try to cling to what you know. Accept what happens. It will take you where you need to go.'

What if I don't like what happens and need to come back? This was not a new consideration. I sat breathing as I had practised, trying to attune to this sheer white surface and the immense sky with stars spinning in spirals, streaks of light dashing through them, dying. The air was from another reality altogether. I must make the attunement inside myself, I thought, and from deep inside me an image will arise and become exterior to me. It will be more actual than anything I'd known. I was now promised that the guide would be there. I would follow him.

The comforting sound of the Primal Mother—the celestial Great Bear made of stars—was tapped like a code, and it rose into my thoughts. I changed my breathing and sang out F-sharp sustained. Nothing happened. I felt incongruous, sitting alone on the summit of a sacred mountain. How could this ever be understood? I laughed, and my padded clothes swelled in and out like lungs. Then the thoughts started: They would come, the assassins, and silence me. Unknown figures, soft-footed in the front, from behind. Shivering, I wrapped the extra quilted coat around me and heard an animal call. A wolf? Did they eat humans? I decided I was scared of wolves. Come to think of it, I was scared of everything. Attuning my thoughts, I chanted through frozen lips sounds only half remembered and then gave up. I should go back, screaming down the mountain for rescue.

Was it because I did try to get up that I fell as though pushed, spinning and tumbling, until I was sliding ever faster like a fairground ride gone mad down a spiral drop and hit the sides and screamed until there were no screams left? Had I gone over the side of the mountain? I whispered to God and saw the tower in the moonlight, poisonous, mocking. Remember the chant, the prayer. And then in an innocent daylight I was in front of a green covered mound like a bunker with what seemed an orifice at its front. Standing beside it was a friend who'd been dead for years and who, alas, I hadn't thought about lately, and he seemed to be waiting for me.

Richard Cobb was one of the most unique and brilliantly alive people I'd ever known. A professor of French history at Oxford, he had always been immediately interested in French life on all levels and had known people from my past who were linked to the Rennes-le-Château story and Spain. Seeing him now, Richard appeared as full of energy and life as ever; and as I watched him he became younger and then older, jumping to and fro boyishly. This jumping seemed to fill my mind too much, and I understood that the orifice at the green mound was itself the portal. I must have gone through its dark, pulsing entrance, because I then sped down a curving tunnel with rocks and thin trunks of trees

315

close together on either side, reminding me of Dali's painting of Perpignan station; and, scared, I opened my eyes and heard someone say, 'She is not ready.' Determined or foolish, I closed my eyes, an action that was in fact part of the process of letting go and created the opportunity for the portal to allow what came next.

The next experience came speedily. Sitting now in a café in Paris opposite José, I knew that I was very young, and I also knew that I could never, by mere memory, have seen him as he was in that instant—the raven, rich black gleam of his hair, the vibrant olive of his skin, and that particular expression on his face that had vanished years ago.

I could never by will alone have recaptured this place, this time. I was there. I was in the café in Les Halles, 1956, with its long-forgotten smell and the large, chipped coffee cups, and Richard was giving me messages by thought, not spoken words: 'You had no choice. He was everywhere.' And I took him to mean that I had had no other option but to leave my husband years later, as I did, and go to José with the children and cause so much pain. I'd spent the rest of my life trying to sort that out—to make amends—and living with the torturous fact that in breaking up my family I had made an unthinkable mistake and so closed off my true destiny. Yet now Richard was showing me another reality.

Then suddenly I was present in the chamber of a man with a white wig from which powder rose and settled on his shoulders. He wrote with a pen at the end of a white swan feather, and I knew this was a sign of an initiate. When he offered me the swan feather, Richard was excited and said, 'I would take it.'

Although I was present in those long-lost places, I was also aware that I myself was separate, a sightseer. I did not want to be taken over by the place, the people. If I had continued sitting at the zinc-topped table in Les Halles, looking at José, at the way his expression changed so charismatically even when giving bad news, and he should have spoken and I replied, I might have been there for good. Was that thought a fear or a hope?

But I seemed to have no choice about where I went. Next I was on Finchley Road, North London, years later, and I'd arrived there with no warning, lurching on to a pavement filled with people waiting for buses. Finchley was not yet a four-lane thoroughfare, as it later became in the seventies, and it was lined with trees on either side and pleasant cafes with tables on the pavement. This was the mid-sixties. It was autumn and dark, and I was going home to my husband and our two small children. My body and legs felt young and light as I walked through wet, sodden autumn leaves that led to the fire escape, which was the approach to our flat behind the shops.

I had been to see the movie *A Man and a Woman*, which only too clearly echoed my own past affair with José and brought back all the longing and terrible nostalgia. Even the French actor Jean-Louis Trintignant looked a little like my lover. As I entered the living room with my husband and our children, it could not have been more real. There was the rush matting that I would never have remembered, worn at the edges, shifting on the floorboards. It was as it had been exactly, made of fibers that I could actually smell and touch. And they were so happy, the three of them. The very room seemed to smile, and I stood there knowing that I could not let José go, that I had to join him, that I had to leave this sweet and innocent room because José was where life was. Yes, he was all around me, everywhere. Even the film confirmed that.

Some days were better than others, but the smell of spring rain brought all my longing for José back, or autumn rain, or a wind from the south, or the smell of wood smoke—that was the worst. My body sat heavily on the bed. I was too heavy with sadness to stay standing up. Undeniably I was present in this room again, which was not something I would have wished to revisit. I had gone back in time or found this time or been obliged to re-enter this period of my life that was somehow extant in all its dimensions beyond the portal. In all the intervening years, I had not thought of that film and that terrible evening once. And my husband put the children on the bed next to me and said he was happy, and I knew—how I did!—that I was a traitor and would leave and go to the irresistible interloper with whom I had those transcendent moments of fusion. Was it the film that brought back all the memories I'd so suppressed? I had made my decision and in the process, as they say, cooked my goose for good. Even in this astral dimension my assessing mind was still with me, making its commentary. I heard Richard speak close now: 'There was no choice. That parting had your name on it from the moment you were born.'

Images, powerful and innocently coloured, rushed towards me, flooding me with their identity until I was part of each and every one. The sound of a steam train, Perpignan station; and then it all slowed and I went to the window and José was there on the platform waiting, younger than I remembered, half smiling as he lit a cigarette, cupping his hand against a southerly wind.

So I visited these episodes and took my place in each, and then without choice was moved on to the next, and the farther back in time the more sharply etched and highly charged the episodes were. José sat on an iron chair opposite me in the sun outside the station buffet, drinking coffee, wearing a black overcoat, his skin olive in tone, eyes grey, hair lustrous, black and long to the white collar. And

318

we laughed and tried to keep the laughter private and so laughed the more and a bird crowed beside him. What language did we speak? I heard a church bell. I realised that his clothes were not from the 1950s; they weren't even from this century, and just by touching the fabric I understood that neither were mine. The skirt was long and ruffled to my ankles. It was undoubtedly José, and yet he was too young and fine; his cheekbones were higher and his voice deeper, so seductive. He was a man of grace. He said he must go back to Rome, and I asked if he loved me. 'C'est le destin peut-être,' he replied and reached for my hand.

And then the café table was snatched away and I was elsewhere and everything smelled of rich earth and mould. I wanted the man in Perpignan station and the skin I could touch and kiss. He was truly exquisite and there was no one like him. I had to hold on. I was losing myself. I was going into another's thoughts. I needed to work it out. It was José, yet José did not smoke. At least he hadn't in Girona. And the farther into the past I was pulled, the more real existence became.

I could hear the sound of earth being dug; the man must be strong. As I walked along the track in the dark towards the tower, the cathedral bell rang midnight sonorously. Through the garden gate I could see the French priest digging deeply beside the royal palm tree. He bent and examined some object, then, irritated, flung it to one side. I could see the carriage of the Frenchwoman by the front door. Then Saunière saw me, and I was evidently a surprise. 'I thought this was a bad day, but at the last chime you have quite changed it,' he said. Who did he think I was? And he carried on with the digging and wiped sweat from his face.

'Are you digging your own grave?' I asked.

He looked at me, assessingly. 'This used to be where priests were buried, so perhaps I am. It's called the "Black

Cemetery". Why don't you sing? I heard you earlier.' The sound of many priests approaching made him drop the shovel and retreat out of sight behind the tree. I asked him what he was looking for: 'Treasure?'

'Oh, bigger than that.'

I was there; I was she, this person who was me and yet was not. My thoughts were her thoughts. I must hold on to my own identity, or I'd slip into her consciousness and be gone. But hold on to what? I had no idea how I looked or how old I was, but I knew how it was to feel, to answer, to sing.

Then there was darkness and the rattle of a train, and I was jolted against my young lover in the airless carriage and could smell the eau de Cologne in his lustrous hair. I knew he was Italian; no argument about that. I wanted to know his name. It was not José anymore, but I was swept on, along with him, into other moments, other places, without choice. Even the darkness was dazzling. He had the documents from Rome. The French priest would be pleased.

'There is evil in this world,' the lover said. 'You just have to look at him. It comes well disguised . . .' and the noise of the train took away the rest of his words. I saw the cathedral; we were approaching Girona.

And a voice said, calmly, 'There was no choice.'

The garden was filled with ladies and gentlemen of high rank. I could hear the diva start the Schubert and see that the chamber group had moved their instruments into the shade. The kitchen was too small for all this preparation, and the swiftly hired serving girls bumped into me as I stirred the drinking chocolate. I knew the priest wanted it perfectly blended. I'd been told that more than once. I poured it into a long glass and added a spoon to the tray. Coming out into the sunlight of the garden was blinding, and for a moment I did not see him. He held out his hand and I saw the priest's ring and the initials B.S.

'Only from a gold cup.' His voice was as rich and as smooth as the chocolate. I had to return the tray to the kitchen and ask the resident maid for a golden goblet. She said I must call the mistress, who for some reason was not with the guests. She gave me a better apron with lace around the edge, and I looked at myself in the mirror. Surely I was more beautiful than the diva?

'Calvé's come from France,' said the gardener. 'Where the priest goes, she goes.'

And the girls giggled.

'But he does come here to this house,' said the cook cautiously. 'He climbs the steps up the city wall at night right into the garden and thinks no one sees him, that no one in this town even knows he's here.'

'Well, he's up to no good. He doesn't come here for a woman; he comes for a tower,' said someone else, and they all laughed.

The diva waited for the applause to end. I was told to find the mistress and ask for a gold cup. I climbed the one flight and could hear sobbing. I looked through the doorway at the bed and saw her lying there, inconsolable. I crept down again and found a dusty gold chalice on a shelf and filled it with the chocolate.

The priest thanked me, his eyes taking in my face, my hips, my breasts. He certainly wasn't giving Benediction. 'Your apron is most pretty. How old are you?'

'What do you think?' I knew all the answers.

'Sixteen. How long have you been a maid?'

I was proud. 'But I'm no maid. I'm a singer. I sing in concerts all around Girona.' I watched the diva.

'I can see from your gaze that you think you can sing better.'

'She can't get the F-sharp pure.'

'Come and be a maid for me. I live in France. It will suit you.'

And then I saw my lover—'the Italian', they called him—talking to the musicians and nearly dropped the tray.

'Why are you the maid?' the priest asked.

'I was called in. A lot of us were, locally. Because Madame Maria is giving this entertainment. There are people from Paris here.'

I could see he was interested in me. I wished my lover was. The diva had now attracted the Italian's attention, and everything tumbled inside me as though my organs had come loose. The jealousy was extreme, and I threw the tray in a bush.

'So you need the money?' The priest had to ask me twice.

'Who doesn't?'

He laughed a genuine laugh. 'Oh, I like you. Go and prepare another chocolate drink—served only from a gold cup. Surely you know that. And I will give you one hundred francs.'

The Italian still talked to the diva. He must love only me. I trailed among the guests, through the musicians, so my beloved would see me. His eyes as they joined mine eased all pain. The lover made his excuses to the diva and stood beside me.

'I will meet you in the alley by Chez Beatrice. I will always meet you there.' And my lover's hand touched mine, and I shivered and could see the French priest's eyes on me. He was displeased.

'Eleven o'clock tonight,' said my lover.

I would go to the last heartbeat, the last clock tick, the ultimate surrender to meet him. His eyes were light and amused; he knew my thoughts. Then he saw the French priest. 'Avoid him. He knows evil. He is Lucifer's servant.'

The musicians prepared for the aria, and the diva moved under the tree.

'But you have documents for Saunière,' I said. 'He will pay you what we need.'

'That much? How?'

'I will give them to him.'

The French priest beckoned to me. 'So you like the Italian who walks on Canigou?'

'He's from Rome and walks on many mountains. He stays in Ripoll with the poet Jacint Verdaguer.'

'Yes, I know who he is. But you like him.'

'Perhaps.'

'*C'est le destin peut-être,*' he said.

'*Peut-être.*' I, too, spoke French.

'He plays music excellently, I hear.'

'At the Vatican,' I said, not without pride. 'He has arranged for me to have tuition at the Conservatoire. I will sing in France and Italy.'

'But you're Catalan. So what do you speak to him?'

'Whatever he likes.'

He laughed, all displeasure gone.

'Alessandro is too lucky.'

I didn't like the way he said 'too'.

'What's your name?' he asked, interested.

'Cecilia.'

'St Cecilia. November 22: the patron saint of music and musicians.'

The diva started the aria that I knew so well. It was overproduced.

'Are you jealous?' the priest whispered. 'Why don't you call down the birds? I'm sure you know magic. Then they'll sing with her.'

I laughed and people turned in dismay.

'Then I'll do it.' He looked up at the palm tree. Nothing happened, and then the big, black, greasy-coated bird started its jarring laugh and the singer's top note failed, and the audience laughed more than any bird.

'Oh, what have we done?' said the priest, transformed by mirth. He gave me two hundred francs and gently took off my lace apron. 'Remember, I like chocolate always from a gold cup.'

I tried to reach Alessandro, but I was spun up higher than the tree and could see a gold staircase below with seven steps and he, the priest, was staring at my lover. Saunière's anger was worse than that of most people because it was all internal and calculating. He kicked the wall savagely, and the stone tumbled down and Saunière cried out, 'But it's here!' He scraped with his greedy, devilish foot, and there was the black sign for the doorway. Some priests of Girona had said it was there, but no one had ever found it. It led to the unimaginable. Even the future. Saunière was beside himself. The buxom woman climbed the golden staircase and applauded. The French priest shouted triumphantly, 'There's the entrance and exit to everything that is.' He called for me. 'Cecilia, you have brought me luck.'

Then Alessandro moved towards the priest, and I so wanted to stop him that I shouted—how I did—that Saunière knew evil, but Alessandro could not hear me.

The old station in Girona was still lit by gas lamps blowing in the mountain wind. This was the last place I traversed. I could see on the crumbling, broken wall that the decaying, chocolate poster was torn. It seemed to acknowledge a time that had been truly alive, a time that was now truly gone.

4	29	12	37	20 **⑥**	45 **⑤**	28
35	11	36	19 **⑦**	44 **④**	27	3
10 **⑧**	42 **⑩**	18	43	26	2	34 **❶**
41	17	49	25	1	33 **❷**	9
16	48	24	7 **⑪**	32	8	40
47 **⑨**	23	6	31	14	39 **❸**	15
22	5	30	13	38	21	46

(SITE – SQUARE)

1. Girona – 34

2. Besalu – 33

3. Ripoll-Gombren – 39

4. Figueras – 44

5. Empúries – 45

6. St Pere de Rodes /
Devil's Cave – 20

7. Collioure – 19

8. Perillos – 10

9. Rennes-le-Château – 47

10. Perpignan – 42

11. Mt Canigou – 7

Figure 20.1. The initiate's journey on the Venus Magic
Square, following the constellation of the Great Bear.

CHAPTER 20

A month after that day on the mountain, I sat with Liliane on Perpignan station outside the buffet. I had my back to Canigou. I was telling her of my experiences—of how the images had begun immediately coming into my mind more brightly than anything I'd ever known and of how they could be instantly recalled later. The journey through the portal had been like a dream too big for my mind to process. It was also as capricious as a dream, and I couldn't hold onto any of it. It must be like a dozen acid trips in one.

'But I said you would have no control,' she replied. 'Anyway, control wouldn't serve you well. So now you know you are a spirit with a body not a body with a spirit.'

I said I was without fear most of the time now. Perhaps it was because I knew that there was not only this world as I understood it but many more existences out there, in here—wherever they were—and I felt part of a vast network. It made me want to do other adventurous things. I felt better in all ways. I wanted to go further into the experience and would do it again if necessary.

'But you don't have to do it again.'

I said I realised traversing the portal was a huge and privileged experience. But one could only revisit and repeat the past, not change it. She said she was impressed with my understanding that the symbols of the sites could be experienced. They were an early, universal language, transferred by vocal sound that in turn caused images to arise in the mind and then in feelings and senses—among others, danger, joy, and caution.

I described Alessandro. Was it José? Perhaps it was a brighter, younger spiritual version of him.

She laughed. 'He'd like to hear that.'

'Let's just say it was the angel inside him,' I decided.

'Let's get on with now.' And she placed the document case on the table.

'What am I on now? If anything.'

'Resurrection.' She ordered a hot chocolate.

What is it about chocolate,' I asked. 'It crops up everywhere. In the past the chocolate company's main office was next to St-Sulpice in Paris. Emma Calvé advertised this chocolate, and her small advertisements appeared in Saunière's house at Rennes-le-Château, Marie's home in Girona, and Emma Calvé's residence in France. Then there was the poster for Torres chocolate fading in the alleyway in Girona. And Saunière had said, "I only drink chocolate from a gold cup." Is chocolate part of a ritual?'

'No,' she replied. 'It's just coincidence.' I sensed there was more but knew she wasn't going to give me an answer, so I tried to draw her out on reincarnation.

'Of course that man from Rome, who walked in the mountains with Verdaguer, has or will reincarnate here or in some other realm. Of course you've known José before. You yourself have felt that many times, and he's in agreement with the sense of familiarity you share. This time you can work through something together but not be together.'

'What work?'

'I think now you can find out.' She gave me a list of numbers and exotic words that I supposed began the next journey.

I asked directly if the Italian in that previous life had been José, and she sighed and said that in order to know we would have to get José to agree to be taken back in a regression into other lives or share those he's already uncovered.

'But in Spain they say if you meet a person you've known in another life, cross yourself, turn and walk away, and say you've seen a ghost.'

She was silent, but I felt she knew the answer. 'Liliane, on this point you are as tight as Fort Knox.'

'I am sure José has his work to do, his path to finish concerning the house with the tower, just as you do. You are not the same as the girl with the lovely voice who served hot chocolate. Similarly, the Italian would be returned here with different aspects from many previous incarnations—such as aspects from his spiritual evolvement and necessary tasks—and with a different genetic line. Moments of his present life might link back to that previous incarnation, but only if there is work unfinished, or something to put right, or he meets a person from that time.'

Liliane was most interested that the priest had found the doorway symbol. That made a great difference to the conclusions everyone had since drawn and explained why the doorway had been successfully closed off. It was not meant ever to be known and available.

'So only Saunière knew of it?'

'But of course. After his death it was closed permanently by ritual.'

She showed me the drawing with numbers 7 x 7 Venus Magic Square and linked up the sites we'd passed through. The result was a design. What did it look like? Nothing recognisable. When she turned it sideways, I thought it was an animal, a bear, a bear in motion—a charming creature, not heavy but eager.

'As I told you, the Venus square comes under the Great Bear constellation.'

'What is the Bear?'

'Ursa Major, the great mother of all things. The Great Bear has seven brightest stars. We are familiar with the number 7. So it is not surprising that this constellation is related to the journey, beginning in Girona—which is under Isis, Isis being 7—and ending in Canigou, number 7 on the magic square.' It relates to passing through the eleven sites that lead to the entry, the portal, through which higher entities from other galaxies and times can approach us.

I said I would like to be her student and work in other aspects and she seemed pleased. And then at last I felt able to turn and look at the mountain.

The effects of the portal journey were not in my case noticeable immediately. The most important, perhaps, was the voice of Richard Cobb saying, 'You have no choice.' It certainly simplified the ambivilance and pain of my past actions, but I felt his words referred solely to the relationship with José and not to my actions in general. I was more harmonious with José, and trusted that, when the time was right, we would remeet. It took other people to notice that I wasn't as afraid of the known, and indeed of the unknown, as I had once been. I did not think so much about my son-in-law, even though the results of his actions were still only too evident in my family. Surprisingly, though, my mind was more filled with new projects.

Had I, after all, given the society what it needed? I now understood that what it had wanted was for Liliane to guide me into learning whether Saunière had found the portal in the Frenchwoman's garden. To discover that he had must have increased the members' knowledge of his activities. To whom had he passed on that information, and how many still knew of the portal's existence?

I did, just to check on things, ask a clairvoyant specializing in past-life regression what she discerned in me. I of course wanted to know about José. She said that in a previous life I had been a singer but was too ambitious for my hometown somewhere on the Mediterranean. I'd gone to Paris and made a career.

Now, in my present life, I am living in new time. Nevertheless, I still sometimes dream of the old railway station lit by gas lamps and the mountain wind blowing the fading poster from a time that has gone.

Figure 21.1. The tower in Girona always faced North.

AFTERW⊕RD

The End and the Beginning

S ince the controversial *Holy Blood, Holy Grail* was published in the 1970s, the spotlight has been on the hilltop parish of Rennes-le-Château. Treasure seekers by the thousands have scoured the area, but the secret of Rennes-le-Château has always been somewhere else altogether, in a little-known city across the Pyrénées in Catalunya towards the Mediterranean. As my guide Liliane said, 'The journey begins in Girona.'

I had long been curious about the impoverished French priest, Bérenger Saunière, who in 1891 between one day and the next became a fabulously wealthy man. No explanation seemed to provide the answer. In the 1890s, Rennes-le-Château was a simple agricultural village scratching out a modest existence. Had the priest uncovered there treasure secreted by the earlier occupants, the Visigoths? Or had he found a stash of gold hidden in the 1400s by the Knights Templar?

Testament suggesting Jesus was not crucified but had come to the area with a pregnant Mary Magdalene was a favourite among Grail writers at the end of the twentieth century. Proof of a deceased Jesus, a married Jesus, a fleeing

Jesus washed up on the shores near Perpignan would have given Saunière enough to blackmail the Vatican. Or had he chanced upon the records of an exotic and little-known sect using sorcery and magic? Had he in the seminary he attended at Narbonne discovered the Cabala? The wealth seemed to follow the finding of the scrolls hidden by his predecessor, Antoine Bigou, in the altar columns of his run-down church. As José Tarres said, 'What he was doing was not about gold bars. Or the Catholic Church.'

The nature of this strange priest is just as enigmatic. The German Cabalist Ingrid has said he was originally a high initiate and quickly understood that his work was to leave a message for those to come, a message hidden in symbolism. But along the way he became drawn to power and material abundance and so fell from grace. In Cabalist terms, he was *Samael* (the willful ego, the force of temptation and rebellion against the Divine), which, the Cabalist said, he would have understood.

Whatever Saunière found, after his discovery at Rennes-le-Château his grail was Girona, and he lost no time in getting there. In 1891, a train from nearby Couixa to Perpignan and then south to Girona would have taken approximately eight hours, and a coach and horses would have been even quicker.

There were four things Saunière needed from this Spanish 'city of passage' between France and Barcelona.

The first was the plan of the tower adjoining the House of Canons, which he purchased and into which he placed the young Maria Tourdes from Quillan as mistress of the property. He needed to copy the Girona tower in Rennes-le-Château exactly and at the exact energy pulse to activate a magnetic path and so mark the central point that previously had been accessible only to the initiated. Secondly, Saunière had to understand and learn how to open this central point, which, thirdly, depended on his acquiring the ritual documents and the power to use them. Lastly, to gain this power he had to take the journey, as had initiates before him. He had to work mentally, physically, and spiritually on this rite of passage to become sufficiently evolved to reach his goal.

Did Saunière know that the end point was at the peak of Mt Canigou? That it was a portal? That the Grail was said to exist in its earthly form as a cup made of the highest material known and that it concurrently existed in its etheric form in the etheric realm carried by the figure known as the Lady with the Cup? And that this object was a key, an activator, to open the doorway to other realms, other realities considered unsuitable and dangerous for any but the highest adepts? To gain knowledge of such matters, he had to be introduced to the secret society that had been based in Girona for generations. This introduction, according to correspondence, he was able to arrange. It was said that he possessed, as had Bigou before him, material of interest to the society.

There were other portal openings at some of the journey sites, especially in Girona at the house with the tower, which Saunière was eager to locate. Had he done so? That was the question the society had always needed answering. All that digging in the Frenchwoman's house and garden. Had the French priest found and understood that site and passed on the information thereof to his paymasters, the Habsburgs? Had he entered a portal? Unlikely as it seemed, he, like many others, had not finished the initiate's journey.

So why Girona? How did this little-known city happen to have the knowledge that must be kept secret for so many years and on such a scale? The initiates have said that certain points on this earth have significant force to do with ley lines and energies and that at these places extraordinary events can happen, events that could not occur elsewhere. For centuries, Girona had housed different religions and mystical practices—the cult of Mithra, the worship of the Sun God, and the worship of Isis brought by the Romans. Other cults and practices from the Phoenicians and Egyptians had made their way to Girona's coast at la Escala. Charlemagne was said to have caused a sign of fire in the sky to appear over Girona, so banishing the Moors. In the twelfth century, a centre of Cabala was founded by a Jewish settlement that had existed in the province since the fourth century AD. The renowned scholar Gersham Scholem said this Girona School of Nachmanides was the most important in history. Not to mention that the Greeks had arrived four thousand years ago. Girona is certainly a nucleus where a great deal of psychic energy has built up. The ritual, along with its documents and artefacts and practices, had been held here by a hidden society keeping a necessary silence through the centuries. As José, one of the society's recent custodians, has said, 'Rennes-le-Château is here in Girona. It has always held the secret. That's why Saunière came here.'

So the secret was the Portal—but what is it, really? And the Lady with the Cup, the Magdalene—what part did her appearances play? Once Saunière had understood the Girona tower, he built a matching tower at the correct distance in Rennes-le-Château. The towers had to be activated in order to charge the chemistry of the path between and at the central point of Mt Canigou. Under these conditions, matter and spirit are apparently able to leave and also reenter our existence. The phenomenon allows contact with layers of realities beyond us and not normally within our reach. This point can reclaim the past existing on the etheric plane. It can facilitate and allow the entry of other entities, beings, knowledge. The calling up of material from the Portal has always been in the care of adepts. In unwise hands, the power of this process could send the planet into unthinkable darkness.

The Lady with the Cup has been depicted in Catalan painting and stories from earliest times, and some medieval art works still remain. Her purpose is to bestow benefit, for which it is not necessary for us to seek or ask. On the primary level, she heals. On a higher level, she leads. She enters our atmosphere always in the vicinity of the mountain portal when called up by a group of adepts powerful enough to reach her. Could she be said to be the guardian of the Portal? Regarding the last sighting of this benevolent figure in 1976 in Girona, the hundreds of witnesses said the experience was a divine healing like no other and never to be forgotten.

Saunière was said to understand Cabala. Was he prepared sufficiently to deal with it? Was the material itself too powerful for him? Was he just out to acquire the earthly Grail cup? Did he mistakenly see it only as a literal concept and fail to grasp its symbolic significance?

José, considered in contrast to be an elevated initiate, feels that as he nears the end of his life he must hurry to finish the path laid out so many generations ago. 'If I don't,' he says, 'if I fail, I'll end up as Saunière did. I have to complete what must be completed. The priest did not.'

On my own journey, I discovered that the hidden society of Girona had been over the years made up of professional and elitist people, individuals from many sectors of life, their purpose being to keep the material secret. Only in the recent past have some of the members felt that this material should be made available to everyone. As Lucia Stilman said, 'Secrets are dangerous. They are elitist.' Conservative members in reply wanted the material all given to the Vatican and the society closed down. According to José, society members finally agreed to keep it private until the world should become a more optimistic place. 'I can't see that this has happened,' he said in characteristic understatement.

It was suggested that after finishing *City of Secrets* I should follow the journey of the initiates as best I could and write about the experience. Some of the conservative members were more against this book than the first one; and I did wonder—as I trod in the steps of the Catalan poet Jacint Verdaguer, the Abbé Saunière, José Tarres, and some hundreds before them—what catastrophe I should perhaps encounter.

The journey at its most obvious form is to slough off the layers of brittle defence and deadness that life has encrusted. It allows you to be who you really are. It opens up experience, puts it on a bigger tapestry, and shouts that what we perceive and pass through is not all there is. It introduces another sense of time, especially the past, which we might think of as irretrievably gone. But as Liliane said, 'Nothing is lost. We just get lost in time.'

This concept is inherent in children's stories, and children would have no problem with transformation and a portal. In fact, some years ago a group of children in Girona talked about an event that was quickly dismissed as imagination. They said they were taken to the doorway of the church of St Nicholas known as the 'portal of the invisible ones'. Here they waited to be drawn up a mountain and through an opening into places colourful and marvellous. The opening there was called a portal. In each case the parents said it was only a dream and the children had been asleep. And then they discovered that all the children had had the same dream. And it happened night after night. Then, unaccountably, the phenomenon stopped as suddenly as it had begun.

What did I need during the portal experience? I would have said control. I remember Liliane saying, 'Forget control. No use there. Trust would be a better ally. Trust the higher consciousness. Because if you don't, my friend, you're lost.'

When the distrust subsides, something else occurs—a sense of true adventure, of being shown the unimaginable, of being in other hands wise and caring, of passing a test, of marvelling at the enormity of it all seen on other levels, if only briefly. In my case, it was at the very least a rebirth. After the experience, I was less fearful. I had been given a deeper sense of life and could see a bigger picture. I could go deeper in my work and was fed by the experience. I could automatically take chances unthinkable prior to the journey. I could feel sometimes that, truly, nothing had been lost. At other times, I felt free. The journey has changed the way I see my life. It has been a privilege.

Later, through the German Cabalist and sometimes quite by chance, I have spoken to others who have taken this or another such journey. It seems that there are certain points in common. In addition to the loss of control at the portal entry, images become ever more vibrant. Some travellers, I have been told, have been taken much farther than I was into spheres previously unknown. Others heard sounds not even guessed at. Perplexing aspects of their lives were quickly understood. Potential initiates gained clarity about their life purpose, seemingly chosen to work here on earth to heal and transform. All felt a sense of freedom afterward, and the usual bad days didn't last as long. Some took up new paths or went further into the portal subject.

Not every seeker I know of reached a portal, but the approach itself, with the required work at each site, was beneficial and freeing. One or two did not experience a resonance with the portal; they could not enter and sat in a state of meditation. A few preferred the transformation of the journey to the portal's challenge of the unknown. Many revisited the experience in their dream state.

Before my journey, I had never heard of portals or of people travelling this path. Students such as I am effect change in themselves, while presumably chosen adepts can effect change on a global level. By their resonance, they can put to right at a high level some of the planetary darkness. Didn't the Cabalists in the Middle Ages do the same in their aim to help God in perfecting this universe? Modern scientists take the portal in another direction, examining it, seeking to understand its energies and its structure, and even righting portal entrances that have slipped with time.

The initiate's journey is a personal one, not a contest. It gives varying outcomes and qualities, depending on the person. Verdaguer, for example, became clairvoyant and gave healing and exorcisms, to the dismay of the Church. But in the end, all such journeys have one thing in common. What value does this ancient practice have for the world in these days? 'Same as always,' says José. 'Enlightenment.'

APPENDIX A

Stages of the Journey on the Venus Magic Square

SITE	SQ.	LOCATION	ATTRIBUTE	SPIRITUAL PRACTICE	CHAP.
1	34	Girona	Portal	Reflection/Enquiry/	1–9
		Baracca		Renunciation, Pt 1	3
		Frenchwoman's			4–8
		Garden			8
		Hotel Centro			9
		Residencia			9
		International			9
		Alley			9
		Jewish Centre			
		Savoy Bar			
		Hotel Penin-			
		sular			
		Romanya de la	Rest Point	Peace	10
		Selva			10–12
		Caldes de	Rest Point	Purification/Psychic	
		Malavella		Baptism (for students)	
2		Palera	Energy Point	Surrender, Forgiveness	13
		Besalú	Energy Point	Purification , Psychic	13
				Baptism (for initiates)	
3	39	Ripoll/Gombren	Energy Point	Acceptance	14
4	44	Figueras	Energy Point	Silence	14
5	45	Empúries	Portal	Receiving	14
6	20	St Pere de Rodes/	Energy Point	Renunciation, Pt 2,	14–15
		Devil's Cave		Gratitude/Rebirth	
7	19	Collioure	Portal	Transformation	15
8	10	Perillos	Energy Point	Abandonment,	16
				the Void	
9	47	Rennes-le-Château	Portal [?]	Humility	16
10	42	Perpignan	Portal	Preparation	17
11	7	Canigou	Portal	Redemption/Initiation/	17–19
				Freedom	

APPENDIX B

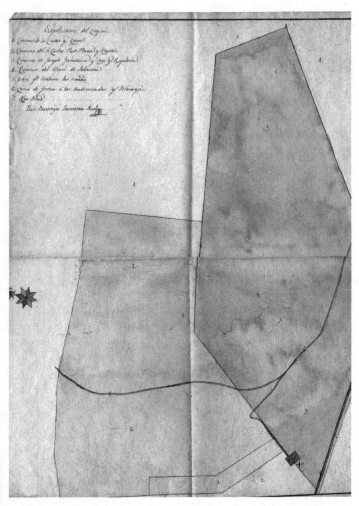

Map of land the society purchased in Girona, circa 1830.

ILLUSTRATION CREDITS

Patrice Chaplin and the publisher wish to thank Christopher Murray for his generous help in assisting Ms. Chaplin in preparing for publication many of her photographs that appear in this book. We also thank those who have kindly given permission for the use of other illustrations, as follows:

Pages xii, 3, 4, 64, 75, 77, 86, 139, 141, 142, 182, 243, 280, and 298, courtesy of Andrew Gough

Pages 5, 130, 185, 194, 204, 206, 211, 232, Shutterstock Images, LLC

Page 238, The Stapleton Art Collection/Art Resource, NY

Page 252, courtesy of Roger M. Erasmy

Page 332, courtesy of the Ajuntament de Girona, Girona, Catalunya

All other illustrations come from Ms. Chaplin's or others' private collections

Quest Books

encourages open-minded inquiry into
world religions, philosophy, science, and the arts
in order to understand the wisdom of the ages,
respect the unity of all life, and help people explore
individual spiritual self-transformation.

Its publications are generously supported by
The Kern Foundation,
a trust committed to Theosophical education.

Quest Books is the imprint of
the Theosophical Publishing House,
a division of the Theosophical Society in America.
For information about programs, literature,
on-line study, membership benefits, and international centers,
see www.theosophical.org
or call 800-669-1571 or (outside the U.S.) 630-668-1571.

Related Quest Titles

City of Secrets, by Patrice Chaplin
Kabbalah, by Ann Williams-Heller
The Kabbalah: Doorway to the Mind (CD), by Edward Hoffman
Mary Magdalene: The Great Initiate (CD), by Pamela Giese
Pilgrimage, by David Souden
The Templars and the Grail, by Karen Ralls

To order books or a complete Quest catalog,
call 800-669-9425 or (outside the U.S.) 630-665-0130.

Praise for Patrice Chaplin's

THE P⊕RTAL

'The Grail mystery: Patrice Chaplin lived it and is now conveying its incredible nature to the reader.'

—**Philip Coppens**, investigative journalist and author of
The Stone Puzzle of Rosslyn Chapel and *Servants of the Grail*

'Chaplin continues the epic literary journey that she started in *Happy Hour* and *City of Secrets*. The reward is an enchanting tale of love and nothing less than the truth.'

—**Corjan**, Singer/songwriter and publisher of
Rennes-le-Château Research and Resource

'Chaplin's work lifts the veil on the mystery of the Holy Grail. Her firsthand accounts of secret societies, initiates, and figures such as Salvador Dali, Jean Cocteau and Umberto Eco make for compelling reading. *The Portal* is fresh, insightful, and more proactive than anything she has ever written.'

—**Andrew Gough**, publisher of
Andrew Gough's Arcadia